Cross Bronx

Also by Peter Quinn

Banished Children of Eve
Dry Bones
Hour of the Cat
Looking for Jimmy
The Man Who Never Returned

CROSS BRONX

A Writing Life

Peter Quinn

EMPIRE
STATE
EDITIONS

AN IMPRINT OF FORDHAM UNIVERSITY PRESS

NEW YORK 2022

Fordham University Press has no responsibility for the persistence or accuracy of URLs for external or third-party Internet websites referred to in this publication and does not guarantee that any content on such websites is, or will remain, accurate or appropriate.

Fordham University Press also publishes its books in a variety of electronic formats. Some content that appears in print may not be available in electronic books.

Visit us online at www.fordhampress.com/empire-state-editions.

Library of Congress Cataloging-in-Publication Data available online at https://catalog.loc.gov.

Printed in the United States of America

24 23 22   5 4 3 2 1

First edition

for Bill Kennedy
Who told me what I needed to know

CONTENTS

FOREWORD

Dan Barry

Imagine being on a New York City bus, lurching and jerking, grinding and sighing. The bus, not you. Imagine this bus lurching and jerking its way through the New York City borough of the Bronx, down Tremont Avenue, along 181st Street, onto Southern Boulevard. Every seat is taken.

But this is no ordinary bus. To your left sits the late New York Governor Hugh Carey, ruddy now and singing a rousing Irish ballad. And to your right is his equally deceased successor, the intellectual bulldog Mario M. Cuomo, orating on Pierre Teilhard de Chardin, the Cross Bronx Expressway, and the sacrifice bunt.

The author Frank McCourt, who long ago joined the celestial beings he once described as "J. C. and Mary M. and the 12 hot boys," is smiling from the back seat, while across the aisle the nineteenth-century composer Stephen Foster gazes out upon the Bronxian blur, dreaming beautiful dreams.

Sitting together are the ageless and beautiful Miss O'Neill, who has been teaching elementary-school art for more than a century now, and executive assistant/guardian angel Helen Ross, forever unflappable. This might have to do with her having been one of four Black students to integrate an all-white high school, where not one white student spoke to her in four years.

Near the front of the bus, a Bronx County judge, enveloped in memories of what might have been, sits in silence beside his proud and loving wife, who casts a cold eye on duplicitous prelates and saint-worthy priests, political rogues and fallen business titans, wily gangsters and wiseacre cabbies. Many are benefiting from the technically dead bus-fare discount, but they are very much alive in the imagination and on the page.

This is because you are on the Peter Quinn Express. It travels from the New York present to the New York past and back again, filling you with so much joy and reflection and admiration for the written word that you will miss your stop, and be glad for it.

As this gorgeous and affecting memoir makes clear, Quinn is not an easy man to categorize, considering all that he is: a son of the Bronx, and proud of it; an Irish American who knows how to parse the profound difference between being Irish and being Irish American; a practicing Catholic who does not shy from calling out ecclesiastical hypocrisies; a historian, speech-writer, mentor, husband, brother, father, grandfather.

Writer.

But how many writers have helped write both a speech that ranks among the greatest in the American political canon (Cuomo's "Tale of Two Cities" keynote address at the 1984 Democratic National Convention) and a classic historical novel (*Banished Children of Eve*)? Who else has written a trilogy of noirish detective novels (the Fintan Dunne series), as well as scores of essays, reviews, and opinion pieces on politics, cinema, faith, history, on and on, each one a model of scholarship and literary engagement?

In these pages, Quinn demonstrates his historical command of New York politics, city and state. Born of Tammany stock, he toiled for many years in Albany as the main speechwriter for two larger-than-life governors, Carey and Cuomo, and his insights into the political world are both clear-eyed and empathetic. He understands the nexus where lofty idealism meets human folly.

He also demonstrates why he is regarded as the poet laureate of the New York Irish-American experience. One moment he is placing the much-maligned Tammany Hall in proper context, and in the next he is explaining how strands of the Irish famine are woven through the Irish-American DNA. But he is also this culture's conscience: He does not shy from calling out the occasionally suffocating tribalism, nor from confronting those who commit the worst of all Irish sins: forgetting where they came from.

Not this mug. The Irish, it is said, forget everything but the grudge—but Peter Quinn remembers *everything*, including the grudge (he maintains particular and delicious ire for the Manhattan tone poems by certain elitist writers who all but sneer at the outer-borough workers who animate the city's pulse).

He remembers every inch of his family's Parkchester apartment. His lifelong failure to connect with his imposing father, that Bronx judge.

His lifelong bond with his twin brother, Tom. The bus rides across the Bronx to high school and college. The decades-long search for his place in the world. The pitch-perfect speeches written on deadline and for paltry credit. That transformational moment when he committed to rise every day before dawn, arrive at his corporate speechwriting job two hours before the starting bell, and write, write, write this story flaming inside him: about New York City in 1863, and the Draft Riots, and a Catholic bishop called "Dagger John," and Stephen Foster.

Quinn's wanderings are not only of the imagination. He has spent time in the underprivileged neighborhoods of Kansas City; the violence-plagued streets of Belfast; the corporate inner sanctums of Gotham's flawed media gods. But wherever he goes, his heart and soul stay loyal to his native borough.

Cross Bronx: A Writing Life preserves forever a central component of the American experience in the second half of the twentieth century: the politics and culture and very feel of its greatest city. But Quinn does so much more than that. He reminds us of yearning, and resolve, and discipline, and honor, and compassion—and, yes, love. You see, there is this willowy young woman he encountered at Hot Dog Beach out on eastern Long Island, and—well, let him tell it.

Just sit back, feel the timeless time travel sway, and enjoy your ride on the Peter Quinn Express.

PROLOGUE

One day I was an impecunious grad student who never wrote a speech. The next, I was in a cubbyhole in the Executive Chamber's New York City office. A state trooper loomed in the doorway waiting for the governor's text. It was too late to run.

Intending to spend a year at speechwriting, I stayed nearly thirty. I wrote for New York Governors Hugh Carey and Mario Cuomo, and five successive chairmen of the shapeshifting, ever-inflating, now-imploded Time Inc./Time Warner/AOL Time Warner. I filled a wall of file cabinets with a modicum of memorable (so I like to think) and myriad utterly forgettable, already-forgotten prose.

When I began, there were no college classes devoted to speechwriting as there were for poetry or novels. I found a few here's-how manuals. If they offered an abracadabra formula, it escaped me.

Speechwriting taught me how to write. It drove home that filling the empty page is a matter of persistence, not inspiration. It gave me the discipline I needed to become a novelist. It allowed me to pay the mortgage, educate my kids, and enjoy a generous pension. No small things.

Speechwriters have special access. The longer you're at it, the more you're around, the more you're like an old, comfortable chair. People don't notice you. People can sit on or in chairs. No matter, chairs might squeak but they don't squeal. Same goes for speechwriters.

I went through an election and a trio of mergers. Except for blood and guts and artillery barrages, they're like wars. Everyone's priority is making it through. The sinking-ship rule of Women and Children First is first out the porthole. People you thought you knew do things you can't imagine. It can go the other way. That callous, shallow cad turns around and offers the old lady from steerage his spot in the lifeboat.

"Tell-all books" by speechwriters and chambermaids are inflated with compressed air. Nobody knows it all. Tell-all books without sex, murder, or something juicy to tell don't sell.

The last interesting tell-all I read was Procopious's *The Anecdota*. After the Byzantine doings of the Emperor Justinian and the Empress Theodora, all the shocking, untold, soon-to-be-revealed secrets by Angela Merkel's dogwalker or Joe Biden's barber are fingernail clippings.

People who buy books to wallow in the latest exposé deserve what they get—a book by the toilet that's out of date before the toilet paper. If you really care about this shit, you should get off the john and get a life.

I never planned to write a memoir. I'd reached a dead end on a novel I was working on and wasn't ready to start another. The involuntary idleness brought about by the pandemic provided copious space for writing and rumination. With no ultimate purpose in mind, I jotted down random notes on what led me to speechwriting and what I found when I got there.

I was held back from giving a full accounting by fear that people I respect might feel I'm violating their privacy, and ones I don't, a deepened animus. An increasing number are dead. *De mortuis nihil nisi bonum.* The more I wrote, the fewer my qualms. Every memoir is part confession, part betrayal.

Bad behavior isn't illegal. I witnessed unbridled greed, treachery, mental cruelty but never a crime or felony, unless evidence comes to light that I'm not aware of, which I will not rule out.

If I wanted to write a book chronicling the crimes and misdemeanors of my employers, I couldn't, unless I wrote a novel. I wrote three about crimes. I incorporated a lot of what I learned about people; the crimes were made up.

I worked with people whose everyday decency and generosity exceeded my ability to reciprocate. I'm indebted to speechwriting for the chance to share the company of writers who offered the solace and support—and laughter—I came to rely on. It's the bad we're likely to remember because the good can be such an ordinary part of our day that we take it for granted.

Has there ever been an insider tell-all book about people who do the right thing?

Speechwriting is like the vice presidency. It's not a position anyone aspires to. Few stay their entire careers. The speechwriters I know fell—or, in my case, failed as well as fell—into the profession.

Jim K. wrote an iconic memoir of the student rebellion at Columbia. A book-writing lawyer and former staff writer for *People*, he's a gifted, versatile writer, and a master of the deadpan. After months (or was it years?) of working together with company executives to compose a Time Warner "Values Statement" (unfortunately, that's not a joke), Jim said to me, "If you have to struggle this hard to come up with your values, odds are you don't have any."

The executive committee for execrable prose would occasionally send suggestions. A favorite was "We are not false." As the company's end time drew near, Jim suggested we change it to "We are no longer in business."

A brilliant and battle-scarred veteran of the profession, Mike W. freelanced a well-received autobiography for a big-time CEO who went on a talk show claiming he wrote every word. Pressed if he'd really written it himself, he answered, "Hiring somebody else to write my story would be like handing my clubs to a caddy and asking him to play for me."

Mike contemplated dropping him a note asking if he wanted his clubs back.

I did my best to make sure any names I drop are essential to the story, not my ego. When it came to identifying people, I followed no hard-and-fast rule. Where I thought people would prefer to maintain their privacy, I've used initials. Where people had a public profile that made them easily identifiable, or their identity was crucial to the story, I used the full name. I've tried not to betray any confidences.

Like us all, I'm eminently capable of rendering pleasing, semi-fictional, self-stroking versions of events, or telescoping or transposing them in what Joan Didion described as "the imposition of a narrative line on disparate images." All memory is a matter of splicing.

In some places, I'm not certain of the chronology. Worse than forgetting what happened is remembering what didn't. My wife calls it Plus-heimer's Disease.

This is a book of personal reflections. Those expecting to find detailed instructions on composing a speech should proceed to the cashier's counter to ask for their money back or contact Amazon Returns.

"Depend on it, sir," Sam Johnson said, "when a man knows he is to be hanged in a fortnight, it concentrates his mind most wonderfully." The strange interlude of the pandemic provided the inspiration as well as the time to write this account.

In a moment of upended expectations and fear-prone uncertainty, the tolling of John Donne's bells becomes perhaps not as faint as it once seemed. Before judgment is pronounced and sentence carried out, I want my chance to speak from the dock. Let no man write my epitaph. In the end, this is the best I could do.

Cross Bronx

PART ONE

The Bronx, Yes Thonx

WE CARRY THE PAST with us like a book. Whether we open it or not, it doesn't go away. Wounds that heal or not, moments of grace and humiliation, are with us until the end. We never get over our childhoods because we never get out of them. "The past is never dead," William Faulkner wrote. "It's not even past."

My father gave the first speech I ever heard. My twin brother, Tom, and I had just started the second grade. Our father took us to the communion breakfast of the NYPD's Holy Name Society. My mother insisted. She thought he didn't spend enough time with us. He was of the opposite opinion. He maintained we were too young. His relationship with us would never be the Sheriff Andy–Opie type.

We took the subway from the Bronx to Midtown. Before breakfast was Mass at St. Patrick's Cathedral. Although I'm sure I was there before, this time it made an unforgettable impression. It's the dull child who isn't awed by vast and reverent spaces. Pew on pew of men in white gloves and blue uniforms made it even more memorable.

I can't say I remember who said the Mass. I suppose the cardinal, but maybe not. When we stood for the reading of the gospel, I felt lost among giant sequoias. I know not every policeman could have been seven feet or taller. It only seemed that way.

Tom was on the other side of my father. I couldn't see him. I glanced around to see if there were other squirrel-sized creatures. If there were, they were hidden among the tree trunks.

We walked from the cathedral to the Commodore Hotel beside Grand Central. In days far off, the hotel's gut-job refurbishment would be the first venture into Manhattan real estate of a neophyte hustler who'd flimflam his way from penthouse to Pennsylvania Avenue.

The third most impressive thing that morning, after the cathedral and the police, was the hotel's football stadium–sized grand ballroom. Midfield, on one side, was a long table atop a platform.

The men at our table had gold bars or silver stars (maybe it was the other way around) on their uniforms. The men were friendly to my brother and me in the condescending way adults are to small children. They asked perfunctory questions about what grade we were in, and did we like school? We most decidedly didn't but lied. The rest of the time they paid no attention.

They chattered with my father. A judge and former congressman, he seemed to be enjoying himself. I knew he wasn't. The stiff way he held himself was a tipoff to his discomfort. Always cordial to strangers, practiced in the art of politics, he wasn't naturally outgoing. Several times he did a quick scan of the room. I guessed he was trying to see if other wives did unto their husbands what his did unto him and saddled them with two small boys.

The room went silent. A priest in a blue uniform—I presume he was the department chaplain, not a desk sergeant—said grace. There were brief remarks by the commissioner and some of the brass. My father was furiously rubbing his hands under the table. I thought I heard wrong when his name was called.

He stood and walked, shoulders back, to the raised platform. I looked at Tom across the space where my father had been. The panic in Tom's eyes was a mimeograph of mine. The seconds my father stood silently at the microphone felt like two or three hours.

In time, I learned that this was a tactic of his. Never start talking immediately. Take a deep breath. Look around the room. Let the audience focus on you. That morning, I had no idea.

The men were all turned in his direction. A current of fear and abandonment ran through my bewilderment. How could my father have left us like this? I wanted to reach for Tom's hand. I was afraid one of the men might notice. I bowed my head so low I could've pulled the tablecloth over it.

And then the laughter started, wave after nauseating wave. I felt about to throw up my fruit cocktail, scrambled eggs, buttered toast, and bacon.

Tom had his hands over his eyes. The waves crested, fell, and crested again, until they stopped. The loud applause sounded like appalling mockery.

I couldn't look at my father until we were on the train home. If we had the kind of relationship we didn't, I'd have tried in some way to let him know that, whatever the audience thought, we were proud of him. I was afraid he might blame my mother when we got home for making us witness his humiliation. They chatted in a friendly way, and that was it. Tom and I consoled each other that no one we knew had been there. We stayed mum.

I'm not sure how old I was before I came to full realization of what had happened. I never brought it up to my father, not even in a humorous way. It's not true that the more you do difficult things, the easier they become. On the occasions when I've walked up to a lectern to speak, the awful sensations of that morning flood back. I have to fight to stop them from overwhelming me.

My father never encouraged us to get into politics. It was never part of my life plan because I didn't have a plan. I knew I wanted nothing to do with politics. I knew I'd be compared to my father, and not to my advantage.

My first week as a speechwriter in Albany I was introduced to Dick Connors, a member of the Assembly since the days of Tom Dewey, or maybe those of Grover Cleveland.

He grilled me. "Are you a son of Pete Quinn from the Bronx?" My father had left the Assembly thirty-five years before. I confessed. He told me the Assembly used to wait to hear my father speak. Even the Republicans enjoyed listening, except when his remarks were aimed at them.

"If you're half the speechwriter your father was," Connors said, "consider yourself lucky." I refrained from thanking him for ruining my opening day.

My friend Joe Wells worked for the New York State Council of the Arts. Generous, urbane, wickedly funny, he died of AIDS. The last time I saw him, he was in NYU hospital. He preferred not to talk. "I'm watching my childhood," he said. "It's all there. I remember everything."

When I think back to my early childhood, most of all I remember brick.

My mother pushed the baby carriage with Tom and me through canyons of brick. Learning to walk, I held her hand and looked up at walls of brick.

Our building was thirteen stories of red brick. All the buildings in Parkchester, a planned community in the Bronx of 12,000 apartments and 40,000 tenants spread across 171 red-brick buildings of seven to thirteen stories, were identical red brick.

We competed to see who could loft a pink rubber ball—"a Spaldeen"—highest against brick walls. On my way to school, a woman stopped me and said she was trying to find an address but was bewildered by the overpowering uniformity of brick facades.

Parkchester rose out of the flatlands of the East Bronx like a mighty fortress, a red-brick bulwark, an Art Deco Stalingrad crisscrossed by Metropolitan Avenue and Unionport Road, with a landscaped oval of frolicking, water-spitting mermen at its center.

Stores lined the avenues. We got our clothes at Cornell's, a father–son shop. My mother always asked for Ira, the son. His father was saturnine and grumpy. Gaunt, sweet, helpful, Ira was the saddest man I ever saw. I constantly expected him to burst into tears.

Years later, my Jewish therapist told me that if you want to make sure a Jewish boy ends up in psychotherapy, have him work for his father.

Alfred Eisenstaedt took pictures of Parkchester for *Fortune* magazine. In one, a traffic jam of baby carriages crowds the sidewalk. To avoid impassable tangles of baby-bearing vehicles blocking building entrances, white lines demarcated parking spaces. Some residents laughingly referred to Parkchester as "Storkchester."

The Metropolitan Life Insurance Company conceived, financed, and built Parkchester on the eve of World War II. A scale model was displayed at the 1939 World's Fair.

Despite its actuarial acumen, even Met Life couldn't foresee the eventual return of an army of sex-starved, baby-breeding GIs. Its investment proved prescient. The postwar city was desperate for housing. In the middle of that desert, Parkchester's supply of desirable apartments turned into a precious oasis.

Parkchester was built on the site of the old Catholic Protectory (full name: The Society for the Protection of Destitute Roman Catholic Children). Spread across 150 acres, the Protectory was founded in 1863 by John Hughes, the Ulster-born hierarch-*cum*-Irish tribal chieftain who established Fordham University, initiated the building of St. Patrick's Cathedral, and wielded the New York Irish into a political as well as religious constituency.

The Protectory housed orphans and abandoned children, mostly Irish, whom the Children's Aid Society had begun shipping out west on "Orphan Trains" to be settled among God-fearing, Anglo-Saxon Protestants, an urban variation on the assimilationist model wielded so cruelly against Native Americans.

It's possible an ancestor of mine spent time in the Protectory. When it comes to my ancestors, lots of things are possible. I continue to discover things, many of which are less than felicitous.

When my father was a boy, a common admonition was, "You better mind yourself or you'll end up in the Protectory." To put it in the nicest way, kids weren't coddled. Mad Dog Coll and Joe Valachi—the latter of Peter Maas's *The Valachi Papers*—spent time there. I don't know whether their lives of crime began before, during, or after the Protectory.

I lived in One Metropolitan Oval from birth through college. My mother lived there for forty-four years. Our apartment looked down on the Oval. In the days of the Protectory, the Oval served as a ball field. It was where the Negro League's Lincoln Giants often played Sunday doubleheaders.

On hot nights, the windows wide open, I heard water splash. On warm evenings during the High Holy Days, Yiddish voices echoed from the benches around the Oval and drifted into our apartment.

The days the garbage was incinerated, ash swirled and descended like gray snow. Windows were tightly shut, and curtains drawn. Beneath the buildings were large, gloomy, dungeon-like storage rooms. Also intended as bomb shelters, they were filled with bikes, baby carriages, and machines whose functions weren't immediately apparent.

Parks and open spaces were strategically placed. The grass was for admiration, not recreation. Carefully spaced islands of green were guarded by knee-high iron chains. The playgrounds and ball fields were asphalt. We played punchball and softball. Nobody attempted to slide into second.

I never doubted Parkchester. At Mass, kneeling between my parents in our tan-brick Romanesque-Byzantine church, when I heard the words "and the gates of hell shall not prevail against it," I thought of Parkchester and the Bronx, not Catholicism.

Parkchester's residents were overwhelmingly Jewish and Catholic (Irish in the main). We lived separately together. I had no Jewish friends and no acquaintance with Jewish girls, except one. We rode the Bx 20 bus together, she to Walton Girls High School in Kingsbridge, me to all-male Manhattan Prep in Riverdale. I sat in the back with my school buddies, she in front with her classmates.

The first time I saw her, I was smitten by her thin and graceful figure, clothes loose and flowing (the style then was tight), thick black curls (the fashion was long and straight), an early blossoming flower child.

It was part of growing up in the Bronx to figure out, as quickly as possible, a person's tribe. I identified her Jewishness in the same way; if she bothered to notice, she perceived my goyishness. We never spoke. And then, one September, she was gone, off to college I presumed. I spent months bereft.

Protestants were regarded with curiosity. On Sundays, octogenarians Carl and Clara Bock quietly shuffled their way to St. Paul's Lutheran church. The Flynns went to Quaker meetings and were quiet about their faith.

Anytime I went past the stony, ancient-looking façade of St. Peter's Episcopal church, the doors were locked. Our Boy Scout leader told us that George Washington had worshipped there, which was unlikely or miraculous since it wasn't built until 1853.

African Americans were free to apply for apartments as long as they knew they wouldn't get one. The Lincoln Giants were the last African Americans to be welcomed to the Oval. Until the 1960s, Met Life enforced the same Jim Crow rule at Parkchester's Manhattan twin, Stuyvesant Town. This was of a piece with the intransigent injustice of residential apartheid that prevailed (and still prevails) across large swathes of the city (and country).

Met Life built Riverton in Harlem for middle-class Blacks. A scaled-down version of Parkchester, Riverton was conceived as a sop to the critics of Met Life's racist practices. The residents of Harlem weren't fooled. They watched Riverton be built, wrote James Baldwin, "in the most violent bitterness of spirit."

Desperate to increase the supply of middle-class housing—at least for whites—New York's progressive mayor, Fiorello La Guardia, didn't make a public fuss. Integrated developments couldn't be profitable, Met Life claimed, which it proved by not building any.

The main means of transportation were subways and the city's extensive system of bus lines. Our subway line was the IRT Pelham Bay line (the one Hollywood hijacked in the 1974 movie *The Taking of Pelham One Two Three*).

Parkchester was an experiment in Americanization, a step in and up from the immigrant's continental toehold. Watching the drooping crowd shuffle up Metropolitan Avenue from the subway at the end of day, it was impossible to tell Gentile from Jew. If we didn't always get close, we mostly got along.

The southern terminus of the IRT local was City Hall. The express ended somewhere in the Orient, in Brooklyn, a destination I wondered about but never visited. When I was five or six, I was on the subway with my sister Sheila. She was nine years older than I. I read aloud a name I saw on a train across the platform: *Canarsie*.

To me, it had a musical sound, foreign, exotic. I asked where it was. Sheila waved her hand in no specific direction. "Out there," she said. "Somewhere."

I was intrigued by her explanation—or lack of it. Canarsie was the world I didn't know—big, wide, unexplored. Out there. Somewhere. I've never been to Canarsie.

⁂

All writing is work. "Ass power," Mario Cuomo once told me. Others see it as a day at the beach. I remember an ad in which a shirtless, bronzed surfer-type, his face stylishly stubbled, sits at a typewriter, the portable vintage kind, and stares at the sea. A woman in a white bathing suit is emerging from the turquoise water.

It could have been an ad for watches, whiskey, or whatever the latest male fetish. Or maybe women's bathing suits. There was a single blank page in the typewriter. If intended to sell the writing life, it was for the life that nonwriters imagine writers live.

I never learned to type until late in the game. I wrote speeches, novels, essays, and student papers all by hand. Handwriting is also something that's acquired a romantic tinge. The hand–brain connection supposedly stimulates the mind in ways typing can't. This might be true, or it might be a Luddite fantasy.

I wrote by hand because I went to a school in which we were graded on penmanship. Once a year a Christian Brother, specially designated to the task, came around to inspect our copybooks. The class with the best penmanship won a banner. It was a big deal.

In high school, there were no typing courses. We took Latin instead, lots of Latin. It hasn't proved as useful, but it allowed me to impress acquaintances by translating quotes incised on stone pediments of courthouses and colleges.

In a bar in Albany that's no longer there (one of many), a drink-sodden, ink-blotted former newsman slurred, "Pencil, typewriter, a goddamn crayon, what the fuck difference does it make? All that matters is what you write, not what you write with."

I didn't know any writers growing up. Bronx neighborhoods were short of them. Don DeLillo, among the country's most accomplished novelists, was raised in the Belmont section. He went to high school at Cardinal Hayes on the Grand Concourse—where Martin Scorsese went and George Carlin was kicked out of—and to college at Fordham, a short walk from his neighborhood.

Edgar Allan Poe lived in Fordham for a period in the 1840s. His teenage bride died there. He made friends with Jesuits at the nearby college. He described them as "highly cultivated gentlemen and scholars [who] smoked, and drank, and played cards, and never said a word about religion."

We had a writer in our neighborhood, Elizabeth Cullinan, whose first novel was the critically acclaimed *House of Gold*. She grew up right outside Parkchester, across Tremont Avenue from St. Raymond's, on Poplar Street. Her novel was an intimate account of the tangled emotions and memories left behind in the death of the family matriarch.

My parents knew her parents. My mother recognized the close resemblance between the real and fictional families. She was aghast at how a family's intimate hurts and sorrows were made public.

After college, Cullinan started out as a secretary. She worked at *The New Yorker* for novelist and fiction editor William Maxwell. He recognized her talent and went from employer to mentor.

She wrote two books of short stories, many of which appeared in *The New Yorker*, and another novel. She taught writing at Fordham and faded from the literary scene. In the way of the world, after her recent death she's been recognized as an important figure in the development of Irish-American literature. I admire her work. I never met her.

Through eight years of high school and college, I made the two-buses, hour-long, borough-spanning, etched-in-memory odyssey down Tremont

Avenue, through West Farms, along 181st Street, onto Southern Boulevard, past the Bronx Zoo, across traffic-clogged Fordham Road to Kingsbridge Avenue, past Poe Park and the poet's landmarked, ill-treated cottage where he lived with his teenage bride, down to Marble Hill and 225th Street, and west under the Broadway El to 242nd Street.

When I started high school in 1961, the area around West Farms was heavily Jewish. On the High Holy Days, streets were flooded with worshippers going to or coming from synagogue. By the time I finished college, the population was overwhelmingly Puerto Rican and Black. Incremental change in the borough's ethno-racial composition had turned tidal.

My rough estimate is that, over eight years, I annually made around 250 roundtrips of at least 15 miles. That comes out to more than 30,000 cross-Bronx miles to acquire an education. I traveled the circumference of the Earth and then some without leaving the Bronx. It's amazing what you can learn by staying home.

We never owned a car and my father never learned to drive. There was a taxi stand close by our apartment building. When we went as a family to Sunday Mass, my father whistled for a cab by inserting his pinky and forefinger into the sides of his mouth. The fierce, piercing pitch made us wince and drew the attention of the neighborhood.

I asked him to teach me, but when it came to things he thought I should master on my own, he didn't have much patience, so I never learned. To this day, I've never heard anything quite like it.

My mother regularly took us to a dentist in Midtown, in the Fuller Building on 57th Street. Mostly we went by train. One heat-seared September afternoon, she decided to spare us an air-conditionless subway ride home and take a cab instead. She gave the cabbie our address.

He said he didn't go to the Bronx. She said we weren't getting out. He said he wasn't moving. She said her husband was a judge. He said he didn't care if she was married to the pope. She said she'd report him to the Taxi Commission. "Go ahead," he said. "Report me to the FBI. I'm not going to the Bronx."

She saw a cop and called him over. She demanded he intervene and instruct the cabbie he had a legal obligation to take us where we wanted to go. He shrugged, "Whattaya want, lady? I should arrest somebody for not going to the Bronx?"

We took the train home. She kept her head high and stared at the opposite wall. I tried not to notice as her lips quivered with indignation and humiliation.

An educated, independent woman, she retained an Irish-Catholic aversion to public displays of emotion. Suffering in all shapes and sizes was to be accepted and turned to a higher purpose. "Offer it up for the poor souls in Purgatory" was her oft-repeated advice. As far as I know, she never complained to the Taxi Commission.

The subways were part of my life from the beginning. An early memory is riding the El from Parkchester to Pelham Bay Park. My brother and I rode the Third Avenue El with my aunt from 23rd Street to 42nd Street. It was sometime in the early 1950s, just before the El was demolished.

Tom and I stood at the window in the first car and watched the towers of Midtown grow more prominent as we approached. I had the feeling of being in a low-flying airplane. Then we went to the Automat. It was a magical day.

▪▪▪

John was my father's older brother. They were very close. They both had degrees in civil engineering from Manhattan College. I have only hazy memories of him. He died when I was five. He worked for the New York City subway. He rose to be head of the budget office or the maintenance department or something in between.

According to my father, my grandmother cradled him in her arms to ride the subway on the day it opened in 1904. I don't like to quibble, but since he was going on four, I think it more likely he held her hand than rested in her arms.

The reason for the convoluted configuration of New York's subways is found in its origins. New York's subways had been built by two private companies and one public. There were endless political squabbles and inter-borough turf wars about where to expand and how to rationalize the system.

Eventually, the city's strapped finances and Robert Moses's monomania for automobile travel put public transit on a starvation diet. The subways stagnated. The superhighways prospered.

My father had his own dustup with Moses when as a member of the state Assembly he proposed acquiring a defunct commuter rail line in the northeast Bronx for incorporation in the subway system.

Moses wanted to use the right-of-way to build a truck route. He wrote my father off as one of those "cheap political fellows" and "smart aleck lawyers" incapable of comprehending the master builder's schemes for the region's future.

My father got into a subsequent tussle with Moses over the building of a connection between Whitestone in Queens and Ferry Point in the Bronx. My father was ready to introduce a bill in the Assembly to build a tunnel under the East River.

Moses quickly batted it aside. He didn't like tunnels. He preferred the soaring monumentality of bridges. It was a bridge that got built. Long before Robert Caro's epic takedown of Moses in *The Powerbroker*, my father regarded him as an insufferable bully.

John thought that with the right investments the city's subway system could be made into a showcase for urban transportation. People in the East Bronx had to ride into Manhattan and transfer at 125th Street to get to the West Bronx.

He imagined a cross-Bronx, east-west subway via Tremont Avenue or Fordham Road that would run from Pelham Bay into northern Manhattan. He said building was only a beginning. Repair and maintenance required eternal vigilance and reinvestment.

The subway's nickel fare lasted for forty-four years. When it was raised to a dime, the public outcry was deafening.

John's was a voice crying out in the wilderness. Without sustained sources of funding, he preached, chaos lay ahead. He despaired at the fecklessness of the city's leadership when it came to public transit. "Does the world's greatest city want to end up with its worst subways?" he agonized.

John died of a stroke at age fifty. My father said the subway killed him. It couldn't have helped.

By the late '70s, the subways were a wretched, graffiti-rife, crime-ridden, breakdown-prone system tottering toward collapse. I wrote Governor Carey's remarks when he unveiled a multi-billion-dollar program to bring the system back from the brink. (Forty years later, another disastrous deterioration testifies to lessons unlearned.)

I went to Grand Central Terminal for the governor's announcement. I didn't put Uncle John's name in the remarks, but I thought of him.

Parkchester's commitment to a "middle-class community" wasn't lip service. Annual income levels for prospective tenants were targeted between $1,800 and $4,800, a plebeian population firmly planted between proles and patricians.

An early enumeration broke it down into roughly 4,200 white-collar workers, 2,700 manual workers (usually unionized), 2,200 service workers, 700 self-employed, 400 retired, and 300 proprietors of small companies. There were significant contingents of teachers, police, firefighters, and Met Life employees.

Parkchester residents developed a reputation as uppity. An exiled Bronxite I met in Denver when I was in VISTA told me, "You Parkchester people acted like your shit didn't stink." The lack of poor and low-income tenants might have helped elevate us, although the Art Deco apartment buildings on the Grand Concourse and neighborhoods of single homes like Pelham and Riverdale ranked far above residences in Parkchester.

We had full-time grounds crews. They polished the place and kept it sprightly. We had the best plumbing in the Bronx, which might account for the theory of odorless feces.

My father was elected to the state Assembly for Parkchester and environs in 1936. He'd met my mother seven years earlier. For the first time, they felt confident enough about the future to get married. The Assembly sat from January to April, when the state budget was passed. Members were paid per diem. He supplemented his income through his law firm at 149th Street, which consisted of himself.

He donated a portion of his time to the Bronx Democratic Organization serving working-class clients pro bono. In 1932, Ed Flynn, the Democratic leader (a.k.a. boss), sent my father to Chicago with a small contingent to keep the New York state delegation from shunning FDR in favor of the much-beloved Al Smith, who'd been thumped in '28. (The delegation stayed with Smith, but FDR got the nod and the presidency.) The hotel room was paid for. His sister lent him the money for the train.

In 1944, he ran for Congress. In a piece published in the *Daily News*, he described his loyalty to the New Deal as rooted in the example of his father, "a coppersmith by trade [who] for half a century stood in the thin front-line of those unsung heroes who led the long, heart-breaking, uphill fight for the rights of the workingman."

For an immigrant's son from the tenements of the Lower East Side, his election was a moment of supreme satisfaction. My mother told me he enjoyed the excitement and spectacle of wartime D.C. He grew close to crusty John McCormack, the future Speaker. Harry Truman banged the piano while my father sang one of his songs.

FDR's address to Congress on his return from Yalta in February '45 was the first time he delivered a speech sitting down. "It was shocking to see how drained and sick he looked," my father said. When FDR died two months later, he was one of the two New York congressmen who rode the funeral train to Hyde Park.

His pay rose to $10,000, a sum that blew through the ceiling of Parkchester's income cap. But the functionaries at Met Life weren't about to ask the district congressman to vacate either his apartment or his seat.

The voters did that for him. He was unseated in the next election. By war's end, after twelve years of controlling the presidency and both houses of Congress, Democrats faced strong headwinds. The odds that my father would retain his seat slipped from probable to highly unlikely when Ed Flynn, opposed to the growth of third parties, prohibited candidates from accepting the endorsement of the left-wing American Labor Party.

The ALP nominated its own candidate. Another independent entered the race. The Republican candidate won with 45 percent of the vote. The unthinkable came to pass. "For the first time," one historian writes, "the Bronx sent an Anglo Republican to Congress." My father's was one of fifty-five seats that changed hands.

After an era hospitable to progressive notions, the weather was changing. In a response to criticism from the American Legion for voting against a resolution turning the House Un-American Activities Committee (HUAC) into a standing (permanent) committee, my father wrote that conferring such status on a body "characterized by merely and solely investigative functions" was "un-orthodox and precedent shattering."

In private, he shared with my mother that "un-American" was such a nebulous term—un-American by whose definition?—it was an invitation to "all sorts of mischief."

The following year the committee considered opening investigations into the Ku Klux Klan but decided against it. Committee member John Rankin of Mississippi posited, "After all, the KKK is an old American institution." The HUAC focused on investigating Communist infiltration of the Works Progress Administration (WPA).

Although he never discussed it, my father's defeat must have been a crushing blow. How could it have been otherwise? A rising star turned into a fallen one. There was talk of appointing him to a federal agency.

My mother said if he wanted to stay in Washington, he had to get a new wife. He joined the law division of the Bronx Department of Engineering (or maybe the Engineering Department of the Law Division) and was again within Parkchester's income constraints.

He was a dedicated Democrat all his life. He banned right-wing publications like Hearst's *Journal American* and Henry Luce's *Time* magazine from our house. (A fact I recalled but didn't divulge when I was hired by Time Inc.)

In 1956, when Tom and I were nine, he took us with him into the voting booth. Adlai Stevenson was running against President Eisenhower, whose wartime reputation helped him make inroads among Northern Catholics.

My father pulled the straight Democratic ticket. He instructed us, "Vote the party, not the man. Each party has its quota of fools, hacks, and scoundrels. But each stands for something, and it's only with a majority can it pass legislation that makes a difference in people's lives." It was one thing to respect and cooperate with people on the other side of the aisle, he said, and another to be cowed or to capitulate.

Redrawn several times over the past seventy years, the congressional district currently represented by Alexandria Ocasio-Cortez includes parts of my father's. An up-and-coming political presence, she resides in Parkchester, close to the apartment where my Aunt Gertie lived and where my grandmother was waked.

Today, Rep. Ocasio-Cortez's district is home to many immigrants and people on the low-to-lowest rungs of the income scale. It suffered one of the country's worst outbreaks of COVID-19. Passionate, angry, eloquent, and a socialist, she put forward the far-left, whacked-out proposition "No family in America should worry about not having enough to eat. No person in America should be too poor to live."

Among her severest critics is Fox News's Tucker Carlson, who ranks foremost among the network's blathering reactionaries, which is saying something, given the intense competition. In his inimitable, sneering, snide, condescending manner, Carlson referred to Ms. Ocasio-Cortez as a "former Bronx bartender." Given this is Fox News, where facts never matter, Carlson had no way of knowing she tended bar in Manhattan.

I'm not sure Tucker Carlson knows where the Bronx is. Raised in La Jolla, California, the son of a former ambassador, he is a favorite of reactionary billionaire Rupert Murdoch and his servile heir. They pay him millions a year to sit in a chair five nights a week and attract eyeballs to advertisements for cars never stuck in traffic and overpriced pharmaceuticals, while spitting venom at minorities and immigrants and the people who represent them.

Since Rep. Ocasio-Cortez owns no property, and her student loans cancel out her savings, "Her current net worth," according to one source, "is likely around $0."

Environment is given a lot of attention. It's not a word I like. It's fussy and fancy, and I never heard it as a kid. Ecology lay in the far, far future. In school we studied geography, a word that predates environment by 300 years. Geography wasn't complicated. There was no need to drag in biology, chemistry, or zoology.

Geography was the multicolored orb on the desk of Mrs. Hoctor, my indulgent, forbearing fifth-grade teacher. It was a decorative prop, not an instructional aid. She didn't use it to teach. The national boundaries dated back to the Spanish–American War.

It was wonderful to look at, bright splotches of reds, yellows, and blues backgrounded by a blackboard as coal dark as outer space. We loved to spin it on its axis and imagine how our planet was turning the same way. We wondered how we couldn't feel it, how solid and still was the ground beneath our feet.

The globe told us where we belonged, a litany of locations that grew more particular as we homed in: Earth, America, New York. I could cover the entire city with the tip of my pinky. The Bronx and Parkchester were subatomic particles.

Geography was big and small. It was the world and our place in it: the El rattling above, the ground-shaking subway beneath; the sprawling zoo and botanic gardens; the imposing red-brick bulk of the Kingsbridge Armory; the palatial Loew's Paradise on the Grand Concourse.

The Bronx is the only borough on the mainland. There are hills and valleys. The land rises as you move north and west. Glaciers did their carving. The continental drift did whatever it does. Outcroppings of rock pointed at geologic time.

We gave little thought to terrain or the peaceful Lenape Indians who lived for millennia in intimate relationship with the land until the Dutch and English drove them out and bulldozers and steam shovels obliterated any trace.

A middle-class agglomeration of apartment houses, single-family homes, and small businesses sprawled between the marshlands of Long Island Sound to the east and the Hudson River to the west, the Bronx was (and still is) a so-called bedroom borough whose north–south subway lines transported its inhabitants to and from jobs in Manhattan.

The borough was a small-scale Yugoslavia. Ethnic enclaves were interspersed amid areas in which, though physically mingled, groups lived psy-chically and culturally apart. We thought of ourselves in terms of neigh-borhoods and parishes.

The Grand Concourse was the Jewish Champs-Élyseés, the tony stem of Jewish neighborhoods that branched out to the east and west. The Bronx was overwhelmingly Jewish, 650,000 out of a population of 1.4 million.

Irwin Horne, a senior clerk I worked with in Bronx Housing Court, grew up in the South Bronx. He reveled in torturing uppity, condescending Midtown lawyers. He told me he spoke Yiddish until he went to school. "There were so many Jews in the neighborhood," he said, "even the anti-Semites were Jews."

Highbridge, Kingsbridge, and Woodlawn were heavily Irish. Belmont, on the southern border of Fordham Road, was a tight-knit Italian village of modest apartment buildings and meticulously tended one- and two-family homes. Centered on Arthur Avenue and Our Lady of Mount Carmel church, it had the best pizza, the best Italian bakeries, the best aromas, the best butchers, and restaurants.

Belmont gained a permanent place in American popular music thanks to Dion (DiMucci) and the Belmonts, the Italian-American quartet whose doo-wop style was the leitmotif of the borough's street life.

The cavernous acoustics of the Fordham Road IND subway station provided a popular practice space for rock 'n' rollers, like gifted, lyrical, died-too-young Laura Nyro, who followed Dion into the Rock and Roll Hall of Fame.

Riverdale, in the borough's northwest corner, felt like an appendage of suburban Westchester County. Home to Arturo Toscanini, Carly Simon, and the elite Horace Mann Day School, the Fieldston neighborhood was a privately owned enclave of privilege and wealth.

In the far east was Orchard Beach, which the WPA built when it wasn't promoting Communism. City Island, an anomalous rustic fishing village connected to the Bronx by a narrow causeway, was where many of the America Cup winners were built. It looked as if a hurricane blew it intact from Boothbay to Pelham Bay.

The marshland to the west was a leading candidate for the city's mu-nicipal airfield, which was eventually located in Queens and christened La Guardia Airport. In the early '60s, Freedomland, a multi-million-dollar American history–themed amusement park, opened. It featured attrac-tions that simulated the Chicago Fire and the San Francisco Earthquake, disasters that presaged the park's rapid descent into bankruptcy.

The area is currently occupied by Co-op City, the country's largest residential development, which was built to help stanch the outflow of the middle class from the Bronx. At times, the swamp it was constructed atop has threatened to swallow it.

Bordering Parkchester, Morris Park to the west and Zerega Avenue to the north were heavily Italian. A step behind in terms of assimilation and economic advancement, Italians generally preferred houses with small gardens to apartments. Parochial schools brought us together.

Friendships blossomed, and so did fights. I remember our schoolyard as an asphalt Serengeti where the weak were bullied and Irish toughs battled tough Italians. (Pugilistically inept, I did my best to blend in with the bricks.) Sometimes the rivalries were humorous. Cancro Carting emblazoned on its garbage trucks "We Cater Irish Weddings." When I heard talk of "intermarriage" it referred to Irish–Italian nuptials.

It wasn't until later that miscegenation escalated into ethnic meltdown and bred a new strain of Hiberno-Mediterranean offspring notable for their good looks.

There was a big dump just north of the Whitestone Bridge. It was unsightly and smelled. The city talked for years about transforming it into a park. The remediation finally came about in 2013 when it debuted as a golf course: Trump Links. There were people who wanted the dump back. After the January 6, 2021, assault on the Capitol, the city fired Trump but kept the course.

I waited for the Bx 20 bus by a perpetually locked public toilet in West Farms. The farmers of West Farms long ago followed their Native American predecessors into the obliterating mists of history.

Across the road was a ditch piled with carcasses of abandoned cars, rusted washing machines, twisted shopping carts. Beneath the accumulated detritus of the industrial age was the Bronx River, which makes the borough the only one with a real-live, freshwater river running through it. Except in the Botanical Garden, where there was a waterfall, we ignored it.

At the terminus of its twenty-four-mile journey, the river flows into the wide mouth between Hunts Point and Soundview into the East River, which, unlike the Bronx, isn't a river but an arm of Long Island Sound.

My father, who knew a lot about the Bronx, told us that in the American Revolution the British were so impressed, they imagined they could sail warships up it.

I haven't been back since a boyhood adventure when we were set upon by a foaming junkyard dog, inspiration enough for me to postpone my next visit indefinitely. Today, the river is undergoing an extensive process of remediation, which is a cause for celebration.

Jonas Bronck was the first European settler. He was from either the Faroe Islands, or Denmark, or the Netherlands, or Sweden. Murky roots also have a long Bronx pedigree. He removed his family to Nieuw Amsterdam, bravely left the confines of the fort to cross the Harlem River (which is a tidal strait, not a river), and settled by the river that eventually took his name.

The Bronx River in turn gave its name to the surrounding environs, which is why, alone among the boroughs, *The* Bronx sports the definite article before its name. There are people who dispute this explanation. Many people in the Bronx will dispute anything.

Flora belonged to the Bronx Botanical Garden, the flower beds and landscaped bushes in Parkchester, and carefully tended front yards. My Uncle Jay, head gardener in a tony housing complex in Washington Heights, had a habit of naming any flowering thing that came into view. I had a habit of not listening.

Dogs weren't allowed in Parkchester. Cats never left their apartments. Mice and rats were largely absent. Squirrels zoomed and roomed where they wanted. Raccoons occasionally strayed from the woodlands of Pelham and Van Cortlandt Parks. Fauna gathered from around the globe were jailed in the Bronx Zoo.

We gawked at the big cats as they angrily prowled the cruel confinement of their bare, concrete cells. They glowered back. We trusted we'd never have a face-to-face outside the zoo. We waited until they took a piss. It was like turning on a firehose. We laughed at the uninitiated who stood too close and went home perfumed with tiger urine.

Some blocks were devoid of trees. Others had plenty. I knew what a pine tree looked like. The difference between an oak and an elm was another story. The one tree I admired was the one Betty Smith claimed for Brooklyn. The ailanthus punched its way out of concrete cracks and prospered in barren lots and asphalt schoolyards. Its greenish flowers smelled—not in a nice way.

Tom and I had a favorite. We were court officers in the Bronx County Courthouse. Some days we drove to work on the Cross Bronx Expressway, a road fatal to any living thing not in a car. Poking out of a battered concrete divider was a scrawny ailanthus. It boldly grew where no other tree grew before, or wanted to.

We watched it survive a stifling, exhaust pipe of a summer. Rags and bits of McDonald's bags and shreds of newspapers clung like poisoned blossoms. At one time it hosted a hubcap. We called it "the ass-kicker tree," a fearless Bronxite that took no shit from nobody.

It lasted until winter came and a semi-trailer crashed into it. We were sad to see it go.

Geography is the place we're grounded, the place we never leave, the mind's terrain, our native land. Hedy Lamarr, perhaps the most beautiful and brainy star in Hollywood's constellation, fled her native Vienna to escape the universal death sentence the Nazis mandated for Jews. Long after, she said that though she never returned, she never left. I don't live in the Bronx anymore, but I'll never leave.

Before it was feared for its poverty and crime, the Bronx was laughed at as a synonym for lower-middle-middle class blah. Ogden Nash quipped superciliously, "The Bronx, no thonx." Some disdained it. In his spirited, celebrated, and misnamed 1949 essay *Here Is New York*, E. B. White gave the Bronx the bum's rush.

What he meant to say was, *Here Is Manhattan*. According to E. B., like Caesar's Gaul, all Gotham is divided into three parts. On the bottom is the "desk-bound" commuter, the "queerest bird of all," a weekday drop-in spewed "out of the mouths of tubes and tunnels."

Tops are the just arrived. This adventurer class, E. B. gushes, "accounts for New York's high-strung disposition, its poetical deportment, its dedication to the arts and its incomparable achievements"; "the girl from small-town Mississippi" who flees "the indignity of being observed by her neighbors" and "embraces New York with the intense excitement of first love"; the Corn Belt kid who arrives with "a manuscript in his suitcase and a pain in his heart . . . Each generates heat and light enough to dwarf the Consolidated Edison Company."

The least interesting, according to E. B., is the lifer, the native, the subway schlub—a kind of urban wallpaper—"who takes the city for granted and accepts its size and turbulence as natural and inevitable."

Contra E. B., not all "incomparable achievements" were distilled and bottled elsewhere. A pathetically paltry list of the city's native-born high achievers includes Herman Melville, Jimmy Cagney, Irving Berlin, Spike Lee, Tony Bennett, Martin Scorsese, Woody Allen, Barbara Stanwyck, Barbra Streisand, Lady Gaga, Fats Waller, Eugene O'Neill, Lou Gehrig, Ira and George Gershwin, Snoop Dog, the Marx Brothers, James Baldwin, Bobby Sanabria, Stanley Kubrick, on and on and on, writers, artists, and actors without whom American culture—high, low, in-between—would be about as rich as Guam's.

A good portion of the metropolis's working-stiffdom was identifiable by its uniforms, many civil service: cops, firemen, and sanitation; doormen too, some in getups worthy of the Hapsburgs; and the elevator operator who whisked E. B. to the offices of *The New Yorker*; and the waitress who served him coffee and a donut at Chock full o'Nuts.

Unionized workers greased the city's machinery and clambered in and out of manholes to repair Con Ed's Rube Goldberg pipe-and-wire maze, so that there was electricity enough to keep the lights on and heat enough to make sure natives and newcomers didn't freeze to death.

E. B. picks out Parkchester for a Bronx cheer. Among the "high in purpose, low in rent" housing projects, some public, some privately owned, sprouting around the city, "One of them in the Bronx," he writes, "accommodates twelve thousand families, sky acreage hitherto untilled, lifting people high above the street, standardizing their sanitary life, giving them some place to sit other than on an orange crate."

Parkchesterites were no strangers to the flush toilet. If my mother wondered where she left her orange crate, I wasn't listening. What they shared with the rest of the Bronx was attitude. It was hard to reach the age of six and not have already been told "You're full of shit." People were phonies, dickheads, empty suits—take your pick—until proven otherwise.

Along with etched-with-acid sarcasm, an arsenal of profanities, and a withering sense of humor was a hatred of snobs, an underlying decency, a sympathetic grasp that what separated haves from have-nots weren't genes but birth, circumstance, and luck. The people of the Bronx remain the funniest, earthiest, in-your-face truth tellers I ever met.

When I began as a speechwriter, I got a last-minute invite from the governor to a black-tie event. I didn't have a black tie or the outfit that went with it. I called my mother to see if she still had my father's tux.

She didn't but told me to call Marvin's Formal Wear on Castle Hill Avenue and mention that I worked for the governor. I did, which is as far as I got before Marvin, in his admirable, inimitable Bronx-Jewish fuck-you drawl, said, "G'won, I'm impressed."

Few Bronx neighborhoods were without a gang. These varied from loosely organized social clubs to tight-knit, turf-conscious, ethno-centric groups that fought (rumbled) with rivals from nearby neighborhoods. Atop the food chain were the nasty antisocial criminals-in-training who pilfered and intimidated and were branded with the opprobrious appellation "juvenile delinquents."

Richard Price, a native Bronxite and highly accomplished novelist and screenwriter, wrote a novel about the Wanderers. The most ferocious of the lot were the Fordham Baldies, a bad-ass wolfpack of marauding, penitentiary-bound juvenile delinquents. Heads shaved Mohawk-style, they raided schools, pushed aside nuns, wrecked classrooms, and robbed teachers and pupils. The police absented themselves at word they were coming.

We lived in terror of the Baldies, only we never saw them or knew any witness to their depredations. They resided in the same fourth dimension as the neighborhood kids who climbed down the sewers to retrieve a ball or coin and were dragged away by alligators, never to be seen again.

There are those who continue to insist that the Baldies were real. They remember times and places. A friend had a cousin whose cousin's cousin was a member. I have a cousin who saw the Loch Ness monster. He can tell you the exact day and place.

The borough had only one real hotel, the Concourse Plaza. It was often referred to as "the Bronx's Waldorf Astoria," a description more aspirational than exact, which is not to say it wasn't a fine place to spend the night.

A Mickey Mantle home run away from Yankee Stadium, the Concourse Plaza is at the center of the 1956 movie *A Catered Affair*, a tale of working-class Irish-Catholic parents in conflict over their daughter's wedding reception. My wife's parents had their disputation-free reception there several years before.

In an improbable feat of casting, the taxi-driving Irish-Catholic dad is played by Ernest Borgnine, the daughter by Debbie Reynolds, and the mother by Bette Davis, whose attempt at a Bronx accent strays between misfire and weird. (Barry Fitzgerald, her brother, has a rich Irish brogue, a discrepancy left unexplained.)

The movie was based on a television play by native son Paddy Chayefsky. The previous year he won the Academy Award for best screenplay for *Marty*, another Bronx tale with Ernest Borgnine in his Oscar-winning role as an Italian-American butcher.

I recall *Marty*'s getting accolades from relatives and neighbors. Scenes shot in the Bronx and mention of places like Fordham Road and Arthur Avenue sprinkled Hollywood stardust over the borough's prosaic precincts.

As opposed to *Marty*, which had a ring of authenticity, *A Catered Affair* was a blatant attempt to piggyback on the success of its predecessor, with Irish characters substituted for Italian. The screenplay was written by Gore Vidal, who, if pressed, could probably have located the Bronx somewhere between Montreal and the Upper East Side. The movie earned mostly raspberries.

***

I'm the poster boy for parochial. I never set foot in a public school. I went from kindergarten to the last stages of a Ph.D. in Bronx Catholic institutions. I was raised in St. Raymond's parish. I attended the same parish grammar school as my father. He graduated in 1918. Tom and I finished in 1961.

In the eighth grade, I sat in the same scarred oak desk he had. The iron legs were bolted to the floor. It had an inkwell. Charles Dickens would have been at home.

My brother and I spent the better part of a decade trudging down Metropolitan Avenue each morning to our parish school. We were taught by the Sisters of Charity and the De LaSalle Christian Brothers.

The nuns wore black bonnets and habits. The laminated collars worn by the black-robed brothers resembled the tablets of the Ten Commandments Charlton Heston hauled down from Mount Sinai. Laywomen teachers filled in the gaps.

My art teacher, Miss O'Neill, was one of the three maiden daughters of Bronx Sheriff John O'Neill. Her white hair pulled back in a bun, her immaculate white blouse and same gray suit freshly pressed and meticulously clean, she was pretty with lively blue eyes. Her face was wrinkleless. She seemed ageless.

She taught my father nearly fifty years before. I did the same color wheels he did. A generation later she taught my niece, who did the same wheel. On the improbable chance she's still alive, I wish her the best.

St. Raymond's had a new school and an old school. The old school, on the corner of Metropolitan Oval and Castle Hill Avenue, dated back to the beginning of the century. It had all the charm of a precinct house.

The yellow-brick new school was built in the early '50s. Cardinal Francis Spellman and my father were the main speakers at the dedication. In private, my father was contemptuous of the cardinal's barely disguised Republican sympathies.

I have no idea of the cardinal's estimation of my father. My guess is it wasn't entirely favorable. In public, their relationship was cool but respectful.

Boys and girls spent two years in the new school under the care of the nuns, then the boys moved to the old school and the Christian Brothers. We knew nothing about the backgrounds of the nuns and brothers who taught us. They took religious names when they made their vows.

What we didn't know we invented. We pictured Sister Liguori as a café singer before entering the convent. We never heard her sing, but she was lovely enough to have been. We imagined Brother Robert as an ex-prizefighter who killed another fighter in the ring, and his self-imposed penance was to teach arithmetic to boys in the Bronx. Maybe he was too hard on himself.

Class sizes were between forty and fifty students. We were either smart or stupid. There was no special-needs teacher or assistance for those with emotional or cognitive challenges. (I'm told public schools weren't much better.) I had a sister with eye problems. Even with my parents' support, she was traumatized by the treatment she received.

Harried, often undertrained, overwhelmed by class sizes, teachers varied from kind, understanding, and compassionate to brutal martinets with no business in a classroom.

For families registered in the parish, school was free. In some cases, the church was in a basement and the school above. Through most of grammar school, I was bored. Creativity wasn't a priority. Passing civil service tests was.

The schools provided the education parents wanted. We aimed for decent salaries, job security, and reliable benefits, not the stars. Given their limited resources and proscription of public funding, parochial schools did a remarkable—and largely unheralded—job in creating the city's middle class.

It was a lucky break for the public schools, since without parish schools, they'd have been hard-pressed to serve all the students.

Although I know people whose lives were permanently damaged by abuse that resulted in the rape and abuse of thousands of children and has done so much to discredit the clergy—especially the hierarchy who did their best to keep it secret—I was never a victim. In those days, the subject was tightly under wraps. Laity and clergy alike were faithful to the code of *omertà*. As far as I knew, priests and brothers were asexual, free of temptations and transgressions.

Like Dostoevsky's protagonist in *Notes from the Underground*, "I mainly used to read. Reading was a great help—it stirred, delighted, and tormented me." The torment came from the exotic worlds reading and my expanding imagination conjured up.

I heard kids talk about "dirty books." I knew they existed the way I knew sex existed. I knew I wasn't going to handle them anytime soon. My bookworming focused on historical fiction and nonfiction.

There was a series of histories under the Landmark imprint aimed at young readers. I peeked in the window of Womrath's, our local bookstore, with an addict's fretful ache for the next fix. My parents' rule was, unless I was sick, I couldn't stay in the house on a sunny day.

I remember a summer on Shelter Island feigning maladies sufficient to finish a series of Civil War novels but not raise my parents' suspicions. When my mother threatened to whisk me back to the city to see a specialist, I knew I had been unmasked. Often enough, the books I chose were above my reading level. That only fed my habit.

I was an athletic nonentity in a parish and neighborhood where ball-playing stardom—especially basketball—wasn't merely an avocation but an apotheosis. My brother, Tom, got into basketball and became good at it. I never did.

It didn't make any difference to our relationship. Tom and I are fraternal rather than identical. Heavier and taller than I, he's always been more athletic. His hair didn't start thinning until he was in his sixties; mine in my thirties. Physically different, in our souls we're nearly identical.

Being a twin circumvented the childhood search for a close friend, which some find problematic, even traumatic. When Tom and I were small, people noticed how we interacted in our crib, cooperated as we played, and ganged up on neighbors' children who had been left with us.

My mother said that when we babbled our incoherent babytalk, it seemed we were conversing with each other in our own secret language. (Maybe we were.)

Our bond hasn't been the Corsican Brothers' type, Alexandre Dumas's fictional twins who felt the other's physical and emotional distress. We preferred to think of ourselves as Sicilian Twins, a quasi-clandestine, blood-bonded brotherhood.

We were put in different classes in the sixth grade. The teacher explained to my mother that we behaved like "co-conspirators." She wasn't wrong. We conspired—in its original meaning, breathed together—since we left our mother's womb.

We made our own friends, but whoever became friends with one became friends with the other. The bond between us, I think, had a centripetal pull, drawing others in. Instead of referred to separately as Peter and Tom, we were often identified collectively as "the Quinn twins."

It turned out that we both made our livings as writers. Maybe what motivated us was genetic. But given how few famous authors have sired equally famous progeny, I'm doubtful about any connection between genes and writing.

Our shared childhoods had something to do with it, although I know twins who, despite almost identical upbringings, have gone in entirely different directions.

When we were kids, my father placed a stepladder in front of the stand on which he kept his hefty unabridged Webster's dictionary. Whenever we asked about a word, he told us to look it up.

Mounting the steps felt like approaching an altar. The dictionary had the feel of the missal from which the priest recited the Mass. Words took on a sacredness, a way of defining not just language but ourselves. Maybe that's the best explanation for why words and writing have always been central to Tom and me.

Founded in 1842, St. Raymond's was the first Catholic parish in Westchester County. (The Bronx became a separate state county in 1914. The five boroughs of New York City are coterminous with state counties.) In the old burial yard in front of the church are three towering Celtic crosses. Monuments to the half-century reign of a triad of Irish *monsignori* who cast a cold eye on the oblivious passersby.

The "new" St. Raymond's Cemetery, which is well over a hundred years old, is run by the archdiocese. It's located in Throggs Neck, which a recent *Times* article described as "an obscure corner of the Bronx," a borough that, for the *Times*, is made up of obscure corners. Among the 500,000 (and counting) resting in its obscure corners are Freddy Lyman, Billie Holiday, and my father-in-law.

The opening scene in Alice McDermott's award-winning *Charming Billy* takes place in a post-funeral gathering in a bar across the street, on Tremont Avenue. The necropolis enjoyed fifteen minutes of fame for its part in the Lindbergh kidnapping. The one time I was inside was on a magical-mystery tour bus with an international band of Lindbergh-kidnapping fanatics. We visited the site where the ransom was paid.

A story floated around about a kid from St. Raymond's who got picked out by a talent scout who whisked him to Hollywood, where he became a star. He was variously recalled as Kelly something—Emmett, Colin, certainly not Grace. Somebody said his name was Murphy. But not George or Audie. Whatever.

Since I never spied *stardom* and *St. Raymond's* in the same sentence, I wrote it off as a side effect of the incurable fame-yearning fever that rampaged through Bronx streets, like wind-lofted pages of the *Daily News* on blowy spring afternoons.

Years later, I read a *Times* obituary that turned Bronx myth into Hollywood flesh. One of thirteen children (some accounts say one of five), Tommy Kelly was a sixth-grader at St. Raymond's in 1937. There was never a lot of luxury in the East Bronx. There was an abundance of dreams that the Depression knocked the wind out of. Kelly's father was receiving assistance through the WPA.

In a not-unusual instance of PR braggadocio, David O. Selznick claimed that 25,000 boys were interviewed for the lead role in an upcoming movie, *The Adventures of Tom Sawyer.* How a talent scout landed inside St. Raymond's is hard to figure. If his car broke down, there were plenty of nearby garages; if he was lost, the sidewalks were filled with passersby happy to tell him where to go.

When Kelly made the cut, Selznick directed a Professor Henry Higgins–style remake. According to his obituary, he "spent an hour a day with a speech coach to de-Runyonize his diction." The reviews for Selznick's 1938 Technicolor adaptation of Twain's classic were good, but the box office wasn't.

Selznick tried again with Tommy as the lead in *Peck's Bad Boy with the Circus*. The result was the same. The next year, Kelly had a small but memorable part in Selznick's history-twisting epic *Gone with the Wind*. Other roles followed, but nothing that led to cement handprints on the Walk of Fame.

As far as I'm aware, Hollywood talent scouts never revisited St. Raymond's. It seems Tommy never reappeared. Maybe he wasn't interested in revisiting a Depression-era childhood with his family on public assistance. Maybe he wasn't nostalgic about the Bronx. Not everybody is, often with good reason. One way or another, there was never a "Welcome Back Tommy Kelly Day."

⠶

Those who forget the past are often happier than those who remember. That was my mother's philosophy. She was an anti-genealogist. "Lost relatives are usually lost for a reason," she said. When my father died, she disposed of the binders in which he kept press clippings, naturalization papers, death certificates, bits and pieces of family history.

When I learned what she did, I exploded, "You had no right. That belonged to all of us." She was unbothered. "It was excess baggage," she said.

Some bags were more loaded than others. My mother's eldest sister eloped with Bill Brady, a milkman. Even in old age, she was striking, erect, elegant. She always kept a picture of Bill on her bureau. He wore his hair slicked back. He had sharp features and wore horn-rimmed glasses that made him look like Joe Kennedy.

Like my aunt, he was the child of Irish immigrants. They were both hardworking and ambitious. Employed as a bookkeeper, she was promoted to manager. He bought the truck and expanded the milk route. She became his assistant. They sold the truck and bought the garage, then added another garage and a warehouse. He made friends easily and formed connections.

He became a bail bondsman. They bought a spacious house on Summit Avenue in Hackensack and had two children. They were preparing for a vacation in Florida when he dropped dead of a heart attack. So the story went.

When I turned eighteen, in a hurry to find my birth certificate so I could get a draft card and stop using phony proof, I made an unauthorized search through my father's papers. I skimmed news clippings about politics and court cases until a front-page banner headline stopped me: "GANGSTER GUNS SPIT DEATH TO WM. A. BRADY; SLAIN FROM AMBUSH AT HIS HACK- ENSACK HOME: KID STEECH SEIZED, CHARGED WITH MURDER."

The story was splashed across the front page of the January 17, 1931, *Bergen Evening Record*: "Thus ended a ten-year saga: From Milkman to Millionaire" . . . "Before he died Big Bill Brady, close-mouth and shrewd in life, had blurted out the names of his assailants to his life-long friend, former Lieutenant Garrett A. Dawson of the county detectives."

The story, which could have been out of *Front Page*, was a gruesome mix of noir fact and noir fiction:

> Brady, having finished supper at 7 o'clock last night, adjusted his derby at a rakish angle, lit a cigar, and announced: "I'm going down to the office."
>
> Then he kissed his wife good-bye and stepped out of the side door. A moment later the smooth hum of his expensive automobile began. Brady was going for a ride, but he didn't know it yet.
>
> The car slid slowly backward down the driveway toward Summit Avenue, Brady peering through the rear window.
>
> As it reached the sidewalk he saw that which made his blood run cold. Two men stood a dozen feet up the sidewalk toward the south, leaning against a long-slung coupe whose engines purred pre- paredness.
>
> Leaving the engine of his car running, Brady opened the door and flung himself out, but as he sprinted for the haven of his door, the first bullets struck. One chipped off a button of his overcoat; another ripped his cigar to pieces. Brady, struck by buckshot in his right leg, started a limping gallop, screaming for help.
>
> Around the house he ran—all the way around—while the gushing wounds in his leg wrote a bloody odyssey behind him and behind ran two crouching men, blazing away. They trapped him at the side door of his house. Unarmed, Bill Brady turned a man at bay, and took what was coming to him. Ten feet away, point-blank, the killers riddled his body with seventeen bullets.

That night, the police arrested Joey Borgiorno—a.k.a. Kid Steech—and charged him with the murder. Thomas and Louis Priori were held as ma- terial witnesses. They put out an all-points bulletin for Joey Szabio—a.k.a. Tony Fabbio/Chicago Fats—and Guillermo Moretti—a.k.a. Willie Ward/ Willie Moore.

They did their best to make sure Bill Brady told no tales. "His right arm was torn to shreds," the *Bergen Journal* reported, "but the wounds that killed him were low in his abdomen." The story left out that my aunt and her two children were at the kitchen door when the final bullets were fired.

She cradled him in her arms until the police came. Her pink dress was soaked in blood. Amazingly, given the riddling he received, he lived long enough to receive last rites and give a statement that named his killers.

I devoured the story. I thought it involved one of my father's early cases. I don't remember when I grasped this WM. A. BRADY was our William Brady. The uncle who died of a heart attack turned out the victim of a classic Prohibition-era rubout. I talked to my older sister. She knew and warned me never to raise it with our parents.

When Moretti and Szabio came to trial that August, Bill Brady's statement had vanished. They went free and enjoyed successful careers as murderers, extortionists, and drug traffickers. Szabio, who earned the alias Chicago Fats working for Al Capone, ran the gambling racket in northern New Jersey. He died peacefully in Italy, in 1947.

Moretti became a member of the board that operated, according to one chronicler, "one of the most fantastic empires in the history of America's underworld, an empire that eventually spread to Southern California, Las Vegas, Miami and Havana."

He's most remembered for plucking Hoboken crooner Frank Sinatra from obscurity. He supposedly served as the model for the mobster in *The Godfather* who sticks a severed horsehead in the bed of a record executive who won't let a singer out of his contract. Sinatra, Dean Martin, Jerry Lewis, and Milton Berle all performed at Moretti's daughter's wedding.

Syphilis ate Moretti's brain. He blabbed in public about mob business. He was shot twice in the head in a Cliffside Park restaurant in 1951. An associate whispered to the press that it was a "mercy killing."

The Brady case lingered in the press a while. Big Bill Brady shrank back to William Brady, 5'10", 170 lbs. Once touted in the press as "Reported King of the Bergen Underworld," he reverted to an unwitting pawn in a game played for keeps.

What his transgression was is unclear. The press speculated it involved a raid on the warehouse he owned and the confiscation of a cache of illegal whiskey. The police scotched the rumor that he was an informer. Whatever it was—real or imagined—it brought down the full firepower of the mob.

I debated writing a novel about the murder. I called the Hackensack police to see if the files still existed. The detective I talked to never heard of Bill Brady or Willie Moretti. I had to convince him I wasn't pulling a prank. I decided I didn't want to spend time with Moretti. He had attention enough. I moved on to write a novel about an unrelated case set in the same era. I occasionally ran across characters from the Brady case in my research.

My aunt's two children both died in their thirties. She married again. It was short and unsweet. I'll always remember her as poised, handsome, and generous to us all.

In my mother's last days, I spoke to her about her sister. My mother didn't ask how I knew. "Your poor aunt," she said. "It was a crucifixion."

Families are entitled to their secrets. That doesn't mean they go away.

Built before the war, Parkchester wasn't wired for air conditioning. Movie theaters advertised "COOL INSIDE" on their marquees. In the middle of a brutal early June heat wave, my father took us for the one and only time to the movies. We saw *The Ten Commandments*. Twice. It was the beginning of my lifelong aversion to Charlton Heston.

Whether for the day or week or whatever they could swing, all who could get out of Parkchester did. Some to the Catskills ("The Jewish Alps"), or the Rockaways ("The Irish Riviera"), or the Jersey Shore, or the Poconos, anywhere there was relief from the stultifying bake of apartments unwired for air conditioning.

Willie Moretti brought us to Shelter Island. The murder of her husband, carried out in front of her eyes, left my aunt shattered. Her mother and sisters cared for the children. She became hysterical at the thought that the murderers might return to kill them. Someone was always with her.

My grandparents resisted institutionalizing her, even in a posh sanitorium. For Irish immigrants like them, institutions, no matter how genteel, retained the stigma acquired in Ireland, the shame and indignities heaped on those put away in poorhouses and public asylums, people whose families were unable or unwilling to care for them. As a general principle, hospitals were where you went to die.

Months went by. Priests and doctors were consulted. One suggested taking her to some remote, quiet place, away from everything that could remind her of the murder. A friend of my father's suggested an island tucked between the north and south forks of Long Island. It was a four-and-a-half-hour drive from the city, through the flat farmlands of Long Island. "You want dull," he said, "you'll fall in love with Shelter Island."

The first time my father saw it, he did. It was the summer of 1931. Hilly and green, sleepy and remote, the island was a place where my father convinced my aunt she'd feel safe. She rented a spacious, rambling Victorian in the Heights, on a bluff overlooking Peconic Bay.

Billy Brady was shrewd with his money. In the depths of the Depression with burgeoning Hoovervilles and growing breadlines, my aunt enjoyed a substantial income. She became a one-woman welfare agency.

She brought along the whole family—her kids, her brother who was out of work, her sisters whose small savings were flushed when the local bank failed, her mother and pension-less father who was still working at seventy, my mother and her fiancé (my father) who was making five dollars a week as a law clerk.

The house was big enough that no one felt crowded. Lena, her German cook, prepared the food, which was plentiful. There were picnics and cocktails before dinner, afternoons lazing at the beach. My mother noticed that for the first time since her husband's assassination, my aunt's taut face began to soften. Cousins and friends came and went.

Shelter Island had been a bustling resort at the turn of the century. There was a boat from Wall Street to the sprawling Manhasset House. Visitors took the Long Island Railroad from the city to its terminus in Greenport. The Heights was founded by well-off Protestant families from Brooklyn as a Chautauqua-style summer camp. Tents were replaced by cottages and substantial homes.

The island gradually faded as a resort. The Manhasset House burned down. The boat from Wall Street stopped coming. Those with the means preferred Europe to the sleepy end of Long Island. The Heights' founding families stayed on. The Crash of '29 was a crushing blow to those dependent on investments. Houses went up for sale at please-take-this-off-my-hands prices. Still, no matter the economic exigencies, the arrival of the first Irish Catholic family was a jolt for many.

A real estate agent explained to my father, "Up until now, most of the Irish have been cooks and maids."

My mother's family was content to be left alone. They weren't eager for anyone to pry into why they'd come to the island. On the other hand, they were stung by the slights, intended and otherwise. They were advised to not bother applying to the Heights Yacht Club, which wouldn't entertain the notion of Catholic members. Bereft of a boat, they had no desire to join. Nonetheless, the "need not apply" rankled.

The beach club was part of the Prospect Hotel and open to all. That didn't mean all were welcomed equally. Half-century later, my normally forgiving mother bitterly recalled a WASP dowager who made a point of turning her head whenever they came into view. Neighbors kept a polite if icy distance.

My mother struck up a conversation with a woman on the deck of the beach club. She remarked on the large number of people at my aunt's house: "Are you all related?" she said skeptically, as if my aunt might be running an illicit boarding house. My mother smiled and said, "As far as I can tell, yes."

My father and Uncle Jay went fishing on a chartered boat. The more beer, the friendlier their fellow fishermen became. One of them asked what my family enjoyed most about the island. My father said, "Everything." The man said they were fortunate to have a Catholic church on the island. It wasn't always the case. "It was built," he grinned, "because the Irish help was too hungover on Sunday mornings to row to Mass in Greenport."

More times than not, familiarity breeds not contempt but acceptance, or at least indifference. My aunt rented houses for the next fifteen years, right through the war. My cousin was drafted. The national emergency eroded old attitudes. My family's arrival each summer became expected, or at least went unremarked on.

The island grew sleepier. The Hurricane of '38 destroyed docks, felled hundreds of trees, and flooded homes. The Prospect Hotel burned down. The volunteer fire department's motto was "We never lost a foundation." My father turned forty. My parents had a second daughter. He was elected to Congress.

In Congress, he became friendly with fellow member Jim Roe, the Democratic leader of Queens. Roe had purchased Westmoreland, a large estate and working farm in foreclosure. There were barns, stables, a manor house, and a brick water tower that was the tallest structure on Shelter Island.

He built a number of no-frills summer bungalows. My parents rented North Ridge cottage. There was no danger of suspicion or disdain or just-under-the-surface resentment of Irish Catholics because practically everybody was.

<hr/>

Despite all belonging to the genus of B.I.C. (Bronx Irish Catholic), we at St. Raymond's Elementary School considered ourselves distinctly different from—and a degree above—our counterparts in the cheek-by-jowl parish of St. Helena's.

An upstart addition dictated by the swollen number of Catholics attracted to Parkchester, the parish had to divide students into morning and afternoon sessions. Devoid of St. Raymond's majestic marble baldachin and magnificent stained glass, the church had the spare, functional feel of a train station or bomb shelter.

St. Helena's had three things going for it. Air conditioning. Friday night dances that attracted teenagers from across the Bronx and boroughs beyond. And Monsignor Arthur Scanlan.

An ascetic stalk with steel-gray hair brushed in the upright style of General von Hindenburg, he swayed up and down the aisles during Mass in a frayed cassock and cracked leather high-tops. He heard confessions every day for hours at a time. He had a saintly air.

When a local Jewish group tried to buy nearby land to build a synagogue, the owner refused to sell. Scanlan bought the land and sold it to them at cost.

In St. Raymond's, nonsexual sins of the type that didn't involve homicide or grand larceny were usually treated mildly. Offenses of the flesh were subject to a rigorous, Perry Mason–type cross-examination.

All who dreaded confessing certain sins or who lived in parishes in which confessors word-whipped penitents with tirades that stirred the confessional's purple curtain poured their mortal and venial sins into the monsignor's ear.

There was always a line outside his confessional, especially long on Saturdays, the day assigned for confessions. Whatever sins he was told, Scanlan forgave, asked the sinner to pray for him, assigned a penance, and sent him on his way.

My most indelible memory of Scanlan is the fall of 1962, during the Cuban missile crisis. I was a sophomore at Manhattan Prep when Brother George, the principal, announced that as soon as the sirens sounded, the student body of 300 pimpled, sex-obsessed, pubescent boys would proceed to the basement—a moldy and windowless chamber—where we'd stay until "the conflict ended."

One student asked at what point we could go home. Brother George, a grim Teuton and dour disciplinarian, replied that if Civil Defense approved, and there still was a home to go to, we'd be notified. The sheer absurdity of my life ending in a hellish cloud of radioactive dust before I had the chance to kiss a girl or travel west of New Jersey left a permanent scar on my psyche.

Greater than dread of nuclear immolation, which had the advantage of being mercifully brief, was anticipation of Hell's endless flaming tortures. Dying in a state of mortal sin meant that hope of a pardon or a sentence reduced for good behavior went up in smoke. Hell was instantaneous and forever.

Wracked by fear that our previous confession(s) might be imperfect or a random impure thought might be held against us, my brother and I went to confession every night of the crisis.

For the duration of the crisis, the line outside Monsignor Scanlan's confessional stretched into the street. No matter. We prayed the bomb wouldn't hit before we had our turn.

My parents were devout and educated Catholics. Both had graduated from Catholic colleges, my mother as a classics major, my father as an engineer and lawyer. They were voracious readers. They made Catholic prayers and rituals an important part of our lives.

At the center of Catholic worship is the Mass. In the days before the Second Vatican Council, it was said in Latin by a priest who faced the altar, with his back to the congregation. The altar was fenced behind a rail that kept the laity at a distance.

Unchanged since the fifteenth-century Council of Trent, the Latin Mass exuded tradition and mystery. It also embodied, as one critic put it, a "recondite antiquarianism" that left many congregants uninvolved or saying the rosary instead of following the rite.

Altar boys had a special place. (Altar girls were a nonstarter.) We alone accompanied the priest as he said Mass. We alone gave the ancient Latin responses. Whether we understood them was another matter. Sometimes laminated cheat cards were available to read from. Other times not.

Both governors I wrote for were outer-borough ethnic Catholics who'd been altar boys. What we had in common involved experience, not ideology or dogma, references that didn't have to be explained, the shorthand of a New York Catholic childhood. The more the Latin rite receded, the more nostalgic—and proud—we became of our mastery of the banished language. It grew into a bond of sorts, the way a vanished past often does.

The *Suscipiat*, a tongue-torturing response to the priest's injunction "*Orate frates*" (Pray brethren), was the great test. If he detected mistakes

or mispronunciations, a priest in my parish instructed us to say it over—
and over—until we got it right.

I accompanied Governor Cuomo up the Capitol's opulent Million Dollar Staircase (back in the day, a million was a lot of money) to the legislative
chamber where he delivered the annual State of the State address. He
started the *Suscipiat*, and I joined in. We made our way flawless through
the thicket of "*ad utilitatem quoque nostram, totiusque ecclesiae suae
sanctae*."

The people with us, non-Catholics and post–Vatican II Catholics,
looked at us quizzically. At the top of the stairs, one of them whispered to
me, "Was that Pig Latin?" I shook my head. "Ixnay," I said.

On a snowy day, I rode on the state helicopter with Governor Carey to
Hyde Park for the commemoration of FDR's centenary. The ground was
icy. I reached up my hand as he got off. "*Introibo ad altare Dei*," he said.
"I go unto the altar of God."

The opening line of the Mass (expropriated by ex–altar boy James Joyce
for the first paragraph of *Ulysses*), it was spoken by the priest as part of
the prayers at the foot of the altar. I responded with words embedded in
the mind of every altar boy, "*Ad Deum qui laetificat juventutem meum*."

"To God who gives joy unto my youth."

The Feast of Corpus Christi paid tribute to the Blessed Sacrament with a
special procession. The priest placed the consecrated host behind a glass
monocle in the middle of an elegant gold reliquary in the shape of a sun-
burst. Hands folded in his cope, he elevated the monstrance.

Four altar boys assigned as pole bearers held the gold-embroidered
canopy above. One altar boy, designated thurifer, swung the gold censer.
Incense billowed into the high recesses of the nave.

I was sent with other altar boys from St. Raymond's to serve in the cardinal's procession in St. Patrick's. We were given our roles. I prayed to share
the relative anonymity of the pole bearers. I was made thurifer. There
was a brief, spur-of-the-moment rehearsal. I was shown the point where
I turned, faced Francis Cardinal Spellman, and swung the censer high
three times.

The day was hot, the cathedral packed. A thousand eyeballs were trained
on the procession. My parents were somewhere in the congregation. The

choir broke in the ancient, moving Latin hymn *Pange lingua*. I walked ahead with solemn step, conscious that if I went too slowly, I'd jam everything up; too fast, I'd leave it behind. I was the only one who could screw it up.

The cool interior of the cathedral turned stuffy. At the designated turning point, I turned to the monstrance-bearing cardinal archbishop. Counselor to popes and presidents, the country's leading Catholic prelate—a Republican-leaning partisan in my father's eyes—he infused a near-bankrupt archdiocese with such financial prowess that the Vatican looked to it for support. He was perspiring heavily.

He lifted the monstrance. I swung the censer. Beads of sweat ran down my sides. I swung it a last time. A puff of smoke rose into my mouth and eyes.

I panicked at the thought I'd have a coughing fit, or stumble, or both. The obloquy would follow me into the next world. I took a gulp of air, planted my foot, and swiveled a perfect pirouette. Sometimes the happiest things in your life are the things that don't happen. The applause I heard was in my head.

***

The Catholic boyhood is often said—especially by Catholics—to be, by varying degree, difficult, painful, intolerable. I don't imagine boyhood is a picnic for Hasids or Baptists. I've no idea about Muslims.

Maybe it's a bump-less ride for the indigenous young on a remote South Seas Island spared the neuroses of modern adolescence. For the rest, it involves the awkwardness and confusion Yeats poignantly described as "The ignominy of boyhood; the distress/Of boyhood changing into man/The unfinished man and his pain."

I was clueless about the how-to component of sex longer than most of my classmates. My parents slept in different beds. Our apartment had one bathroom. I had two sisters but never saw a tampon.

My mother had a private coming-of-age discussion with my sisters. The possibility that my father would do the same with my brother and me was as likely as Dwight Eisenhower's having phone sex with Marilyn Monroe.

My father left the room when a Maidenform bra ad appeared on TV. My mother complained, "Do you want the boys to think their father was the milkman?" If it meant he didn't have to open a can of procreative worms with us, he sided with the milkman.

At school, our introduction to sex was mummy-wrapped in mystery and foreboding. Come a young age, we were required to make an examination of conscience and go to confession, sometimes once a week.

Mulling the sin in your head, deciding if you collaborated and willingly put yourself in "the near occasion of sin," raised the stakes. It was double or nothing. A bad confession, willingly withholding a mortal sin, added a mortal sin to the original.

As necessary as marriage was to continue the human race, it was a step down from celibacy. Sex came up in the context of sinful desires, impure thoughts, unspeakable deeds. We didn't linger on commandment one (idolatry) or six (murder).

Neither seemed likely. Seven (adultery) and ten (coveting your neighbor's wife)—sins of the flesh—were emphasized. I was unconcerned. Our neighbor's wife was Nora Cassidy, a slight, soft-spoken Irishwoman who worked as a waitress at Schrafft's. I was very fond of her but not in the sense of coveting.

As I made my way through the distress of adolescence and alternately welcomed and resisted the luscious succubi and their seductive invitations to impure thoughts and deeds, confession grew more challenging. Despite absolution and the firm resolution to sin no more, temptation trumped intention, biology triumphed theology.

Once a year, we stood at Mass to swear allegiance to the Legion of Decency. Maybe there were brave souls who stayed seated and silent, but I never spotted them. Dedicated to safeguarding the faithful, the Legion required oath takers to "remain away from places of entertainment" that showed films "dangerous to moral life."

The Legion's weekly rating list separated films into three categories: A (morally unobjectionable); B (morally objectionable in part for all); C (condemned). The list was posted at the back of the church and was featured in the *Catholic News*. My father was a stickler for consulting the list.

Each week, the youth of the parish went directly to the C-list to identify the movies we'd choose if we could figure how to fake looking old enough to be let in. Sometimes, when a particularly objectionable film arrived, we studied the posters and still photos displayed in the front of the theater.

The Circle Theater, located across from the El on the fringe of Parkchester, lacked the restrictions on chains like RKO or Loew's, which rarely risked running C movies. Along with independent films and reruns, the Circle spiced its fare with a selection of the salacious.

The titles on the marquee provided a titillating taste of the main course: *Never on Sunday*, *I Am a Camera*, and *The Third Sex*.

One Saturday, the Circle Theater's marquee heralded *And God Created*

Woman, starring Brigitte Bardot. Though her name meant nothing to me, the movie title was immediately recognizable from the C-list. I leaned in for a closer look at one of the photos.

A woman lay on her stomach facing the camera. Her lower half was covered by a rumpled sheet. Her elbows were propped on a pillow in a way that exposed the top of her breasts and cleavage. Her thick blonde hair was tousled and wild. The hint of a smile on her full, pouty lips suggested she was ready to do again whatever she'd just done.

I temporarily froze. Brigitte's voluptuousness, the insouciance of her smile, her tossed and abundant tresses, spoke to me of a world I knew existed but had never been able to conjure in all its fleshy splendor.

In his chance encounter with the young, radiant Beatrice Portinari, Dante saw an embodiment of purity and divine beauty. Mademoiselle Bardot sent my imagination spinning in the opposite direction. I had my first bite of the apple.

It wasn't until five decades later that I saw *And God Created Woman* on Turner Classic Movies. Brigitte was indeed sultry, beautiful, and sexy. The notion that the movie—with its inane plot and peek-a-boo sex—threatened the foundations of the moral order says more about the would-be censors' fear of female sexuality than any threat to public decency.

⋮⋮⋮

The word *masturbation* was mostly avoided. "Self-abuse" and "the solitary sin" were preferred. At first, I had a vague notion what it meant but was quickly filled in by the informal, forthright, clinical program of sex education given gratis on streets and in playgrounds.

Marty D. and I leaned out the window of our fourth-grade classroom. He yelled down into the schoolyard, "Maura is a who-ah." I didn't know Maura and had no idea that *who-ah* was a local pronunciation of *whore*, a word I was equally ignorant of but knew it wasn't something I'd ask a nun or parent to define.

As a high school freshman, I sat on the Bx 40 bus with a classmate. As a cute, preternaturally endowed high school girl got on, he turned to me and whispered, "What a cunt." It was another mystery word that I immediately intuited obscene and unrepeatable.

I was clueless when puberty came on with the same horrifying sudden-ness as Lon Chaney Jr.'s transmogrification into The Wolfman. Unsure what was happening, I spurted sperm in my sleep. Bewildered by hair sprouting in places I never had it, I watched helplessly as assorted appendages—arms, legs, and that other thing—lengthened Pinocchio-style.

If heterosexuality was a scary proposition, mined with opportunities for damnation, the dare-not-speak-its-name variety was a pox fatal to every infected soul. I wasn't sure what contortions boy-to-boy relationships involved but was attuned enough to fear some unconscious behavior on my part might suggest a hidden attraction to the sin of Sodom.

I watched as a boy in my class whose effeminate manner and gentle flamboyance made him an obvious target was ambushed on his way home. Pushed and taunted as "fairy," "fag," he begged to be let go. The crowd that gathered egged on his persecutors. I know now I had classmates who, though they gave no outward sign, watched in terror of being subject to the same treatment.

I stayed an un-innocent bystander, sympathetic but motionless, silently relieved he was sacrificial victim to our classmates' cruelty, not me. The next day, I sought him out to say how sorry I was. He turned and walked away. It's a scar on my conscience I still carry.

We took living in an all-white community for granted. Nobody questioned it, at least in front of me. My parents warned us against using discriminatory language of any kind. My father served in the legislature with Hulan Jack, an African-American member of the Assembly from Harlem, later Manhattan's first African-American borough president.

They enjoyed each other's company. After a political get-together, my father invited Jack to accompany him to a saloon in the Gut, Albany's *demimonde* where insiders spent their off-hours and the respectable rubbed elbows with the questionable.

The bartender poured my father a beer and pointed at Jack. "I'll serve you, but not the coon." My father grabbed a glass off the bar and put it under the tap. "Then I will." He reached around, pushed down the tap, and filled the glass. The bartender picked it up and smashed it against the countertop, spraying beer on my father and Jack, who turned and walked out. My father cursed the bartender and left to find Jack.

Part of me is proud of my father's stand; another wonders why nobody did anything. My father knew many of them. The biggest part wonders at the humiliation suffered by Jack, the iron curtain of contempt not even a member of the legislature could break through.

When my father caught up to him, what did he say? Did he apologize for the bar, the state, the country, the ceaseless injustices, and the indignities of racism?

Scotty was a light-skinned Black man. He periodically cleaned our windows. He carried what he needed in a shopping bag. My brother and I loved to watch the speed and dexterity with which he made a pane of glass glisten. He whistled while he worked. When he finished, he sat at our dining room table. My mother served him a sandwich and a beer.

When I saw Scotty on the street, he was always whistling and smiling. It wasn't till I lived in a Black neighborhood in Kansas City, Kansas, that I understood Scotty's zip-a-dee-ay charade. He was a lone Black man in a whites-only preserve. When he rode an elevator, there were people who wouldn't get on. In a whites-only neighborhood there'd invariably be hostile as well as questioning stares.

He had to calibrate his every move. Being inexpressive or sad could be interpreted as sullen, or nursing a grievance, up to no good; too happy as cocky, looking for trouble. Even if he struck the right balance, he couldn't be sure. The possibility of being taken in on suspicion of shoplifting or burglary—or worse—was always there.

My mother's hospitality didn't change the fact that we lived in a segregated community. For Blacks, the rule was always and everywhere the same: guilty until proven innocent. Scotty used centuries worth of accumulated experience to make his way across a paper-thin sheet of ice that could crack at any moment and swallow him, and he knew it.

People in the parish spoke with increasing dread of a rising racial tide. The word was to get out before the deluge—"before it's too late."

One Sunday in the early '60s, Father John Flynn, a newly arrived curate, spoke at the 11:00 A.M. Mass in praise of Martin Luther King, Jr. and the burgeoning civil rights movement. The name Martin Luther, progenitor of the Protestant Reformation, was never spoken of in a positive way in Catholic churches. Attached to a Black man many regarded as an agitator and troublemaker, it was doubly unwelcomed.

Some parishioners complained vociferously. Flynn didn't back down. He proposed enrolling students from the South Bronx in the parish's Montessori program. An outraged parent lashed out at him: "If you care about them so much, why don't you go live with them?"

Which is what Father Flynn did. He spent the next fifty years as a parish priest in the South Bronx working alongside a cadre of dedicated priests and nuns. In a long saga of callousness and abandonment, they stand out as true prophets.

Most of what we knew about African Americans was from the racist stereotypes on boxes of rice and pancake mix, from TV and the movies, Jack Benny's Rochester, Charlie Chan's Birmingham Brown, the blustery, lazy Kingfish, and slow-motion Lightnin' from the "Amos 'n' Andy" TV show, which ushered radio racism into the Television Age.

The South Bronx started as a specific place. In the late '40s and early '50s, African Americans and Puerto Ricans began to replace Jews and Irish. In my youth, it included everything south of 161st Street; when I was a court officer, it went up to Tremont; by the time I was in graduate school it was lapping Fordham Road.

By the early '60s, humor soured into fearful anticipation. Newspapers stuck the generic label "South Bronx" on crimes committed in neighborhoods we previously thought of as north. I watched as news accounts of Parkchester, which I was raised thinking was in the North Bronx, moved to the "South Central Bronx."

A location morphed into sociological shorthand for a pandemic of urban ruin—poverty, addiction, crime. The virus raged far beyond the Bronx, in Camden, Detroit, Newark, Baltimore, Washington, et al.

In the second game of the 1977 World Series, announcer Howard Cosell and his co-host turned their attention to a fire in the distance. For a while they paid more attention to the fire than the game. Cosell never quite said what legend says he said: "Ladies and gentlemen, the Bronx is burning." (And *contra* the *Daily News*'s famous headline, Gerald Ford never told New York, "Drop dead," although that's what he hoped.)

The previous week, President Jimmy Carter visited the South Bronx. He crossed an empty lot strewn with trash and broken bricks. A few years later, when he was running against Carter, Ronald Reagan made a visit. He criticized Carter's inaction and promised to do something. Good as his word, soon after being elected he cut federal aid for housing.

It was Cosell who made the lasting impression. He introduced a national audience to the borough's fate. Amid the bleakness was the soothing balm that the Yankees won their first World Series in fifteen years.

That summer, a citywide blackout led to riots and looting. There were several thousand alarms in a single night. The worst flare-ups were reported in the Bronx. Most were false alarms. Several years before, firefighter Dennis Smith wrote *Report from Engine Co. 82*, a searing chronicle of a Bronx firehouse pushed to the limit.

My friend Brian M. was a plainclothes cop in the South Bronx when fire and crime rampaged. One day, he saw a three-legged pit bull hobbling down a half-abandoned street ahead of two emaciated mutts. It had a dead cat in its teeth. A thousand-word kind of picture.

As a court officer, I accompanied judges on inspections of buildings in the South Bronx. There were volatile confrontations between tenants and landlords at each other's throats over whether repairs were made and rents paid.

The tenants stopped being statistics. Some were angry and frightening, often rightly so. Most were quiet, respectable, eager to make their case. These were the people, I realized, who never got their pictures taken, never appeared in perp walks featured on the 10 o'clock news, who didn't give up in the face of odds that would leave most people paralyzed, who carried on amid the wreckage and abandonment.

Raised in the South Bronx during its time on the cross, journalist David Gonzalez pointed out how his and other families "were often blamed for the borough's decline, while policymakers and planners reduced entire communities to cold statistics and map lines."

Describing people as "resilient" or "tough" made it seem as if they had a choice. "We were not resilient," Gonzalez wrote. "We were resisting death."

"It's the pimps and drug dealers—the dogs with dead cats in their jaws—that get noticed," my friend said. "It's never the mother with three kids working her ass off to get out of the projects who gets splashed on tabloid covers."

If the South Bronx was dying, the people were vibrant and alive. Along with the violence and addiction and prostitution, there was more struggle, pain, and ambition than in all the tony precincts of Manhattan and the suburbs.

Large swathes of Bronx apartment buildings were thrown up in the early part of the century and the boom years of the '20s. By the '60s, the aging housing stock was increasingly starved for re-investment and repair. Banks stopped lending. Redlining was rampant. A generation coming out of two decades of Depression and war sought greener precincts.

In the wake of city, state, and federal government programs that the Democratic political machine helped put in place, its patronage power was greatly diminished. Slow—and to a degree unwilling—to adapt to changing demographics, the machine grew increasingly relevant to people's lives.

As the South Bronx moved north, the population fled in increasing numbers on the highways the government presciently provided. The roads ringed the Bronx. To the east, the Bruckner Expressway fed into the New England Thruway, the gateway to Connecticut.

The Major Deegan started at the Triborough Bridge, where it was linked to the Bruckner, and swept west and north through Westchester to the New York State Thruway, over the Tappan Zee Bridge and the open reaches on the far side of the Hudson.

At a cost of $150 million—over a decade in the making—the Cross Bronx Expressway cut across the middle of the Bronx, from the Sound to the Hudson. It linked to the Deegan and the George Washington Bridge to New Jersey, and the Bruckner, and the Throggs Neck to Long Island. It was a surgical slash that slit the Bronx's wrists and left it to bleed to death.

Over a span of two decades, the federal and state poured millions—billions in today's money—into building an arterial network that carried traffic over, around, and through the Bronx. People can drive across the Bronx and never know they're in it.

The highways were of a piece with federally guaranteed mortgages that subsidized suburbs dedicated to the proposition that minorities will never be allowed to live there. In 1960, Long Island's Levittown housed 82,000 people. Zero were minorities.

The government put in place an updated Homestead Act. Station wagons full of pioneers set out for the new frontier. When it came the cities' turn, the treasure lavished on satellites and subdivisions went missing. Subways and railroads went begging. Jobs followed people to the suburbs, and people followed jobs.

It can't all be laid at the feet of Robert Moses. Mayors, governors, senators, urban planners, cabinet secretaries, all contributed. Across the country, perfectly designed ghettos were ready to receive and hold the unskilled, impoverished rural masses. Crime soared. Drugs flowed in.

Landlords torched buildings for the insurance. Tenants set fires in the hope of getting public housing. Addicts stripped out copper pipes and anything they thought they could sell. For minorities, a new chapter in American history perfectly repeated the old.

The War on Poverty ended. The war on the poor didn't.

⣿

The Swamp, a jumble of marshland-*cum*-garbage dump, was a favorite place to play, especially because our parents forbade us. It was a perfect setting for fighting our way through the jungle morass of Guadalcanal. There was the added bonus of discarded girlie magazines that I did my best not to look at, not always successfully.

One day, fences went up. Bulldozers and dump trucks got to work. The Swamp was obliterated. Buildings came down. The future arrived in an un-spooling ribbon of concrete. The highway makers sliced through the Gordian Knot of streets, avenues, and parks and gave motorists an open road.

That was the plan. In an endlessly repeated scenario, expressways like the Cross Bronx, built to abolish bottlenecks and speed cars on their way, drew more cars that in no time produced monumental traffic jams, which raised a cry for more lanes, which produced more cars and tie-ups.

The flow of traffic through the man-made ditch of the Cross Bronx was quickly clogged and brimming with traffic. A gray dishrag of gasoline fumes hung over it. Brendan L. and Jeff C., two of my closest friends, were neighbors. The Cross Bronx put them on different sides of the ditch. They had to walk four blocks to the nearest pedestrian bridge to get together.

On Saturday mornings, after he returned from a tour in Vietnam, Jeff and I sat in his kitchen, which looked out on the ditch. His mother nursed our hangovers with scrambled eggs and tea. Outside, traffic roared, brakes screamed, a perpetual cacophony sporadically interrupted by tires' screech, crash, and mash of metal into metal.

We watched as a car stalled and the hapless motorist steered to the side. A gang of teenagers pulled up behind him and removed the tires with the speed and expertise of an Indianapolis 500 pitstop crew.

When I worked as a speechwriter for Mario Cuomo, we rode back from an event at Einstein Hospital, in the north Bronx. We got stuck in one of those massive traffic jams that serve as the Cross Bronx's trademark. The governor playfully fantasized about turning the expressway into a canal. It was a lovely dream. To date, no gondolas have been spied.

Peter M., my oldest friend from Parkchester, moved to New Jersey to raise his five kids. He commuted for decades on the Cross Bronx to the South Bronx high school where he taught. He was sideswiped by a truck, a car crashed into it, and another into that. The multi-vehicle demolition derby backed up the morning rush hour traffic over the George Washington Bridge.

The police opened a single lane to a trickle of traffic and lifted him into an ambulance. A middle-aged woman stuck her head out the window and shouted, "I hope you fucking die!" The Cross Bronx has never been for the faint-hearted.

For nearly a century, the beating heart of the Bronx has been Yankee Stadium. Like any kid who grew up in the Bronx—who wasn't an idiot or a quisling—I was a Yankees fan. Inside its walls, differences disappeared. We were all fans.

From my father's chambers in the Bronx County Court House, home plate was visible. He was raised a New York Giants fan. When they decamped for a fog-bound, gold-rush town on the Pacific Rim, he swore off baseball. A friend gave him tickets to the '60, '61, and '62 World Series. He passed them to us.

The stadium was made holy by the gods of baseball who played there and, for Catholics, the pope who said Mass there. For my brother and me, it was in the blood. Our maternal grandfather, James Murphy, was hired at the Rupert Brewery in 1913 and worked there until 1938, when he was seventy. He dropped dead on his first two-week vacation.

Colonel Jacob Rupert, the brewery's proprietor, and his extravagantly named partner, Tillinghast L'Hommedieu Huston, purchased the Yankees in 1915. If any marriage is made in heaven, it's beer and baseball.

Rupert built history's greatest sports franchise. In 1922, he housed it in a suitably grand stadium in the Bronx. When Prohibition limited his production to "near beer," the Yankees kept him afloat.

He used my grandfather in other capacities besides mechanic. On the theory that a workingman in begrimed overalls and a mechanics cap would be less likely to be overcharged, he sent my grandfather to buy parrots and assorted pets for his menagerie, and on one occasion, a monkey.

My Irish-immigrant grandfather never acquired a taste for baseball. His six children did. They reveled in their access to witness Ruth and Gehrig bat their way to legend. Though my mother didn't follow baseball closely, her Yankees pride made up for it.

People said rooting for the Yankees was like rooting for General Motors. For us, they said attention must be paid. E. B. White could condescend, Ogden Nash poke fun. Nobody could scoff at the Yankees. No other city, county, or country possessed the Bronx Bombers.

Unlike its $1.5 billion replacement with its clubhouse shops, upscale restaurants, and luxury boxes that can rent for up to $12,000 per game (*sic*), the old stadium was just about baseball. There were metal troughs for urinals. Refreshment stands offered franks, soda, Cracker Jacks, and popcorn.

The first time Tom and I set eyes on the field, we were young boys. We looked at each other with wild surmise. There below the towering tiers of seats was a diamond of perfect proportions carpeted by a profound greenness, a stunning, serene greenness we never saw or imagined, deeper than a putting green, far beyond Parkchester's chained lawns or the Bronx's parks. If the game had been called off, I'd have been content to spend the day contemplating the field.

Saturday of Memorial Day weekend, May 30, 1960, a year of Yankee greatness, they played a double-header against the Washington Senators, whose haplessness was the subject of the musical hit "Damn Yankees," in which a fan had to sell his soul to the devil to get them to the World Series.

We took the Pelham Bay Express south to 125th, switched to the Jerome Avenue line back up to 161st Street. We were there in a half hour. Instead of bleacher seats for 50 cents, my mother gave us $1.25 for the better-behaved grandstands.

We knew the lineup by heart. Everyone had a favorite. Mantle, Maris, Kubek, Skowron, Boyer, the universally beloved Yogi. The Yankees lost the first game. In the second, Mantle scored the winning run on Yogi's homer and snagged the final out.

The lights atop the iconic façade were on. The spoor of spilled beer was everywhere. Most of the occupants of box seats were on their way out. Restiveness ran beneath the festive mood. Fans from the grandstands lined the fences, as if waiting to be unleashed. When Mantle caught the final out, they spilled over the top in a human wave that swept aside the thin line of attendants and flooded centerfield.

The players raced for the safety of the dugout. Maris made it just in time. Mantle disappeared amid the swelling crowd.

My friend Peter, my brother, and I stepped onto the field. Programs and pencils in hand, we waited in front of the dugout eager to snag the

Mick's autograph. The crowd was more like a mob. Mantle suddenly broke through. His hat was gone. People clutched at his shirt. His number 7 was half-ripped off.

Eyes bulging with panic, a colossus stormed directly toward us. His closely cropped red-blond hair looked as if it were on fire. I know steam wasn't coming out of his nostrils. In my memory it was.

I stood frozen in place, the last obstacle to the shelter of the dugout. He ran right over me. My brother said he brushed me aside, which my zephyr-weight build made more likely. I prefer to think he ran over me. I lay stunned on the ground. I looked up into the distant lights that I mistook for stars.

My mother always told us that wherever we went we should bring back a story. I had a story to tell friends, acquaintances, total strangers: May 30, 1960, the day I was run over by Mickey Mantle.

My father rarely watched television for more than a few minutes, usually on his way through the living room. The one exception was the summer of 1956. We never had a TV on Shelter Island. But that year the Democratic Convention was in Chicago and there was a chance Senator John Kennedy of Massachusetts would be nominated as the party's vice-presidential candidate.

My father did the unthinkable: He rented a TV. He sat us down to witness Kennedy's name being put in nomination. He wanted us to see an Irish Catholic vie for such high political office. It was less than thirty years since Al Smith's drubbing seemed to preclude the selection of another Catholic candidate.

Smith's defeat was seared in my parents' memory, especially my mother's, whose older brother was mentally maimed in World War I. "I guess we're good enough to die for our country," a cousin observed sarcastically, "but not to run it."

It appeared that Kennedy might win the floor vote, but he didn't. Tom and I hoped the television would stay around after the convention. It went back the following morning. The next time we had a television in Shelter Island was four years later, in 1960, when Kennedy was nominated for president on the first ballot.

A week before the election, Kennedy came to the Bronx. My father was also running that year for the State Supreme Court. (It's a misnomer of sorts. In New York the court of highest jurisdiction is the Court of Appeals.) It was the last of the thirteen elections he participated in (he won twelve).

He sat on the dais with Kennedy at a luncheon held at the Concourse Plaza. Kennedy charmed the audience when he described himself as "a former resident of the Bronx." He claimed he lived there for "five or six years." In fact, it was two years, when his father was wheeling and dealing on Wall Street. The family home was a twenty-room mansion in Riverdale.

"I do not know the last time that a candidate from the Bronx ran for the Presidency," Kennedy said, "but I am here to ask your help as a former resident of the Bronx. No other candidate for the Presidency can make that statement." The filled-to-capacity ballroom exploded in laughter and applause.

Afterward, Kennedy traveled up the Grand Concourse. We stood among the wildly cheering multi-ethnic throng in front of the Loew's Paradise as he went by enthroned on the back of a Cadillac convertible. Tanned, hatless, in a black camel's coat, he awed us the way Cortés—mistaken for a demigod—must have impressed the Aztecs when he entered Tenochtitlán on horseback.

The image of Kennedy riding unprotected on the back of a Cadillac seems separated by decades from the fatal Dallas motorcade three years later. His assassin, Lee Harvey Oswald, spent a part of his childhood in the East Bronx, in a tenement near West Farms, far from Riverdale. Except for the Cuban missile crisis and President Kennedy's funeral, my father kept to his practice of never watching television for any length of time.

The Great Trek Tom and I made back and forth across the Bronx to high school and college was at my father's insistence. He felt indebted to the Christian Brothers for the encouragement and support they gave him. As a young boy at St. Brigid's, on the Lower East Side's Thompson Square Park, and then at St. Raymond's in the Bronx, the Brothers recognized his intelligence and pushed him.

Since we attended the same schools, there were great expectations. We followed him to Manhattan Prep, where he was a star. He started the debate club. We were drafted onto the team. If there were two more hapless debaters, we never debated them. He won the math medal. We didn't shine. Sometimes we barely twinkled.

He studied civil engineering at Manhattan College. He founded the college newspaper and dramatic society. He won the Grady Oratorical Medal. After college, he worked as an engineer building the IND subway and paid his way through law school at night. He was one of those who made equal use of the right and left hemispheres of his brain. Whichever hemisphere Tom and I used operated below full capacity.

As we grew older, Tom grew defiant. He talked back. He disobeyed curfews. He failed geometry because he wanted to. He dropped out of college. He was demanding attention, and he got it.

My father never lifted a hand to us. His furious, window-rattling verbal blasts could scorch paint off the walls. He predicted Tom would amount to nothing. He was like his own Uncle Richie, my father said, a man of squandered potential who put the ne'er in ne'er-do-well and ended up living on handouts from relatives.

My father expected excellence. It was nothing to be congratulated for. He focused on failures. As he saw it, he started with nothing, we with everything. He did everything with his nothing, and we were managing to do nothing with our everything. He had a long stride. We stumbled out of the starting blocks and kept stumbling thereafter. We couldn't keep up, and then we didn't try.

He intervened in my life three times that I remember. When I was in the eighth grade, he stopped me from going to the minor seminary to begin study for the priesthood. He had studied briefly to be a monk in his early teens. He thought making a lifetime commitment at such a young age unwise. A priest from the parish said he was denying my vocation. My father said if I had it at fourteen, I'd have it at eighteen. At eighteen, I knew I didn't want to be a priest.

Years later he directed me to take a civil service test, which I did. When I wanted to leave the courts, he warned me not to. That was the sum of his career advice.

I hated Manhattan Prep. Like my grammar school, it was boys only. All the courses were required. We studied Latin, Spanish, algebra, trigonometry, chemistry, biology, English, history, and religion. Our Spanish teacher, a layman, was a certified sadist.

Other students credited the Prep with being a positive formative influence. I credited it with giving me a knot in my stomach I'm still trying to unravel.

One teacher made a difference. Brother Aquinas had a passionate love of literature that he conveyed to us. He told me I should be a writer. "Don't get stuck in a job that means nothing to you," he said. It was the only encouragement I ever received. I'm deeply indebted to him.

I didn't apply to any college other than Manhattan. My father wouldn't hear of it. My brother tried applying to Boston College. My father wouldn't hear of it. Except for being all male, the college was an entirely different experience from the Prep. In the 1950s, the college had adopted the great-books program Robert Hutchins introduced at the University of Chicago.

The four-year curriculum at Manhattan required reading the classics (in translation) from ancient to modern, Aeschylus, Marcus Aurelius, Aquinas, Marx, Nietzsche, Joyce, et al. There were no electives until junior year. The Brothers were open-minded and well-educated. The lay faculty was excellent.

Professor Frederick Schweitzer was a child in Nazi Germany when, unlike the poo-bahs of European diplomacy, his working-class, non-Jewish mother recognized that Hitler was intent on war and fled with her son to the United States. Equally at home lecturing on the Peloponnesian War as the Franco-Prussian, Schweitzer had a panoptic understanding of history. He established the first center for Holocaust studies at a Catholic college. I took every course with him I could.

The object of the curriculum was whatever cultures we studied in graduate school—and a large proportion of students went on to advanced degrees—we'd be grounded in the foundations of Western civilization. Although it's a course of study that's fallen out of favor, and it might be impolitic to say so, I benefited greatly and am grateful.

Eighty percent of the students (all male) commuted from around the city. The closest we had to foreign-study students were boarders from Albany and New Jersey. In a majority of cases, my classmates were the first in their families to go to college.

Drawn from the top ranks of the city's Catholic high schools, they were smart, skeptical, unpretentious, and full of enthusiasm for the texts we read. I've stayed close with many. They remain the most intellectually engaged people I know.

James McCourt—no relation to Frank—was several years ahead of me. His novel *Mawrdew Czgowchwz*, about a fictional opera diva, is considered a classic of gay literature. His book *Queer Street*, about gay life in New York City, was praised by Susan Sontag and Harold Bloom.

I was in the same freshman rhetoric course with James Patterson, the world's very, very bestselling author. The professor took the two of us out of class for special instruction. Patterson generously blurbed a novel of mine. As I pointed out at an alumni gathering, together we've sold 300 million books worldwide (and counting). I didn't break out the numbers.

Also ahead of me was Rudy Giuliani, who graduated from the college the year I graduated from the Prep. A member of the ROTC, he passed up serving in the military for a law-school deferment, obviating the need for a bone-spur diagnosis.

Former U.S. Attorney and New York City mayor, Giuliani ran a spectacularly unsuccessful campaign for the Republican nomination for president in 2008. His supporting role as snarling presidential attack dog and co-fomenter of the attack on the Capitol led some to speculate he suffers from an undiagnosed form of rabies.

⁑

It was 1968. I was in college in the north Bronx. I felt I was missing the upheaval shaking the globe from Paris to Prague to San Francisco. I wanted to see the world. I wanted what I couldn't put into words.

My philosophy teacher that year had been raised in Florence and had a face like Dante's. He was from the rigorist wing of the academy. The course consisted of three texts: Bishop Berkeley's *A Treatise Concerning Human Knowledge*; Baruch Spinoza's *Ethics, Demonstrated in Geometrical Order*; and Immanuel Kant's *Critique of Pure Reason*.

I think I read the first two, or at least tried. I vividly recall the cover of Kant's book, black, the title in bold red. That's about as far as I got.

We were graded on class participation and a final exam that consisted of one question. If he found we were parroting outside commentators, we lost one grade. The question concerned Kant's tome. I scored zero in the first category and zero in the second. I didn't lose a grade for relying on outside commentators.

Failing philosophy meant I had to go to summer school. Tom and I worked as doormen at the Tower East, on 72nd Street, and attended school at night. Kant made no more sense the second time than the first. Somehow I passed.

On the last night of school and work, we attended a Richie Havens concert with friends in Central Park. For some reason I can't remember—it might have had to do with what we inhaled—we decided to share a ride out to the Hamptons.

The plan, if that's what you want to call it, was to see if we could find people we knew to crash with for the weekend. It was an era filled with high hopes and impossible dreams. We slept in the car on the side of the Long Island Expressway.

The major, but not only, problem was none of the car windows opened. Waking roadside on a baking July morning, I felt the imminent asphyxiation that threatened the protagonist in Poe's *The Premature Burial*.

We parked at Hot Dog Beach, in East Quogue. The sand was covered blanket-to-blanket with the beautiful and otherwise. The smell of the sea, suntan oil, and lust filled the air. We wandered the shoreline until there seemed no reason to continue. It was Tom who sighted Chris and Betty, two girls he'd encountered a few times in a bar in the Bronx.

They were extremely pretty and very welcoming. They invited us to sit with them and their friends. We made no mention of our shelter-seeking intentions. I glanced at Chris's sister standing on the far side of the blanket, then glanced again. She was willowy with long, shimmering auburn hair that framed a lovely face. I felt something stir inside me I never felt before, something beyond physical attraction.

I don't know if there's a force in the universe—call it fate—that even if we're unaware, even if we resist, we can't avoid. Luck is a lighter word, which we all recognize as part of our lives, whether good or bad.

Maybe, if I'd paid attention, I'd know if Kant offers insight into the existence or nonexistence of fate. An acquaintance with a doctorate in philosophy assures me he does. I'm too old at this point to care.

In the course of novel writing, I frequently draw on characters, events, and places from my life. Dressed in the motely of fiction, they allow me to describe what I'd otherwise have to guess.

I think it was Tolstoy who said, "True arrogance is quoting oneself." (I'm fairly certain it wasn't Yogi Berra.) If I could avoid it, I would. But there's a passage in *Banished Children of Eve* in which I put into the protagonist's head what I felt that moment on Hot Dog Beach:

> [He] was unsure of what to do next, unsure in a manner difficult to explain. It was if the weather had suddenly changed, although it hadn't, or as if the air itself was somehow different than before, although it wasn't, and he kept feeling like that, unsure, even when he went his way, and stayed that way all day and the next . . .

I don't believe there's only one person with whom we're meant to find true love. Love is part chance and part choice. It's reserved for no particular duo. Yet there's only one person who, no matter how content or happy we are with someone else, we're destined to think about from time to time, wonder where they are at this moment, if they're happy with the life they've found, what would have happened if things had been different.

What began on Hot Dog Beach led to a long, tumultuous, on-and-off courtship that wouldn't reach its denouement until a far-distant evening in Albany when I missed the last train to the city, wandered into a bar not far from the Capitol, and spotted that girl from Hot Dog Beach by the door with a friend. Fate doesn't follow calendars or clocks. Love's not time's fool.

The vocational wanderlust that followed my college years was part of a generational drift. The shorthand account of the '60s was a Baby-Booming carnival of self-indulgent, overprivileged, self-righteous hedonists, the epigones who spoiled and squandered the legacy of the Greatest Generation. As with all caricatures, a measure of truth lies within a carapace of simplifications and exaggerations.

The Greatest Generation bequeathed unprecedented domestic prosperity and global power. The American Century was at its apogee. It also passed on a society of entrenched racism and fetishized conformity, political paranoia, and superpower hubris.

Dwight Eisenhower, not Jerry Rubin, decried a "military-industrial complex" whose "total influence—economic, political, even spiritual—is felt in every city, every State house, every office of the Federal government."

One generation fought a war that, until given no choice, a large majority of Americans insisted on staying out. Their sacrifices were great. They fought bravely. Half a million gave their lives. The war instilled a sense of national purpose.

Thanks to their sacrifices, the next generation grew up in a period of unprecedented prosperity. The worm in the apple was the probability of a nuclear holocaust that subverted any sense of personal as well as national purpose, and an awakened awareness of what Michael Harrington called the "other America," the millions left out and left behind, ignored, excluded, barred by visible and invisible walls of race and class from the "Happy Days" fantasy of Potsie and the Fonz.

The new generation joined the civil rights movement and forced the country to stop pretending racial injustice wasn't ingrained into every facet of American life. It spurred the women's movement, which challenged a system that routinely denied gender equality. A process was set in motion that eventually freed millions of gay people from lives ruled by fear of ostracism from their families, loss of their jobs, and physical harm.

After a century of the ruthless exploitation of natural resources and thoughtless pollution that turned majestic rivers into toxic sewers, there was an awakening to the poisonous consequences for generations to come. The environmental movement was timely, necessary, and long overdue.

At the same time, the harsh, sometimes savagely contentious debates over the Vietnam War divided the country more deeply than at any point since the Civil War. One side regarded the other as war-mongering anti-Communist ideologues. The other pictured its opponents as naïve—sometimes traitorous—scum. In one form or another the antagonisms, angry and envenomed, are still with us.

Opponents of Communism weren't wrong. The war was. It was driven by the "domino theory," which posited that if South Vietnam fell, the door would open for North Vietnam and its puppet master, the Red Chinese, to swarm over Asia.

Why, amid a global surge of anti-colonialism, we paid a billion dollars to support France's nine-year war to re-establish its colony; why we decided to take up the fight after the French and their allies suffered 55,000 dead and ignominious defeat; why we kept fighting after the leadership in Washington recognized there was no path to victory didn't—and still doesn't—make a lot of sense.

Great Power hubris and American naïveté played major parts. In the end, it was the Vietnamese Communists, not the Americans who lived out JFK's call to "pay any price, bear any burden, meet any hardship, support any friend, oppose any foe to assure the survival and success" of their cause.

However ill-conceived, some say the war could have been won. Others ask, "At what price?" How many more dead would have been added to the 58,200 Americans and the 3 million Vietnamese killed in the thirty-year war from 1945 to 1975.

The war began in deception and ended in defeat. We did things we were ashamed of. The Viet Cong and NVA committed horrendous crimes they still don't admit to. We abandoned the Vietnamese who fought with us and left behind a legacy of unexploded ordnance that continues to kill and maim. "Winning the war" would have meant guarding a border that half the country didn't want.

Today, the Vietnamese Communists look to us for support against an expanding Communist China. In the final analysis, nationalism outsells other isms.

I was shielded by my draft-deferred status at Manhattan College. John G., a friend since grammar school, dropped out and joined the Marines. The last time I saw him was at a football game in Gaelic Park. He confided he was afraid of dying in a war he didn't believe in. He was killed in the Mekong Delta. He was an only child. His father was a cop.

My friend Max also dropped out of Manhattan. He fought in Khe Sanh and Hue. When he came back, he told us the war wasn't worth it. I recently asked him if being in combat cured him of fear. He said after witnessing the random indifference of death, a part of him has stayed afraid.

In 1969, when I finished senior year, the war was raging. American troop presence peaked at over 500,000. My brother and I applied to be 1-AOs, willing to serve as conscientious objectors. Father Flynn, whom we knew from his time at St. Raymond's, supported us, as did Brother Patrick Stephen McGarry from Manhattan College.

Michael Patrick Jordan, who owned Parkchester's largest liquor store and was a vociferous supporter of LBJ, headed the local draft board. He was less skeptical than confused, more perplexed than hostile. He cited Cardinal Spellman's full-throated backing of the war.

How did Irish-Catholic kids like us, he wanted to know, from St. Raymond's no less, find themselves on the side of hippies and peaceniks? At one point, he blurted, "What the hell does your father think?"

An FDR Democrat, my father supported intervention in World War II before most of his family and friends. He felt Truman made the right decision in Korea. He was an enthusiastic supporter of LBJ. He was careful about taking public positions that might call his impartiality as a judge into question. In private conversation, it became clear that he came to regard the war as a tragic waste.

Except for observing that the decision was ours and we had to live with the consequences, what he thought of us as 1-AOs he kept to himself. My mother, whose shell-shocked brother never fully recovered, thought we should do whatever necessary to stay out.

We passed our physicals in the fall of 1969. Soon after, Nixon canceled the draft and announced a lottery, which seemed a bizarrely random way to choose who'd risk being killed or wounded and who wouldn't. We watched the lottery in the Pinewood Bar on Broadway. It was shoulder-to-shoulder with potential winners and losers.

We got a high enough number to ensure that unless the war went on for another thirty years, we wouldn't be called. A classmate got a ridiculously low number. He was drafted and was sent to Vietnam. It was a weird night. We all got very drunk.

I bumped into him a year or so later on a Long Island beach. He was thin and tanned. We talked a few minutes. I asked him what it had been like. He shrugged and moved on—whether out of contempt for those like me who were spared or because he didn't want to talk about it, I'll never know. I never saw him again.

Willing or not, brave young Americans died in Vietnam. The opponents of the war included those who stood by their beliefs, even when it meant going to jail. Then there were those like John Bolton, Richard Perle, Paul Wolfowitz, Rudy Giuliani, Rush Limbaugh, George W. Bush, Mitch Mc-Connell, Dick ("I had other priorities") Cheney, and Donald Trump—the Bone Spur Brigade—who supported the war but finagled ways not to go.

At the outset of the Iraq War, there was talk getting over the "Vietnam syndrome." If the syndrome includes not using lies and magical thinking to take us to war in a country whose complexities we don't understand, traps us in a tunnel with no end or light in sight, kills and wounds thousands of American soldiers as well as hundreds of thousands of civilians, strains the capacity of our armed forces, and wastes trillions of dollars we need at home, maybe it's a syndrome to be heeded, not cured.

The debacle in Afghanistan indicates we still have a way to go before the moral of the story hits home.

The girl from Hot Dog Beach was starting college. I was going into my senior year. It took some time for me to mount the moxie to pursue her. Distance was an impediment. I lived in the East Bronx. She lived in the West, on Valentine Avenue, south of Fordham Road, on the long blocks parallel to the Grand Concourse.

It required either two buses or two subways to reach her apartment. I wished my Uncle John had got his cross-borough subway. I adjusted to the trip. What I hoped would happen, happened. We became a couple.

Her childhood lacked my privileges. She and her two sisters grew up in the South Bronx, in St. Angela Merici's parish, a short distance from the Concourse Plaza and Yankee Stadium. She was nine when her father died.

Her mother went back to work. The three daughters were latchkey kids before the term existed.

She went to a Catholic girl's high school on Third Avenue and 147th Street. Along with academic studies, the focus was on secretarial skills. In the afternoons of their senior year, the students worked in downtown offices, gaining practical experience for paltry pay.

Each year, St. John's University offered a scholarship to the top student in each of the city's Catholic high schools. She was a runaway winner.

Gentle and forbearing, qualities that would serve her well in her work as a rehabilitation counselor, she had a confidence and independence I lacked. My family turned nonconfrontation into a high art. It didn't take much for supercilious clerks and imperious salespeople to reach my marshmallow center. She and her sisters Chris and Patti spoke their minds. The steel beneath the silk was quickly revealed.

I was taken with her intelligence and quick wit, her unrestrained laughter, her lithe form, long auburn hair. She had a sorceress's way when she danced. A Puerto Rican friend at St. John's offered the high compliment, "You don't move like a white person."

There was a song at the time, un-destined for the Rock and Roll Hall of Fame, with a lyric that lodged in my head. I knew it reeked of teenage naïveté. It didn't help getting rid of it: "I know the only one for me can only be you/My arms won't free you, and my heart won't try."

I was silly to think long term. She was starting college. I was getting out. I wanted to explore the wide world outside the Bronx. Still, however apart, I thought she and I would stay together.

I joined the Peace Corps and was assigned to a training program for Libya. Halfway through, a cabal of young military officers, led by the unmourned Muammar Gaddafi, tossed out the king and the Peace Corps. I returned to the Bronx jobless and equipped with the unmighty credential of a B.A. in history.

Her sister Chris was the head assistant in the personnel department at Compton, a staid agency on Madison Avenue. Chris arranged for me to take a test for a job as a media buyer. The basic requirement, she said, was proficiency in math. I mentioned that mine ended at long division. (I'm being kind.) Out of the goodness of her heart, Chris did the *mitzvah* of providing the answer sheet. She told me to be sure to get a few wrong.

In delicious revenge for years of degrading marks in arithmetic, and to honor the memory of Brother Robert, my put-upon arithmetic teacher, I got them all right. The powers-that-be were impressed, and I was enthusiastically welcomed to my first job out of college, a position for which I was utterly unqualified. I was assigned as a media buyer to the Ivory Liquid account.

The work involved consulting the Koran of TV advertising, the Nielsen Ratings, for how many people were watching a particular show in a particular market, then bargaining with a salesman from the networks about what ads to buy, where, at what price. A day spent placing ads for Ivory Liquid across the melodramatic wasteland of daytime soap operas stretched the meaning of drudgery.

Adding to my plight was the advent of the computer age, a sea change in which I felt, and would remain, barely able to stay afloat. Our calculations were poked into punch cards (which only we fossils from the Pleistocene Era will recall) and fed into refrigerator-sized computers that regurgitated printouts we used to calculate the most advantageous deals.

I had a far simpler approach that didn't require consulting IBM. I interred the printouts in my desk's bottom drawer, closed my eyes, prayed to the Prophet, stuck a pin in the ratings book, and made my buy.

The work wasn't all ratings and pin sticking. These were the Don Draper "Mad Men" days. The two-hour martini lunch was no myth. Neither was the three- or four-, nor the lunch that bled into dusk and beyond, nor the unchecked sexism, incessant cigarette puffing, and rampant philandering.

Free of the ambition to be a lifer, and engaged in little more than pin sticking, I became close friends with Kevin M., a fellow outer-borough Irish Catholic. I didn't share Kevin's movie-star good looks or athletic prowess but took endless delight in his *punji*-stick wit and depth-charge sarcasm that required a minute or two before it detonated.

Kevin and I enjoyed many a garrulous, bilious lunch in the Coral Café, conveniently located around the corner from Compton. Sometimes Chris and Linda D. joined us. An Italian American from Borough Park, Linda had a devastating sense of humor that blended a Dorothy Parker sensibility with a Don Rickles delivery.

After our apportioned two-hour, two-drinks *déjeuner* (we drank beer, not martinis), we returned to the office, draped our jackets over our chairs, shuffled a Potemkin spread of papers across our desks, and headed back.

The crowd was gone. The mood was mellow. As the afternoon grew older and shadows shimmied up the façade of the buildings across 59th Street, we chatted cordially with Carlos, the Argentinian bartender. He filled us in about Perón. He was a fan.

He said any woman who couldn't tango wasn't worth dating, never mind marrying. We argued about the Vietnam War. He was a supporter. We weren't. We filled him in on baseball. He wasn't a fan. He said it was like "watching grown men stand around in their pajamas." Soccer was the only real sport.

What I remember most about my days at Compton, beyond my bottom drawer's capacity-testing supply of printouts, are those soft autumn hours in the Coral with Kevin. It was the glorious apogee of the '60s. Our lives were still ahead. "Bliss was it in that dawn to be alive/But to be young was very heaven." Dusk was closer than we imagined.

One afternoon in the Coral, a man with a tan somewhere between cocoa and burnt Sienna sidled up beside us. There was a hint of menace in his mournful, droopy eyes. He struck up a conversation with Kevin and bought us a round of drinks.

I recognized Roy Cohn, Senator Joseph ("a Red Under Every Bed") McCarthy's *consigliere* and, unknown to us at the time, a cynosure to an on-the-make real estate huckster destined to be the forty-fifth president of the United States.

Wingman for "Tail Gunner Joe," Cohn was at one time the most influential Jewish political figure in the country—Jared Kushner with balls and brains and without need of a blood transfusion.

Cohn and his boss inspired the patriots who saw to it that the proto-sitcom *The Molly Goldberg Show* was driven off the air. Wise, sweet Molly Goldberg, played by Molly Berg, was the big-hearted matriarch of a striving Jewish family in the Bronx. It was innocuous, chicken-soup schtick.

Her TV husband was accused as a real-life Red. The show was canceled. Blacklisted and unable to land another job, he committed real-life suicide.

Roy's father, Al Cohn, a well-known Bronx Democrat and State Supreme Court judge, had been a friend of my father's. My parents were at Roy's *bar mitzvah*. My father said that Al was despondent over his son's role as assistant Grand Inquisitor. As soon as I mentioned our fathers' friendship, a wall went up. Roy left abruptly.

A closeted gay man, maybe he was cruising. Maybe I brought up a time filled with memories of repression and shame. Maybe he remembered an appointment. Who knows? The conversation ended there. I told my father I met Roy. "Poor Al," my father sighed.

I was sitting alone in the Coral, in solitary contemplation of my future, when Kurt Vonnegut came in. He sat close to the door and ordered a gin and tonic, or what looked like a gin and tonic—maybe it was just tonic—which doesn't matter unless you think drinking what a great writer drinks will help your writing, which, take my word for it, it won't.

The bar was mostly empty. The few people there didn't notice him. If Carlos recognized him, he was too much the pro to show it. I was at the opposite end of the bar drinking beer, which I suppose writers great and small have at one time sipped or guzzled. I toyed with going over and introducing myself.

I might tell him what a fan I was and ask him about *Slaughterhouse-Five*, which had come out the previous spring and I and several million people were in the process of reading. I might mention a short story I was thinking of writing. I wasn't looking for tips, though if he had some, I'd be grateful.

He paid for his drink and left a dollar tip on the bar, a lot for those days. He dismounted his stool and walked outside. I watched him hail a cab. I was proud of myself for not bothering him and derailing his train of thought.

It's a New York thing to pretend you don't notice celebrities, which is why many of them live here. I've thought of compiling a list of all the celebrities and stars I've bumped into on the street or in a bar over the last seven decades. Some went dark long ago. I shared an unmemorable elevator ride in the Graybar Building with Andy Warhol. I have better ways to waste time.

It was the autumn of 1969. The bitter taste from the year before—MLK's and RFK's assassinations, the civil war in Chicago, the Soviet winter that ended the Prague spring—hadn't disappeared.

Yet the afterglow from Max Yasgur's farm still hovered. "Hair," the hirsute anthem of a not-yet-balding generation, was in the first phase of its 2,000 performances. The Beatles' *Abbey Road* album was just released. Americans walked on the moon. The Mets were on their "Star Trek" journey to boldly go to the pennant and beyond.

The day they won the World Series, there was a joyous, city-wide eruption unseen since V-J Day. Cabs stopped in the middle of Madison Avenue.

Strangers hugged on the sidewalk. The swell of exuberant fans swept Kevin and me out of the office into the street, then into the Coral, then back out, and so it went.

Kevin went on to become a top copywriter at Leo Burnett. I accepted my unsuitability for any job involving numbers and computers. After six months, I turned in my barstool and quietly canned those pesky print-outs. (I never heard so much as a discouraging peep about my pin-sticking methodology.) I was glad to get out of advertising. I'm sure the feeling was mutual.

Each morning and night, I traversed 59th Street between Lexington Avenue, where I got the IRT subway home, and Madison, where Compton was located. I lived at home, in my parents' Parkchester apartment.

Occasionally, before I got the train back to the Bronx, I stopped at the Argosy Bookstore, a six-story townhouse filled with first editions, antique maps, and assorted arcana. Having survived the great extinction that did in venerable booksellers like the Gotham and Scribner's—which in an example of a fate worse than death was turned into cosmetics emporium—the Argosy is still in business.

Until I read Patti Smith's *Just Kids*, I had no idea that while I was browsing the Argosy's shelves, she was stocking them. She came from the hinterlands of New Jersey with no job and no place to stay. She was a total noncelebrity at the time.

She and her boyfriend, photographer Robert Mapplethorpe, rented an apartment near the Bowery with all the amenities available to a typical family of cave-dwelling Neanderthals.

Stretching below 14th Street, from Broadway across the Bowery to the East River, once home to immigrant Irish and Germans, the Lower East Side became a New World *shtetl* filled with persecuted, *pogrom*-fleeing Jews whose progeny climbed over the ghetto walls and burst into the mainstream with a creative force that vitalized the entire culture.

Over time, along with the arrival of new generations of immigrant poor, the wrecked, decrepit precincts become synonymous with drugs, crime, prostitution, and abandoned factories and tenements.

My memory of the Bowery was a wintry *Walpurgisnacht* when my Aunt Gertie took me to a Catholic men's mission around the corner, on Bleecker. Gertie was delivering clothes collected from her fellow telephone operators for, as she put it, "the bums."

Tattered men huddled around barrels of burning scrap wood, or lay in doorways, or staggered out of brightly lit evil-smelling bars. She said when you gave someone a handout, you always stopped and looked in his eyes, so he knew, however down and out he might be, that you weren't blind to his humanity.

The Bowery's fabled history as the Plymouth Rock and Jamestown of American popular culture was hidden beneath a half-century's worth of grime and neglect. I was distressed by the destitution, but Gertie, who had grown up nearby, was unfazed.

If powerbroker Robert Moses hadn't had a Humpty Dumpty fall from his role as Shiva, the god of destruction, he'd have blitzed the Bowery and its environs with trademark mercilessness and replaced it with highways, high-rises, and stadium-sized parking lots.

For a Jersey refugee like Patti Smith and a rebel like Mapplethorpe (an Irish-Catholic former altar boy from Queens), the risk of moving in was offset by the reward of impossibly low rents and a nascent community of like-minded fellow travelers intent on lives of inventive, culture-changing dissent.

They scrambled to find shelter. Most had no idea where subways went once they traversed the bridges and tunnels out of Manhattan. They were as likely to go into the civil service as an astronaut training program.

Those of us with homes to go to in the outer boroughs knew the turf and felt safe. We patronized bars where everybody knew our names (some we preferred didn't). Even those who stopped going to church identified themselves by parish. It was where they were married and, when the day came, commended to eternity.

Civil service jobs were sought after and revered. They anchored people where they were. If we got our own place, the rent was reasonable, and if we moved to neighborhoods in which law and order were shaky, cheap.

Most Bronxites were immigrants or their children, if not from Europe, from Manhattan neighborhoods whose names told you all you needed to know: the Gashouse, Hell's Kitchen, the Bloody Fourth, the Tubercular District.

The Bronx proved more way station than destination. Pulled by the white middle class's rising standard of living and the attractions of the suburbs, and pushed by crime, the decay in city services, and racial paranoia, the outbound momentum didn't have to be debated or discussed. It was in the air.

For my parents, the Bronx was home. They never thought of moving out. Eventually, when I got married and became the father of a baby girl, my wife and I told my mother that we were moving from our Manhattan apartment to Park Slope, Brooklyn, where we could afford to buy a co-op (those were the days) and have a small backyard.

She was incredulous. For her, Brooklyn was a giant step (or two) backward. It was the one-bedroom cold-water flat on Herkimer Street her immigrant parents left for the Bronx and, eventually, New Jersey.

To her, newly fashionable brownstones evoked old-fashioned rooming houses, speakeasies, and places where women did things they shouldn't.

My mother lived in Parkchester for the bulk of her married life and raised her children there. She was saddened to see her neighbors move away. Her wish, as she put it, was to "exit feet first."

Her wish went unhonored. When the neighborhood grew less safe and her health more delicate, she and her sister were prevailed upon to move to a Westchester apartment beside my sister's. She wondered about her son in Brooklyn. "I only had one child," she said, "who moved away."

***

In 2000, I published *Looking for Jimmy*, a collection of essays, some of which touched on family lore and the history of Michael and Margaret Manning, my paternal great-grandparents. I garnered a few fragments from my father. I speculated when I wasn't sure, sometimes incorrectly.

I received a letter from Kate M., a cousin in Virginia I didn't know I had. She read my book. A patient and practiced genealogist, she was of immense assistance in filling in gaps, correcting mistakes, and turning guesses into facts.

Sometime before the Civil War, Margaret Purcell and Michael Manning emigrated to New York from Kilkenny. They were children during the famine. There's no record of what they saw and suffered. "Those who survived," writes Fintan O'Toole, "usually did so by emigration."

They left from Liverpool, once Europe's largest slave-trading port, since given over to importing cotton and exporting emigrants. Michael's brother Robert left around the same time on a ship that, whether he knew it or not, was headed to New Orleans. They never saw each other again.

Their passage was paid by relatives named Lee who had left a decade before, at the height of the famine, and helped them settle in the village of Fordham, in what was then the southern part of Westchester.

Chain migration like this, the willingness of one wave of immigrants to pay the fare of the next, was taken for granted among many Irish families. Some observers were surprised. The British colonial secretary marveled that "such feelings of family affection, and such fidelity and firmness of purpose, should exist so generally among the lower classes."

Research proved true what I'd been told. Margaret's cousin Anastasia was married to Patrick Lee. The Lees lived in Fordham and had eight children, of whom I know nothing. Patrick's trade was shoemaker, which added weight to my father's story about his grandfather's helping cobble the shoes of the Jesuits at Fordham.

Other discoveries came as revelations. Great-grandfather Michael Manning was baptized Micheal (Me-hall) Mangan. Over the years, he variously gave his name as Mangan, Mangin, and Manning. Maybe he was no good at spelling. More likely, he settled on the more English-sounding Manning because it didn't immediately identify his ethnicity. The process of Anglicizing Irish names had been going on for centuries.

He and his wife, Margaret Purcell, my great-grandmother, sailed in steerage from Liverpool in January 1860. Given the cold and rough seas, winter voyages were the least desirable. Her first daughter, Marianne, was born in August, which means she was pregnant throughout the voyage in the crowded bottom deck of an emigrant ship.

I was told Margaret had five children. It turns out that between 1861 and 1876, she had ten. In that fifteen-year period, she was pretty much constantly pregnant. Four of the children predeceased her. Michael died before he was five. It's uncertain where he's buried.

Anastasia and Catherine both died at age one. They're buried without tombstones in Calvary Cemetery, beside the Queens side of the Midtown Tunnel. In all the times I passed by, I was ignorant that my two great-aunts were interred there. Peter died at twenty-five from tuberculosis.

My grandmother, born on April 17, 1863, in Fordham, was baptized in the nearby chapel of St. John's College (now Fordham University) the next day, which indicates her health was precarious. Her name was recorded as Margret (*sic*) Mangan.

Her father, Michael, worked at the Johnson Ironworks, on the Harlem River, close to the Hudson. According to an unsubstantiated story my father told, Michael took a job as a deckhand on a scow that transported captured Confederates from Newport News to imprisonment on Governors Island.

Unbeknownst to him, his long-lost brother Robert, who shipped to New Orleans, was among them. The story, a neat reprise of the Civil War as brother against brother, has the whiff of an O. Henry story. What's known is that he died in a cholera epidemic in New Orleans in 1873.

Robert sent a daguerreotype of himself to Michael. It was inscribed "To my dear brother." I saw it as a child. It's since been lost or discarded. Whether Robert married or had children is unknown.

By 1865, the family lived on the Lower East Side, where they moved about for the next fifty years. The censuses list great-grandfather Michael in various jobs: laborer, blacksmith assistant, locksmith, etc. Margaret was recorded in one census as unable to read or write. Ten years later, she could.

Maybe she was lying. Irish immigrants had an instinctual distrust of prying officials. My cousin offered the more uplifting possibility that as her children went to school, they shared with her what they learned.

The state census of 1905 said a great deal about the childhood my father mostly kept to himself. There are eleven relatives living together in a tenement on East 12th Street. Along with his grandparents was my father, age one, his parents and brother and sister, three uncles, and a nephew.

Uncle William was a widower. His wife, sick with "pulmonary phthisis"—that is, tuberculosis, a disease common in the tenement districts—died in childbirth. Alice, the baby, died five months later of "enterocolitis," a form of malnutrition suffered by premature babies. William and his son came to live at 12th Street.

William was a heavy drinker. He collapsed outside a saloon on Tompkins Square in August 1914. His death certificate lists the cause as "chronic nephritis and heat exhaustion." My grandparents raised his son.

Uncle Richie, another resident in the tenement—the charming ne'er-do-well my father accused my brother of resembling—owned and lost a saloon. He died in the Bronx several decades later from cirrhosis. My grandmother's loathing of saloons wasn't theoretical.

My grandfather Patrick's frequent absences from home on union organizing trips may have involved living conditions at home as well as dedication to the labor movement.

By 1910, my grandparents had moved with their three children to 296 East 7th Street. My grandmother was the family's designated caregiver. Her parents, Michael and Margaret, lived with them. Both my father and my Aunt Gertie spoke fondly of Michael.

He was almost eighty. He'd gone blind. He was caring, quiet, and gentle. My father remembered that the sole time he mentioned Ireland was when he said he wouldn't go back until "they hanged the last landlord." He died that same year.

Oddly, my father and aunt never mentioned his wife, Margaret Purcell Manning. She outlived Michael by two years. It's possible, I think, that she suffered from dementia. It was the type of infirmity that would have been a closely held secret.

At age fifty, I developed epilepsy. I didn't have a brain tumor or suffer a head trauma, the two most common causes of late-onset epilepsy. One specialist asked if there was any history of it in my family. I almost laughed. It is the very last shameful, disgrace-tainted malady immigrant families would have acknowledged.

I've thought about Margaret Purcell Manning a great deal. As a child she lived through the worst catastrophe in western Europe between the Thirty Years' War and World War I. In a ten-year period, Ireland lost a third of its population to hunger, disease, and emigration.

She spent two weeks on a winter voyage, in steerage, pregnant with her first child. She had the last of her ten at age forty-four. She lived most of her adult life in crowded tenements. She buried four of her children, two of them infant daughters. A son died as a small boy. She cared for her infant grandniece as she withered away. Two of her brothers were alcoholics.

I have no mementos of her, no heirlooms, no rings or brooches or rosary, not a stick of furniture. I didn't inherit a single anecdote or story about her. There are no pictures. I have no idea what she looked like nor any way to measure her joys or heartaches. I can only guess.

What can be said about her except she wasn't alone? Her life has been replicated to one degree or another by generations of immigrant women. Her portion in life was that of immigrant women, now as well as then, who do their best in the face of grimly discouraging odds, who endure.

What can I say except I owe her my life?

In my final days on Madison Avenue, I was accepted into VISTA—Volunteers in Service to America. (VISTAS, as we were called.) Created as part of LBJ's War on Poverty, VISTA was intended as the domestic version of the Peace Corps. We were assigned to economically distressed areas to help organize community groups, run summer camps, work in settlement houses, and serve in capacities where needed.

When I flew to Denver in January 1970 to begin VISTA training, the War on Poverty was going about as well as the one in Vietnam. Nixon was president. He put Donald Rumsfeld in charge of the Office of Economic Opportunity, which oversaw VISTA. It would be another thirty years before Rumsfeld revealed the true depths of his war-making ineptitude amid the sandstorms of Mesopotamia.

The training program was run by Howard Higman, a chain-smoking miner's son who became one of the country's most famous—and iconoclastic—sociologists. The first session, he made us pick a topic we knew nothing about and speak on it for three minutes.

I had a broad range to choose from. Except for being terrified and talking from total ignorance, I've no idea what I said. Higman congratulated us on our bullshitting prowess. When it came to poverty, he said, no matter what courses we took in college, as the children of the middle class, the best we could do was bullshit.

We shouldn't be fooled, he added. The war in Vietnam, an undertaking that no matter how fruitless it proved, was backed by a government willing to spend whatever it took in money and manpower to achieve its aims. The War on Poverty we signed up for was a visit to the shooting range.

Experts and academics talked endlessly among themselves about poverty, he said. Theories about poverty took precedence over the poor. We white, middle-class Americans didn't have to look into the face of poverty because we'd done such a good job of containing it in ghettos and barrios where we didn't think to look.

According to Higman, the poor had been examined under a microscope. It was time to turn the microscope on ourselves. People on top and in the middle needed someone on the bottom. When they talked about tackling poverty, they meant ensuring the poor were well behaved. It wasn't a matter of welcoming the poor to the neighborhood.

The rhetoric about erasing poverty ignored that most of the country was fine with things as they were. Poverty didn't have to be erased as long as the poor adjusted to their poverty and stayed out of sight.

The poor weren't going to be lifted up by anybody, least of all by us. They were going to be empowered to take control of their lives and communities, or we were involved in one big sham.

The structures that kept people poor took centuries to build. It would take a long, determined process to dismantle them. If the poor weren't an integral part of the process, all that would happen is that new structures of oppression would be put in place.

Higman told us our role was to stop seeing poverty as an abstraction that could be erased like words on a blackboard. Nobody knew more about poverty than the poor. We were to go where there was a need and do as we were asked.

If we didn't stand apart as observers, he said, if we were present to those we were with, if we learned to see the world from their perspective, we could make a difference. I was assigned to work out of a settlement house in Kansas City, Kansas, which is not to be confused with its famous cousin next door, Kansas City, Missouri, which I didn't know until I got there.

The two Kansas Cities are split by size, industry, reputation, wealth, and an imaginary state line. Fifty years ago, Kansas City, Kansas, felt more like a southern town than a city. For one thing, it was dry. Kansas City, Missouri, home of the Chiefs, the Royals, the National World War I Museum, and the country's best barbecue (according to the natives), was where, in Wilbert Harrison's oft-sung lyric, "They got some crazy li'l women."

On the Kansas side, the women appeared sane and sober, although I didn't meet a sufficient number to pass definitive judgment. On our second day in Kansas City, we were stopped by the police. Alert to the presence of outside agitators, they asked for our licenses and IDs, and queried us about our reason for being in Kansas City.

President Nixon was scheduled to speak at Kansas State University in Manhattan, Kansas. We were visited by a duo who identified themselves as with the Kansas Bureau of Investigation. They were quietly surveying for potential disrupters. We told them we didn't plan to go anywhere near. We went anyway.

I had two roommates. Bill M. was from California, Mike K. from Michigan. One of the benefits of VISTA was meeting people my age from across the country. We were raised differently but shared a great deal. I asked Bill a not-atypical New York question: "Where are your grandparents from?" He looked a little puzzled: "Arkansas. Why?"

We worked out of a settlement house. We tutored and helped with homework. Bill and I escorted a contingent of twelve-year-olds to a sun-baked summer camp. The first morning we had them put on their bathing suits and told those who couldn't swim to gather for swimming lessons at the pool's shallow end.

In the time-honored fashion of twelve-year-olds, they jumped en masse into the deep end. It was a scene worthy of *Titanic*, except this time no souls were lost at sea.

The little kids couldn't seem to get enough of us. The teenagers, aware of who we were and where we came from and would return, mostly regarded us with indifference. A few were actively hostile.

Bill J. was a large, imposing Black man who peered at the world over the dark glasses perpetually parked on the tip of his nose. He helped run the settlement house. He grew up in Mississippi.

One of his earliest memories was wandering from his grandmother into a drugstore. The cashier seized him by his collar and dragged him outside. "Keep this little pickaninny out of here," he scolded Bill's grandmother. "Or he'll be sorry you didn't."

Bill took me with him to the shopping district along Minnesota Avenue. He told me to follow him into a drugstore. He went down one aisle and signaled for me to go down another. In an instant, the cashier came from behind the counter. He ignored me and unsubtly eyed Bill. On the way out, Bill said to me, "Welcome to Mississippi."

Reverend Cecil "Chip" Murray, the charismatic pastor of Trinity A.M.E. Church, was a universally respected community leader. We frequently crossed paths. He invited us to come to his church anytime we liked.

My churchgoing sputtered and stopped in college. I was too apathetic to apostatize. Chip Murray was, in every sense, a revelation. Fiery and compassionate, he preached the gospel with an intensity that made it seem he was an eyewitness. He was unremitting in his denunciation of racism and insistent that Jesus required hate not be returned with hate.

More often than not, music in Catholic worship felt more like an afterthought. The chanting had an ancient sacredness. It wasn't part of ordinary worship. The post–Vatican II hymnal was frequently less than inspiring, occasionally tipping over onto Kingston Trio–ish schmaltz.

"Music," said Rev. Murray, "is the first language of prayer." The choir at Trinity A.M.E. was made up of at least thirty singers. The spirituals they sang, joyful and sorrowful, resonated with the power, pain, and glory of the faith that sustained African Americans through centuries of unrelenting oppression.

They sang and sang, and if it went on all day, I wouldn't have minded, a feeling I wasn't used to having in church.

Dick Parsons, the last chairman I wrote for at Time Warner, was an accomplished attorney and Nelson Rockefeller's lawyer. Physically imposing, Dick was arguably the country's most powerful African-American corporate executive.

Except for a few mild anecdotes, he never mentioned the inevitable racial slights, intentional and otherwise, he encountered on the way up. I was constantly amazed at the lack of bitterness on the part of people like Chip Murray and Dick Parsons.

They possessed a willingness to grant whites the benefit of the doubt, which whites only reluctantly granted them.

The Time Warner 2003 annual meeting was at the Warner Bros. Studio in Burbank. The next day, I tagged along with Dick Parsons when he met with community leaders in South Central L.A., at the First A.M.E. Church. The pastor was Chip Murray.

He spoke movingly about rebuilding L.A. in the era following the Rodney King riots. "Ghetto walls are built of more than bricks," he said. "You can't tear them down unless you're willing to rebuild the country." He'd lost nothing of his passion and eloquence.

I went up and told him that three decades ago I attended his church in

Kansas City. He took my hand. He said to Dick that he remembered me. I knew he didn't but was trying to elevate me. I told him he re-ignited a faith I thought I'd lost.

He hugged me. He said that if he touched one soul, his years of ministry were worth it. I excused myself, hurried to a bathroom stall, and wept.

Toward the conclusion of my year, a fellow VISTA set up an adult literacy program. She asked me to be a tutor. I said she should find somebody with experience. "There isn't anybody," she said, "and you're better than nobody." With that ringing endorsement, she gave me a manual. She said it had all I needed to know. We both knew it didn't.

I was introduced to Mr. M. He was in his late forties, brown-skinned and sharp-featured. He appeared part Native American, a mix common in many parts of the South. I recognized him from the choir at Trinity A.M.E. Church.

It was a summer of acute heat slathered with Midwest humidity. He wore a starched and pressed checkered shirt buttoned to the collar.

I made small talk as best I could. Formal and reserved, he was hard to draw out. He was born in Mississippi. His parents left after the war, part of the Great Migration that brought 6 million African Americans north and was just ending. He thought of going to Chicago, where most of his family was. "For now," he said, "Kansas City will do."

We met twice a week. He was functionally illiterate, which surprised me. I thought I'd be building on basics he already had. We started with phonetics. He was hesitant and reluctant to speak. I understood his fear that I'd judge him not unschooled but stupid, all the while silently indulging a white man's amused condescension.

I was moved by his determination. His interaction with whites was as a janitor. The condescension of whites, even when benevolent, was always there. He had no reason to trust me. He kept coming. Learning to read meant more than anything I might feel.

Our progress was small. One week I brought in the hymnal from church. I picked out a hymn. I asked if he knew it. When he said he did, I pointed out the words as he sang them. "Lord," "Adam," "Moses." I asked if he owned a Bible. We sounded out the lines of Genesis, "And God said . . ." He was intrigued. For the first time he seemed to relax and engage.

It was my time to leave. A more experienced tutor took my place. Mr. M. was in far better hands. We said our polite goodbyes.

Over the year, friends moving west to California and Colorado stopped for a night. They were finished with New York and looking to start over. As one put it, "The city's had it. It's a sinking ship." The news was decidedly grim. Crime was rising. Businesses and industries were moving out. The streets were dirtier than ever. The suburbs were filling up with ex-urbanites.

I seriously considered a fellow volunteer's offer to follow him to California and apply for a teaching job. The thought of starting over somewhere new had its attractions. But the heart has a compass of its own. I returned to New York. If the ship was going down, I was going with it.

My roommates and I planned to meet for a fiftieth-anniversary reunion. One had been sick so we moved it up. Turner House, the settlement house where we worked, was closed. The row of houses across from where we lived was gone. Kansas City had a significant Hispanic population that hadn't been there in our day.

Once-bustling Minnesota Avenue was pocked with empty storefronts. The drugstore was gone. The diner where we'd go for breakfast was boarded up. We ate at McDonald's, the only eatery available. The man at the urinal next to me swigged from a pint bottle of gin.

I don't know what we thought we'd find. We weren't deluded enough to expect that the year we spent made any difference. We listened and learned, did as we were asked, and went on with our lives, more aware than before.

###

I returned from Kansas City to the Bronx with no more idea of what I wanted for a career than when I left. The girl from Hot Dog Beach and I called it a day. At least, she did. I lied and told her I understood. We were apart for a year. She had every right to the life she wanted to live, and if I didn't fit in, so be it. I was mature about it. Heartbroken isn't a medical condition. Sometimes it only feels that way.

I went to the job placement office at Manhattan College. I had a nice chat with the pipe-smoking counselor. He'd graduated a few years ahead of me. He asked if my year in VISTA inclined me to social work. I said it inclined me otherwise.

We discussed other options. He said that with a B.A. in history, I was essentially qualified to apply to law school, or grad school, or become a teacher. I didn't ask about job counselor. The teaching option included a salary, which was a nice thing to have.

I was hired at an all-boys Catholic high school in New Jersey to teach religion and the humanities. I accepted the religious part not out of apostolic zeal. It was a pre-condition of taking the job. Since I didn't own a car or know how to drive, I had an hour bus ride from the East Bronx to meet a fellow teacher at the George Washington Bridge who drove the rest of the way. It was a dreadful commute to a dreadful job.

The *ancien régime* I endured as a youth had given way to more progressive approaches. Gone were compulsory dress codes, mandatory retreats, and unrestricted (sometimes perversely inventive) corporal punishments. The inmates were drunk on their new freedoms (sometimes on the lager consumed in the woods behind the school).

Immersed in the *Lord of the Flies* world of pubescent boys in the maelstrom of hormonal transmogrification, I sometimes marveled at the unfolding, however uneven, of their minds. Over a year, flashes of engagement with ideas would grow bright, intense.

Having experienced twelve years of hard-edged, unremitting discipline, I had no capacity to hold the line. There were times I yearned for the old-time arsenal of rulers and straps, and sobering slaps across the face.

It should be noted that parents endorsed the prevalence of physical rebuke in parochial schools that they had undergone and that grew out of the desire of generations of uneducated immigrants to instill in their children the discipline needed to forge ahead into the middle class and beyond.

I learned a lesson as well—subsequently reinforced by long experience in corporate life—that an hour teaching high school equals six hours in the office.

I was given the school's list of required reading, which included *The Red Badge of Courage* and *Kon-Tiki*, the same I was assigned at their age. Years later, Frank McCourt told me that one way to ensure a book was read but rarely enjoyed was to land on assigned reading lists.

I called him when my daughter's reading list included his eloquent, moving, mega-selling memoir, *Angela's Ashes*. I asked what he thought of reading lists now. "Better read than dead," he laughed.

I assigned Eldridge Cleaver's *Soul on Ice* and my old friend from the Coral Café Kurt Vonnegut's *Slaughterhouse-Five*. The principal, a moderately conservative, not unreasonable Brother, questioned but didn't overrule my choices. I took my students to see the movie version of Vonnegut's book. In one scene, a woman was in a pool with her breasts exposed.

The next morning, I was summoned to the principal's office. His face burned with the same indignation as his voice. He'd spent the previous afternoon taking calls from incensed parents who learned of their boys' reckless exposure to the naked upper half of a woman's body.

No one mentioned the movie's focus on the firebombing of Dresden and the mass incineration of thousands of innocent civilians.

The principal warned me that though it was too close to year-end to fire me, I had no chance of being rehired. In the future, he advised, I should find a job that didn't require commonsense or good judgement. I took him at his word and tried, with some success, to follow his advice.

I deserved the rebuke. He stretched his boundaries to accommodate me. In a time when he struggled to adjust window-shaking, wall-rattling change, and keep the roof from falling in, I set off the parents. The rest of my life might have been different if he overlooked my transgression and let me keep the job.

Decades later, I was contacted by several students who claimed to be grateful for the books and music I introduced them to. One said that the Dylan album I gave him changed his life. I like to believe it. I know that I learned I had neither the talent nor endurance to expend myself dragging wild, adolescent ponies to waters they had yet developed a thirst for.

⁂

Post my teaching debacle, I had one of the happiest, fulfilling periods of my life. I became a messenger, first for a real estate brokerage that specialized in high-end (unaffordable to all but the rich, very rich, and forget-about-it rich) Upper East Side apartments and townhouses.

My boss was sorry to see me go. I was one of the best messengers the firm ever had, she gushed. I never delivered a package to the wrong address, or got the lunch orders backward, or showed up drunk. She gave me an expensive bottle of Scotch as a going-away present. I waited until I was home before I indulged.

Experience has its privileges. I moved up to a better messenger position at a Wall Street law firm, with better pay and lunch on the firm. Instead of spending my time shuffling leases and deeds around the tony *arrondissements* of the Upper East Side, I traveled across the city filing court documents and serving papers.

Sexism boomed along with the market. Exiting the subway at the corner of Broad and Wall, secretaries were met with lewd and demeaning shouts and hoots from free-market chauvinists.

As long as papers were filed properly and on time, the day was mine. I rode the train to Coney Island and lunched on a hot dog at Nathan's. I read the paper on a decrepit pier where the great ocean liners once docked. The ride over the deteriorating Manhattan Bridge offered a sweeping view of the capacious harbor that I never tired of.

On howling, frost-bitten, Moscow-winter days, I warmed up in the main reading room of the New York Public Library. I was introduced to it in college. Although faded and frayed—its restoration decades in the future—its majesty remained.

I searched the rows of well-thumbed card catalogues for no particular book. I imagined the literary figures from the past who might have done the same. I sat at the long tables with washed-and-worn old men who looked like exiled Mensheviks or escapees from Nazi-occupied Europe. They wrote in tiny script on scraps of paper.

The girl from Hot Dog Beach moved to Colorado. I thought of her less and less, except when I passed the corner of Central Park where on a sweet spring afternoon we picnicked on wine, cheese, and bread and lay silently next to each other and studied the sky, and I kissed her in a way I never had before.

There were times that I paid a visit to the visitors' gallery above the trading floor of the New York Stock Exchange. With 9/11 still far off, it was practically open admission.

It seemed to me the floor hadn't changed much since the frenzy of the Roaring Twenties. There were no screens, no computers. Clerks and traders shouted, waved slips, gesticulated wildly in a writhing, frenetic, mesmerizing scene worthy of the inmates in Peter Weiss's *Marat/Sade*. Unlike a lot of Wall Street office jobs, it was never boring.

The pre-computerized volume of paperwork meant the market closed at 3:00 P.M. to deal with the backlog. The 1973 Yom Kippur War and oil embargo set off the worst decline since 1929. On a particularly grim day, the bars quickly filled.

Stricken if not entirely sober faces crowded the Killarney Rose. The few patrons who enjoyed themselves were the bears who bet against the market and looked forward to feasting on freshly butchered bulls.

One day, I was told to put on a tie and jacket and go to court to answer a calendar call, the pre-trial meeting in which attorneys for the opposing parties appear before a judge to be sent for trial or to seek a postponement. The opposing side had already agreed to an adjournment.

The rules were clear that only a lawyer could answer. But it was a busy time for the firm. They didn't want to waste a lawyer on a perfunctory chore.

Although it made me uncomfortable, I did it once or twice before without a problem. It was pre-arranged that the other side would ask for a first-time postponement, and I'd agree.

I arrived on time. Outside the courtroom white letters on a black background spelled out: Part I: Mr. Justice Peter A. Quinn Presiding. My fight-or-flight mechanism kicked in. I was ready to sprint out of the building across Foley Square. No one at the firm would blame me. They'd be in deep trouble if I were exposed.

Why I didn't turn and run, I'm not sure. Maybe I was being defiant, something I never was before. Maybe I was testing his loyalties. Maybe I was being stupid. We don't always know why we do things, which is why we so often keep doing them.

The clerk called the case. The lawyer for the other side and I stood at the table before the bench. He requested a postponement. There was a pause of seconds that dragged like minutes. I was ready to hear my father pronounce the death sentence. The rubber soles on my shoes felt as if they were melting.

"Counselor," he said, "do you agree?"

I didn't look up. I shuffled papers on the table in front of us. "Yes, Your Honor," I said in a dry croak.

"Granted," he said. "There'll be no more postponements." The barely restrained fury in his voice wasn't hard to detect. I'd heard it before.

Rather than wait, I called him that evening. We rarely talked on the phone. Longer and louder than I expected, the verbal scourging is seared in memory. The firm should be held in contempt and fined, he bellowed so loudly I moved the phone away from my ear. I should be indicted for impersonating a lawyer. His anger turned to exasperation. Did I have any idea of the serious consequences if I'd been recognized?

I punctuated his pauses with "I know. I'm sorry."

My mother had been pressuring him for some time to do something to pull me out of what she worried was a destructive vocational spiral. He offered a command, not a suggestion. "There's a court officer's test coming up in a few weeks. You'll take it."

I took the test with my friend Peter at Washington Irving High School, on Irving Place. We placed near the top. We were appointed as Uniform Court Officers to Bronx Civil Court.

I was assigned to Bronx Landlord & Tenant Court, which had recently been renamed Housing Court, although everyone went on referring to it as L&T. Once a sleepy corner of the city's court system, in a borough of middle- and working-class solidity, it was front and center in the spiraling urban crisis.

L&T was in the basement of the imposing limestone Art Deco Bronx County Courthouse, familiar to baseball fans as the gray hulk brooding over Yankee Stadium's centerfield. I was glad not to be assigned to Criminal Court, where officers were required to carry guns.

In Civil Court we were classified as peace officers, but it was up to us. Since I knew I'd never use it except to accidentally shoot myself or a colleague, I chose not to.

In later years, when the city courts were taken over by the state, a court officers' academy was established to provide professional training along the lines of the police department. Our training was essentially unchanged from the nineteenth—or perhaps eighteenth—century. We were given our blue police uniforms, badges, and a hunk of leather-covered lead known as a slapjack.

A veteran court officer took us around and showed us the basics. He advised we cover our slapjacks in Vaseline. It seemed an odd suggestion. Given his years of experience, I presumed he knew what he was talking about.

A fellow recruit asked him about it. "Well, you see," he said, "when you smack the 300-pound weightlifter coming at you on the head, and it has no effect, it won't hurt so much when he shoves it up your ass." I never used Vaseline. I hoped for the best, which is how it turned out.

My first assignment was to Part 17, where the daily calendar of cases was called and sent out to one of five windowless, claustrophobic minicourtrooms where a hearing officer did his best to settle the dispute.

Part 17 was a battered, barn-sized space that could hold up to 200 people. About 100 cases were called per day. Some days it exceeded 200. I was told the record was 300. Tenants and lawyers haggled in the hallway to see if they could resolve their dispute sans trial. If things seemed headed to something worse than imprecations, we intervened.

There were rumors that the Young Lords, the Puerto Rican version of the Black Panthers, were going to try to take over L&T. The Lords had won fame for their takeover of the nearby Lincoln Hospital, a dilapidated wreck of an institution that they forced the city to close and commit to build a new one.

The Lords occasionally accompanied tenants on a rent strike. There was slogan shouting, but that was it.

Felipe L. was one of the Lords' leaders. He was handsome, articulate, and charismatic. Frankie G., a fellow court officer whose father was a famous Latin band leader, was a friend of his and introduced me. Felipe was a wonderful conversationalist and seemed genuinely interested in what you had to say.

Our paths crossed years later when he was a TV commentator for the local Fox outlet. He was still good-looking and easy to talk to. We reminisced about the Bronx and got nostalgic.

Film crew from French or German or Japanese TV wandered into the court. They were in search of dramatic footage to let their home audiences see for themselves the wretched state of America's dying cities.

By the early '70s, dispossesses for nonpayment of rent topped an annual total of 100,000. As the Nixon recession took hold and unemployment reached nearly 10 percent, they soared to 130,000, equal to the population of Albany.

There were 1,600 murders citywide, nearly 400 in the Bronx. In the morning, prison-filled Department of Correction buses lined up along Walton Avenue. Newcomers and the uninitiated who walked too close found themselves subject to a shower of expectorant.

If the work was less than exhilarating, the pay was rewarding. Mine doubled from my former employment to $10,000. The boast of young professionals at the time was that their income kept pace with their age. I was in my mid-twenties. Though I didn't measure up to that standard, a five-figure income brought a novel level of comfort.

I lived with my brother, Tom, who was also a court officer, in a one-bedroom apartment on upper Broadway, in the north Bronx. Split two ways, our rent dropped from low to subterranean. Our only other fixed expense was a used Volkswagen. The rest was discretionary income that we indiscriminately lavished on meals, movies, drinks, dates, clothes, and shares in a summer place in the Hamptons. We didn't have to bother opening savings accounts because we didn't have any savings.

My first day in L&T, Herbie L., a fellow court officer, said in an accusatory voice, "I know how you got here." I guessed what was next. "Your old man fixed it." I told him I took the same test he had. In the improbable event my old man intervened, I said, I'd be stoking the boiler in the sub-basement.

A lawyer approached me. He confided he didn't want to wait around for his case to be called. Could I move it up? He handed me his papers. Inside was a $5 bill. I confided that he was lucky I didn't spit in his face, and if the day came when I found it necessary to sell my soul, it wouldn't be for $5. His was the last case called.

My father's chambers were on the courthouse's top floor. The few times I rode the elevator to pick up or drop something off, he was cordial in a formal way. He never invited me to linger or stay for lunch. He avoided even the semblance of elevating my brother and me above our peers.

If someone thought they could curry favor by giving us special treatment or jumping us to the head of the line, they were quickly disabused. He'd inherited his father's chipped-shouldered conviction that inherited privilege was the enemy of equality and individual achievement. We'd get what we earned.

The salary notwithstanding, the routine wore me down. The same cohort of lawyers fought day after unending day with the flow of disaffected tenants. The court felt less a Band-Aid than a scene from one of Samuel Beckett's darker plays.

I took the elevator to my father's chambers to tell him I intended to quit. He was visibly upset. He laid down the law: "You never quit a civil service job." He related a story I'd heard before about how in the depths of the Depression, fresh out of law school, he couldn't find a job. He rode the subway to Foley Square and found it mobbed with applicants for a small number of court officer positions. He recognized some of his classmates.

Put in your twenty years, he told me. Go to law school at night. Work your way up to a clerk one. When you retire you'll have a pension. Law firms will welcome someone with deep experience in the intricacies of filing papers and navigating the bureaucracy.

The unspoken subtext was you won't find yourself adrift again. You'll have a steady income and the security to provide for a family. He couldn't order me. But I stayed, mostly from inertia. I took the Bx1 bus up the Concourse after work and began course work for an M.A. in history at Fordham University.

Two days before Christmas 1974, my father died of lung cancer. He never liked Christmas. He became testy and morose, a hangover perhaps from his childhood. He was waked in the Castle Hill Funeral Home on Christmas Day. It was a holiday setting, I thought, he'd have found appropriate.

What hadn't been said between us remained unsaid. In the film *I Never Sang for My Father*, Gene Hackman's character reflects, "Death ends a life but it doesn't end a relationship." A reckoning was still to come.

I left the courts not long after. The city fell into a financial crisis. It got so bad, there was talk about paying city employees in scrip. On paydays we stampeded across the Grand Concourse to the Bronx Savings Bank to cash our checks. Layoffs were threatened.

For the first time, civil servants were eligible for unemployment benefits. Before court officers with families and kids were laid off, a call was made for volunteers. I was single and glad to make my escape. The prospect of collecting unemployment was irresistible. I was among the first to volunteer. I put the whole court experience behind me. I was free. And adrift.

I received a small inheritance from my aunt, who worked for almost fifty years as a telephone operator at Ma Bell. (It was Pa Bell when it came to management jobs and fat salaries.) It was a nice supplement to unemployment insurance, which, because of the rotten state of the economy, was extended from six months to a year.

The income was significantly less than what I made as a court officer, but my financial obligations were few, and what I lost in pay was more than made up for by the priceless gift of free time. When the unemployment benefit ran out and the inheritance was exhausted, I contemplated my options.

I'd done enough of doing what I had no interest in doing to be sure I didn't want to go to law school. I applied to the doctoral program in history at Fordham. The Loyola Fellowship I received allowed me the chance to study with Dr. Maurice O'Connell, the Dublin-born great-grandson of Daniel O'Connell.

Daniel O'Connell was a towering statesman of Irish history. He created the first mass political movement in European history, summoning "monster meetings" of more than a million people to win enfranchisement of Irish Catholics and agitating for repeal of the union with Britain. Revered by the Irish masses as "The Liberator," he has streets and squares across Ireland named after him, including Dublin's main thoroughfare.

I became Maurice's graduate assistant. Deeply learned, a respected scholar, he bore his distinguished ancestor a distinct physical resemblance, but the public-speaking gene hadn't been passed down. He was a raconteur outside the classroom, but his lecture style was to put his head down and read his notes.

His kindnesses were many. He involved me in his work on the multi-volume collection of Daniel O'Connell's correspondence and introduced me to the skill of in-depth historical research. With his support I went to Dublin to finish writing an article on W. B. Yeats and spent a summer at University College Galway.

The first day of class, I sat next to a lovely student, a Basque from Bilbao. We spent more and more time together and less and less in class.

We both roomed with families, so there was no chance, not back then, of spending the night in each other's rooms. We walked to the beach at Salt Hill and through country lanes. She sang Basque folk songs. The words were unintelligible, yet her ardent, lyrical voice created the mood, and the mood conveyed the meaning. She shared her passion for her Basque homeland—*Euskadi*—her hatred of Franco and her loathing of religion.

I remember best of all the times after dusk, a secluded lawn, her black opal eyes, her hair the color of midnight. At the end, she made clear she was returning to her fiancé in Bilbao.

I thought about following her but didn't. I knew she wouldn't change her mind. I wasn't going to relocate to Spain. We parted friends. I didn't regret the post-dusk lessons we shared on soft, yielding grass. I scrambled to make up for all the studying I hadn't done.

As well as a graduate assistant, I taught as an adjunct at Manhattan College and worked as the archivist at the New York Botanical Garden (the borough's natives and those interested in geographic accuracy refer to the "Bronx Botanical Garden").

Afternoons, I roamed the top floor of the Beaux-Arts administrative building and peeked in cartons of files, some of which hadn't been opened since the sinking of the *Maine*. It was a job I loved, although my combined salaries hovered south of a living wage.

Some days I left the cartons untouched, watched the breeze stir the sea of green treetops, and thought of the girl from Hot Dog Beach. She moved back from Colorado and lived with her sister Chris and friends in Westhampton. We re-ignited our relationship. The flame was fleeting.

She went north to attend graduate school in Albany. I didn't hear from her. I tried to console myself that our long, tortured relationship was finally over. I found no consolation.

I crossed over the line into my thirties. Friends were already onto a second marriage or had a second kid. Almost everyone I knew was a few years into their careers and enjoying promotions and bonuses. Yale professor Charles Reich's bestselling prediction of *The Greening of America* turned out economic rather than ecological.

I was bunking in South Yonkers, a short hop over the Bronx border, with Tom and our friend Jeff. The area was what the word *unsavory* was coined to describe.

Tom worked as a cook/bartender at the Colonnades, across yet-to-be-revitalized Lafayette Street from the Public Theater. The owner was a cocaine addict who sometimes slept with his head on the bar. Jeff, a multi-talented graphic designer and playwright, bartended at an after-hours club.

Our friend Nora S. dubbed us "the island of lost boys." She was partly right. We were lost but no longer boys. A feeling of being left behind was no longer a premonition.

I became friends with several Jesuits. I greatly admired the faith and scholarship of priests like George Hunt and George McCauly, their un-cloistered intellects, their ease and openness in navigating the secular world. I considered joining the order.

The flirtation was very brief. I was sitting in a carrel on the second floor of Duane Library. The warm, green, expectant fragrance of April wafted through the window. Outside, the lawn was littered with male and female students studying or sunbathing. One couple was in a tight embrace. I knew a vow of celibacy would always be a bridge too far.

In my last semester at Fordham, the economy was in a punishing reces-sion. Oil was in short supply, but not professors. College enrollments were down. The Baby Boomer tidal wave crested and crashed ashore. Schools of would-be academics lay flopping on the sand, struggling to breathe.

It was 1979. Ten years out of Manhattan College, I was treading water, which is sometimes a prelude to drowning. The state Education Depart-ment convened a meeting for Ph.D. students in the humanities—"loser studies," a fellow graduate assistant mordantly put it—from schools around the metropolitan area.

The intent was to help us switch to M.B.A. programs and have a shot at something more than a stitched-together existence of adjunct positions salaried at a dishwasher's level. I'm not sure if I was the most depressed person in the room.

Like suspects in a "perp walk," we kept our heads sunk low. We avoided eye contact. We were being arraigned for failing to choose a career that would allow us to be productive citizens. We wasted time and money. It was a serious offense. We had no choice but to plead guilty.

I left more depressed than when I came. I knew I'd fail at a business career without really trying. I went to a grungy bar around the corner, on Broadway. There was a young woman from the meeting. We stopped pretending we didn't recognize each other.

She was from Denver. Attractive, articulate, and funny, she was studying for a Ph.D. in French literature at NYU. We laughed at our predicaments. Then we got sad and cried in our two-for-a-dollar beers. The price was right. We had more than planned. We agreed to meet again. I took her phone number.

I waited a week to call. The number was no longer in service. I wondered if she'd gone back to Denver. I couldn't blame her.

PART TWO

The Capital Years

I PASSED MY ORAL EXAMS and began work on my thesis. I wrote a series of personal reflections for *America*, the Jesuit weekly. The editor, Father Joe O'Hare, a Bronx-born erudite, urbane Jesuit who became the president of Fordham, was very generous to me.

A close associate of Governor Carey contacted me. He read one of the articles and liked it so much he passed it on to the governor. He said the governor liked it too. He told me the governor was looking for a speechwriter. Would I be interested?

Yes, I said, as I tried to tame the desperation in my voice. The only problem was that if the governor wanted a sample, I couldn't provide it. I'd never written a speech. All I had were a few articles and two long pieces from academic journals.

My father told my brother and me that all we'd inherit "is my good name and the whole world to conquer." The first part proved true. Whether he read the materials I sent or not, I knew the governor gave me a chance in large part because of my name.

The governor and my father knew and liked each other. They were the same kind of New Deal Democrats. I was friends with his sons from Shelter Island. I was also aware that he didn't suffer hangers-on. If I couldn't do the job, I'd be lucky to get a provisional position in the Rensselaer County Department of Motor Vehicles.

I was called down to a Midtown office on the Friday of Memorial Day weekend and asked to write the Fordham Law School commencement speech for that Sunday. I knew it was a test. What was I like under pressure? How fast could I write? How well? I had nothing to lose. I did my best and turned it in late that afternoon.

The governor used it. The next week I was asked to write the John Jay College commencement. I went to Carnegie Hall to hear him give it. It was the first time I ever heard my words spoken in public. The governor had stage presence. He knew how to take over a lectern and deliver a speech. The following week I was hired.

On my way to the job, I was warned by a cynical veteran of state politics, "The Executive Chamber is a shark pool. They'll eat you up and spit you out. You won't last a month." The sharks turned out to be an entirely different kettle of fish—helpful, thoroughgoing professionals who remained friends long after I left the Executive Chamber. I lasted almost six years.

I quickly learned lessons that stayed with me for the rest of my career. Speeches came in all sizes and styles. Sometimes more care and attention went into three pages than fifteen. Speeches I thought significant, the speaker approached casually, and vice versa. Speeches by committee were the type of cruel and unusual punishment the Eighth Amendment was intended to exclude.

Sometimes, I was bereft of directions. Other times, the directions kept changing, and endless hours went into revising and rewriting. There were times the speaker didn't know what he wanted to say until he read what I wrote and realized he wanted to say the opposite.

There were "security-blanket speeches" whose purpose was to provide a fallback if the speaker's attempt at extemporizing flopped. There were speeches added and canceled at the last moment. Speeches that came with relative ease or that didn't come at all.

Over the years, I was told on more than one occasion that I had a "knack." When it comes to speeches, I'm not sure what exactly constitutes a knack, but if it implies the ability to do effortlessly what others find difficult, I'm knackless.

For me, the day-to-day challenge was the search for a central idea or story to thread through a speech and sew together what would otherwise be a hodgepodge.

In my first weeks on the job, a high-ranking member of the governor's staff came by my office. I was two hours and fifteen cigarettes into looking at a blank page. The deadline loomed. She said it seemed I wasn't doing anything. Could I help her with a speech?

"Right now, Irma," I said, "I'm sitting in the Garden of Gethsemane. If my sweat turns to blood, I won't be surprised." I don't know if she thought I was being flip—I wasn't—but she left in a huff.

The shock of adjusting from the semi-glacial pace of academics to the velocity of major-league politics engendered an initial period of vertigo. When I arrived, it was summertime and the speech calendar appeared relatively light. That week a major contributor died. The governor was asked to deliver the eulogy. The press office gave me names to call "to get some background," which I did. The governor liked what I wrote.

It turned out to be a season of requiems. There was a memorial service at Lincoln Center for A. Philip Randolph, a giant of the labor and civil rights movements who organized the March on Washington. The governor was the main eulogist. I stayed up to the wee hours writing it. The *Times* covered it. The governor liked it.

The following week, another labor leader died. The governor was requested to speak. I was afraid I was being followed by the Angel of Death.

The governor was asked by Pat Cunningham, the Democratic leader of the Bronx (he eventually went to jail, but that's a whole other story), to fill in as keynote speaker at their annual dinner. The governor laughed that, being a native son, this should be easy for me. Then he spoke three words I dreaded to hear: "Make it funny." There's nothing easier to flub than comedy. I did my best and recycled some Bronx political lore.

A speech on insurance reform was added at the last minute. I knew as much about insurance reform as I did about Fermat's polygonal number theorem. Since time was short, I was told to speak directly to the insurance commissioner, who'd fill me in on what the governor needed to say.

The commissioner's office reported he was too busy to be of assistance and passed me off to a mid-level functionary. "Insurance reform?" he yawned, "It's a favorite topic of mine. Blah, blah, blah." I found a lawyer in the Executive Chamber who took pity on me. With his help, I got by.

After a contentious dispute with the governor, a colleague asked if I'd write his resignation letter. Despite their disagreement, he wanted the governor to know that he admired his leadership and was proud to have served in his administration.

Several days later, the governor called. He'd received the resignation letter that impressed him as "generous and honest." He instructed me to write a response "in that same spirit." My friend got in touch to thank me. "The governor wrote back," he said. "I appreciate he took the time." I appreciated that he didn't ask me to re-respond.

I was assigned Helen Ross as my assistant. The office manager told me Helen's primary skills were typing and answering the phones. In other words, don't expect much.

Helen was in her late forties. She was stout with a modified Afro. She had such a small, soft voice that when she answered the phone, callers imagined she was just out of her teens. She'd been born in East St. Louis and had grown up in Chicago, in the notorious Cabrini-Green housing project.

At first impression, she was quiet, distant, and standoffish. It took a while to realize how deeply shy she was. Politically, she was a law-and-order conservative. Her sister had been murdered by a boyfriend who got a laughably light sentence. Her father was wounded and robbed while sitting in a car outside their apartment building. It was unwise to argue with her about the death penalty.

She was one of four Black students to integrate an all-white high school. No white student talked to her in her four years. She came to New York by bus, lived in a hostel, and worked her way up from a filing clerk in a state office in Harlem to the governor's office. "I've never asked for a handout," she said in answer to a question I didn't ask but that she, as a Black person, suspected was on most white people's minds.

She was punctilious and unflappable. Once, while she was still typing, a state trooper and the press aide raced down the hallway. They shouted at her that they needed the speech immediately. The governor was about to leave. Unruffled, she typed with complete sangfroid, as if they weren't there. They got their speech in time.

A dictionary maven who wore out Webster's checking spelling (never one of my strengths) and self-trained grammarian, she read every speech aloud with me. When she deemed phrasing awkward or unclear, I knew better than to argue.

Working out of two cities meant my congenital state of disorganization became a danger to my continued employment. My briefcase and pockets were stuffed with notes, receipts, miscellaneous scraps with barely legible reminders of appointments that may or may not have already passed. My desk was a mare's nest of books and papers.

Helen kept meticulous files of speeches and memos and even provided me with an index. She organized a calendar and alerted me each day to meetings and deadlines. Endowed with a sharp intellect, she had organizational skills worthy of the Prussian General Staff. Helen became my rock and my foundation.

The governor was scheduled to be the main speaker at a national conference on public transportation at the New York Hilton. The speech was done and okayed by the commissioner of transportation and various program associates. Then it was announced that President Carter was coming. The speech was flushed.

Under the best of circumstances, relations between a Brooklyn pragmatist who cast a cold eye on political purists and moralists and a country-bred president who prided himself on not being a "professional politician"—and was cursed with an unfortunate penchant for speeches that sounded like sermons—were destined to be rocky.

Years before, Ed Flynn, a professional politician par excellence, warned, "Beware the amateurs." As he saw it, next to fanatics—which some of them turned out to be—they ran the gamut from ignorant (think Jesse Ventura) to inept (think Arnold Schwarzenegger) to dangerous (think real estate mogul–turned–reality TV star).

To those who made a career of getting elected, "professional politician" was a sobriquet of distinction. Getting elected time after time meant staying close to constituents, serving their needs, earning their trust, building majorities, not waving magic wands.

As my father pointed out, opportunists were never in short supply. Both sides of the aisle had their share of schemers and knaves. But at their best, they stood by the policies their party espoused yet weren't partisans of a whole loaf or none. They cared about results. They recognized the distance between what opponents demanded and what they'd settle for.

They weren't above taking revenge, but only to teach a lesson, rarely for the sport of tasting blood. They lived by the truth that there are no final victories in politics. Far from perfect, and not immune to corruption, they tried to avoid stalemates and dead ends.

Tip O'Neill famously said, "All politics is local." Most of the time, it's also personal. The names and faces change, but not the dynamic. Jimmy Carter prided himself on not being one of the capital's pros.

He proved that in short order by employing a staff of young, arrogant aides whose superciliousness antagonized Speaker O'Neill and Democratic Whip Dan Rostenkowski, the last two men in Washington you wanted to piss off.

Where the Democrats saw their post-Watergate landslide as a chance to pass universal health care, institute a major jobs program, and reward members by funding favorite projects, Carter tightened the purse strings. Part preacher, part technocrat, he was comfortable with machines except when they were of the political type.

For his part, the governor expected the Democratic president to shower the kind of largesse on New York he'd had to beg for from the Republican administration. When it didn't, he came to share the same opinion of the president as his longtime friends in Congress.

In his speech to the transportation experts, the governor told me, he wanted the president from Georgia to hear his frustration. I did my best to give him what he wanted: "When it comes to New York, there are those in D.C. who share the sentiment of Scarlett O'Hara's lover Rhett Butler: 'Frankly, they don't give a damn.'"

I was standing in the service entrance of the Hilton with the governor, his press secretary Mike P., and trusted assistant Tom R. when the president and his retinue pulled in. The impressive swarm of vehicles, aides, and Secret Service agents was like the Shah's sweeping in to accept obeisance from a satrap. The only one unimpressed was the governor. He offered the president a polite if perfunctory greeting and escorted him inside.

When the governor spoke, he dropped the most critical lines and extemporized a far more conciliatory speech. I wasn't entirely surprised. He got out the venom in the speech he had me write. He was too much a pro to attack the president of his party in such a public venue.

The night Carter lost to Reagan, I was among those invited to watch the returns in the Governor's Mansion. The news of Ronald Reagan's landslide victory over Carter came early. It was plain that if the governor wasn't thrilled by who won, he wasn't overly disappointed by who lost.

Most times, I tried to stay away from events at which my speeches were delivered. When there was no way out, I felt my stomach tighten and palms turn wet, as if I were watching a race with a horse I'd bet heavily on.

Instead of following the horse, I focused on the delighted, bored, excited, apathetic faces of the spectators. Their applause or lack of it told me how the race was going and either lifted me up or left me crushed.

A well-crafted speech was no guarantee of success. Sometimes, a speaker's zombie-like delivery could suck the life out of the text; other times, the speech itself was the problem. There were audiences that wouldn't be moved by the Sermon on the Mount. I decided that my job was to produce a horse worth riding. The rest was up to the jockey.

My first flight on the state plane was on a dark, gray winter's morning to gray, dark Buffalo. The governor and the weather were in the same mood.

The governor sometimes reminded me of my father. He was always charming in public. Out of public view, he was susceptible to what my mother called "the Irish blues." There were times when nothing anyone did was good enough. He expressed his angry frustration at being surrounded by incompetents. This was one of those times.

Along with the advance team was Communications Director Bill S. and the head of his security detail, Captain Marty B. of the State Police.

They referred to trips like this as "a visit to the Eastern Front." Those who could avoid it, did. Bill and Marty sat across from the governor. He berated them for so long about the arrangements, I thought he might ask them to step outside. I hid with members of the advance team several seats behind. The governor summoned me. He disliked the speech.

Buffalo was more bereft than I'd imagined. Among the fastest-growing cities at the turn of the twentieth century, it was now among the depressed and depressing. The governor went to meet with the mayor and local and state officials. The audience was small. He made a point of tossing my text aside and extemporizing his speech.

He repeated to Bill and Marty how dissatisfied he was. He intended to get to the bottom of who thought up this stupid misuse of his time. He went off to lunch with the mayor. We huddled with the advance team in a coffee shop next door.

When I'm nervous, I can barely keep down a glass of water. I nursed my water while they ate cheeseburgers, fries, and chocolate malteds. Somebody moaned about the flight home still in front of us.

I tried to console. Suppose this was the 1820s instead of the 1980s, I said, and the Erie Canal hadn't been built nor the railroad nor the Thruway, and we were accompanying Governor DeWitt Clinton on an eight-day, 600-mile stagecoach roundtrip from Albany. Think how much worse that would be.

The others shrugged. If they found any consolation it was in another round of burgers and malteds. The flight back was tense but uneventful. I promised myself to go on future flights only when required.

I'd attended the St. Patrick's Day Parade since I was a boy. My father took us to the reviewing stand. He was chief judge of the City Court. We sat next to Mayor Robert Wagner. He and my father had served together in the state Assembly and were old friends.

There were a lot of bands and bagpipes but no floats. It was very cold. I remember thinking it would have been better if St. Patrick's Day were in May.

Governor Carey was equally proud of his Irish as well as his Brooklyn roots. I enjoyed marching with him in the parade. He sometimes got heckled over his refusal to sign the death penalty bill. One year it got nasty. A group of harassers followed him up Fifth, yelling "fucking pussy," "cocksucking coward," the full Anglo-Saxon lexicon. He seemed not to notice. He went on waving and smiling. The tone got increasingly menacing.

Captain Marty B. said he was going to take him out of the parade before someone threw a bottle or worse. He went up to the governor, who waved him away.

Carey was a decorated officer who landed in France soon after D-Day and was in combat until it reached the Rhine. He married a war widow whose husband had perished in the war. They were the parents of thirteen children. Two teenage sons died in a car accident on Shelter Island. His wife died of cancer. He knew all about death.

If he was bothered by the hecklers, he gave no sign. They fell away. He went on marching. He could be verbally abused and threatened. He couldn't be intimidated.

∷

As well as speechwriter, the governor made me advisor on "The Troubles," the woefully inadequate moniker for the conflict in Northern Ireland.

Along with Speaker Tip O'Neill and Senators Ted Kennedy and Daniel Patrick Moynihan, the governor made up the quartet of Irish-American elected officials—"The Four Horsemen"—determined to help break the tit-for-tat sectarian violence and build a permanent peace.

Together, they employed their considerable political heft to oppose Irish-American support for the IRA, overcome the time-honored Anglophilia of the U.S. foreign-policy elite, and convince the British that the only real hope of changing the equation was to admit a role for Dublin and Washington. This is exactly what transpired in the Good Friday Agreement that ended the fighting two bloody decades later.

At the governor's behest and with the encouragement of Consul General (later ambassador) Sean O'hUiginn, I traveled in early 1981 to the North with John Hume, who led the Catholic civil rights movement and headed the Social Democratic Labor Party.

Hume dedicated his life to peaceful resolution of the conflict. Eventually, after years of heroic persistence and at risk of his own life, he shared the 1998 Nobel Peace Prize for his central role in bringing about the Good Friday Agreement.

I didn't get much sleep on the flight from JFK to Dublin. When we arrived, Hume went off to confer with members of the Irish government. I wandered Dublin. I stopped in Davy Jones Pub where Leopold Bloom lunched on a gorgonzola cheese sandwich and a glass of red wine. I had shepherd's pie and skipped the wine. We picked up a rental car for the three-hour drive from Dublin to Derry.

When Hume informed me he didn't know how to drive, I reluctantly took the wheel. In all my times in Ireland, my fear and loathing of driving on the left side of the road never left me. I always felt one wrong turn away from vehicular homicide (or suicide).

Once we were out of Dublin on the road north, Hume fell asleep. The angst of left-side motoring kept me alert until we crossed the border and neared Derry. I began to nod and drifted to the wrong side of the road as a truck barreled toward us.

Hume suddenly jolted up in his seat, grabbed the wheel, and steered the car to the right. If he hadn't wakened at that moment, the consequences for the both of us—as well as for Ireland—would have been tragic.

This was my first time in the North. In the Republic, except for a core of committed Nationalists, I mostly encountered benign indifference and active disinterest—sometimes outright hostility—toward involvement in the conflict in the Six Counties. The general attitude was that the situation was intractable and it was useless to get drawn in.

Northern Ireland felt more like a different country than a separate province. Poisoned by decades of misrule that empowered an economic and political monopoly by the Protestant majority and embittered the disenfranchised Catholic minority, the sense of besiegement, resentment, and an unbridgeable divide was everywhere. The British army was waging war, not keeping the peace.

I had a cordial lunch with an official of the Presbyterian church. He had a ruddy face and thick, wavy gray hair. He'd have looked at home in any New York Irish bar. He confided that the problem in the North wasn't political or religious, but racial. Catholics and Protestants were from two distinct gene pools.

On the Falls Road, the heart of the Catholic ghetto, a supporter of the IRA told me that Irish Americans who didn't get behind the armed struggle were either dupes or collaborators who did far more harm than good. People like me should stay away.

A short time later, along with John Hume, I attended an off-the-record meeting at Ditchley Park, a stately eighteenth-century English country house used for conferences to promote international relations, especially between Britain and the United States.

Sponsored by the British Foreign Office, the conference brought together representatives of the North's Unionist and Nationalist parties, the Irish and British governments, and the Four Horsemen.

Sir Humphrey Atkins, Prime Minister Margaret Thatcher's Secretary for Northern Ireland, opened the conference. He wore a tie emblazoned with the Red Hand, the symbol of Northern Ireland. Beneath was the date 1607, the founding of the plantation designed to displace and subjugate the native population.

He was followed by Hume, who good-naturedly pointed out that, since Catholics regarded 1607 the way Native Americans did 1492, Sir Humphrey might want to reconsider his choice in neckwear.

The Secretary's harrumph was peevish and dismissive. Arrogance is the eternal prerogative of empires. That's what makes them empires, even when the empire itself is no longer there.

The conference participants sat at four long conference tables formed in a square. I sat next to Harold McCusker, a no-surrender Unionist M.P. I saw him once on TV when I was in the Republic. He struck me as a classic anti-Catholic bigot and intransigent Unionist.

I took an immediate dislike. I assumed he did the same toward the meddlesome Irish American next to him. When he spoke, he offered a blow-torch denunciation of supporters of a united Ireland and gave a special scouring to "ignorant, naïve meddling by outsiders" (i.e., Americans).

He turned to me at the end of the session. I anticipated a furnace blast. I disagreed with everything he said. I braced myself to tell him the "mass support of Irish Americans for the IRA" was fantasy. It was in the best interests of all sides to make use of the desire of Irish-American political leaders to help bring about a peaceful solution.

He surprised me. He didn't touch on politics. He asked in a good-natured way where I was from. "You don't sound like most Americans I've met," he said. I hesitated before I told him I'd been raised in the Bronx. I thought it might set him off. He had to know that NORAID, the American arm of hardcore IRA supporters, was headquartered there.

He didn't bring it up. He wondered about the larger picture, "the Bronx" as shorthand for urban jungle, a synecdoche for an out-of-control wasteland of drugs and crime, and entire neighborhoods in flames. He was curious: How could anyone from the Bronx imagine he had advice to offer on conflict resolution?

I told him we had a Bronx word for it: *chutzpah*. We couldn't offer solutions but could offer sympathy. Maybe that's where all solutions started. For all its economic and racial problems, I said, "the Bronx was a no-bullshit place: According to the *Oxford Book of English Usage*, it's the only place in the English-speaking world where 'Have a nice day' is pronounced, 'Why don't you go fuck yourself.'" He laughed. I wasn't entirely kidding.

Maybe he was humbugging me. I didn't think so. I was among the conference's least influential participants. There were far more significant players to schmooze. We stayed up late drinking and avoiding politics. He liked *noir* movies as much as I did.

He professed to admire people unabashedly proud of where they came from, especially from wounded, stigmatized acreage like the Bronx and Northern Ireland. He said he knew what it was like to be looked down upon on account of where you came from.

He visited New York sometime later. I took him to dinner at Reidy's (now closed), an old-style Irish-American Midtown cocktail bar of the kind wiped out by faux pubs and posh purveyors of Bellinis and appletinis.

We barhopped from Costello's (now closed), with James Thurber's drawings on the wall, to the Village's literary den, the Lion's Head (now closed), on Christopher Street, where he cast a suspicious eye on the voluble, biblious clientele.

We touched on politics only once. It was almost 2:00 A.M. We were outside his hotel. The river of bitterness and bloodshed in the North was too deep to be bridged, he said. Ulster's Protestants would never be forced into a united Ireland. If the fighting stopped, and the wounds had time to heal, and people stuck to local issues, maybe in a century or two things might change. That was as optimistic as he could be.

"History has its own momentum, and goes in directions we can't foresee," I said. We left it at that. He changed none of his views. I changed none of mine. What we had was a fleeting, unspoken truce that put our gaping differences aside.

I promised that the next time I was in the North I'd look him up. I didn't. He said he wanted to return to New York. I said when he did I'd give him a tour of the Bronx. He said he'd love that. I don't know whether he returned or not. I never heard from him.

I read of his death in the papers a decade later. The obituary said that he had long suffered from cancer, but, according to friends, his will to live was broken by the Good Friday Agreement, which couldn't have happened without U.S. intervention in the form of President Bill Clinton.

He decried it as a sellout that dishonored the Unionist dead and would end with surrender to Irish nationalists. It was an agreement I enthusiastically and vociferously supported.

There are things that bring people together and things that pull them apart. I regret not having had the chance to show him the Bronx.

On summer weekends Governor Carey helicoptered to his home on Shelter Island. I was free to come along. Mostly I didn't. I enjoyed the train ride to Greenport. I read, drank a beer, savored the flat farmlands, and welcomed the salt taste and first glimpse of the sea.

The ferry ride was a physical separation from the world of work and obligation. The first time I rode it I was three days old.

The Republicans helped see Tom and me into the world. After they unseated our father from Congress, he traveled with my mother to close his Washington office. He was forty-three and she forty. She did her best to take his mind off his loss.

Over the years, my mother made obliquely jocular reference to Tom and me beginning life in a hotel near the White House. It never failed to irk my father and drive him out of the room.

The baby's arrival was predicted for August. My parents decided to go to Westmoreland until the time arrived to return to the Bronx for the baby's birth. My mother grew so large, she told the doctor on Shelter Island she felt she was having either an octopus or a baby elephant. He sent her to Greenport Hospital for an X-ray, which revealed there were two of us rather than one.

He didn't think it wise for her to travel and admitted her to the hospital, a medical facility that was state of the art circa 1910. It was originally wood, and a brick wing was added just before the war. A separate delivery room was a recent addition. There was no air conditioning.

Several days later, we made the one-way slide down the birth canal. I debuted at 3:00 A.M., at 7 lbs., 6 oz. Tom came out three hours and forty minutes later, at 8 lbs., 8 oz., a baby-pachyderm total of 15 lbs., 14 oz. My mother wasn't given anesthesia because they were unsure when the second labor would come.

It became family lore that her hair turned white from the long ordeal of the delivery. If it did, it returned to its natural color soon after. No matter, the story persisted, the way oft-repeated stories do.

We spent our first weeks at Westmoreland and were baptized at Our Lady of the Isle church. My mother's sister Marion, who usually drove my parents and sisters to and from Shelter Island, stayed to help. That's the way it was for the summers that followed.

When do we first wake to our surroundings? For me, there was no one moment. My earliest memories were of Parkchester, my sweetest of Shelter Island.

I sensed Westmoreland before I recognized it: the airiness of North Ridge cottage, which though smaller than our apartment felt far more spacious; the laxness of time and absence of urgency; the mid-day, post-lunch torpor, naptime for kids and adults alike; the informality of meals; bedtimes while it was still light.

A special part was having Marion with us the whole summer. She shared our care with my mother. She packed sandwiches and took us to the beach. I lay my head in her lap when she read us to sleep. She never showed a parent's impatience, even when justified.

Marion was the first in the family to go to college. She worked as a secretary at St. Vincent's Hospital in Greenwich Village and attended the Fordham School of Education on lower Broadway at night.

She became a second-grade teacher in the Edgewater, New Jersey, public schools. By the time she retired forty years later, she'd taught most of the town. After my grandfather died, she and an older sister stayed at home to support my grandmother, which they did until she died.

She was stylish, intelligent, and educated. She had her beaus and suitors. The only male I knew her to be interested in was a Jesuit priest, Father Daniel Ryan, S.J.

He taught Marion psychology at Fordham. They shared a love of books, theater, and New York City. They became intellectual soulmates. Did their relationship go further? I sincerely doubt it. Skeptics will scoff. It was a different time. Their faith meant everything to them. Human nature doesn't change. How people act and think does.

Marion never showed the slightest sign of being unhappy as a single woman. She approached every moment with expectant joy. She was like a second mother. Having her with us was a special grace.

Those Westmoreland summers blended into one blithe, rainless blur.

Nights, the rain fell like musical notes on the rooftop. Dawn was dewy and full of promise. A breeze shuffled the calico curtains in the window beside our beds. We woke eager to discover what the new day would bring.

Tom and I ran onto the porch. The morning sun glistened on the wet grass. Across the way, West Neck Creek mirrored fresh daylight. We hurried our cereal, threw on shorts and tee shirts, and ran out to meet Westmoreland's jack of all that needed to be jacked, Clint Walker. He reached down, pulled us up onto the cracked leather seat of his truck and circled the farm collecting trash.

We begged him to drive over the roughest, rutted terrain. We bounced up and down. He answered our squeals with laughter. We stopped at the farm's kennel. We lay on the ground as a pack of ravenously playful beagle puppies pawed, and crawled over us, and licked our faces. One fell asleep on my legs.

We went shoeless. The grass tickled the soles of our shoe-accustomed feet. They gradually grew tough and callused until we could walk stony beaches without flinching.

We didn't appreciate how recently the penumbra of Depression and war had lifted. But the relief and joy were palpable. The McCaffreys had four sons in the war. Two were captured, one wounded, all were home safely. They carried us on their shoulders, played ball, caroused late into the night, and kept the war to themselves.

Col. Roe patrolled in his jeep. He didn't smile. We mostly avoided him. He gave us canteens covered in canvas attached to canvas belts. We wore them everywhere. We slept out in canvas tents. Wet canvas had a military smell. We told ourselves the canteens and tents were used at Bataan and D-Day.

We roamed with a freedom unthinkable today. Parents trusted in fate, God, the saints. I don't remember learning to swim. I can't recall not being able to. Tom, Frankie, Gordie, and I went where we wanted. We got lost in a cornfield. We made a fort in a far corner of the woods. We built a dam that flooded a whole meadow before it broke.

Gordie inadvertently wiped himself with poison ivy. We stood outside his window as his mother applied calamine lotion and did her best to soothe his moaning misery.

Baseball games were played on Saturday mornings. Col. Roe made Tom and me the team mascots. We had our own uniforms.

There were clambakes. Old-time island clammers dug a pit on the beach, lined it with large stones, set a fire until the stones were red hot, lay on clams and lobsters, layers of seaweed, potatoes, and corn.

We ate at wooden tables and wore paper bibs. Lobster juice and melted butter dribbled down our chins. Rowboats were filled with beer and soda covered in ice. Our hands went numb as we fished for our favorite.

At the beefsteaks, we wore the same paper hats and aprons as the adults. There were no knives or forks. The rare beef was sliced and lay on pieces of bread that soaked up the juices. Platters of sliced tomatoes, ripe and salted, were passed around. At night's end, there was the murmur of songs we didn't know but made some adults sigh and grow sad.

The costume party was held in the barn. My brother and I went as farm hands. We used rakes for pitchforks. Brown shoe polish substituted for beards. Adults we thought stiff and formal came as clowns and giant clams and Raggedy Ann.

Col. Roe stored up a supply of fireworks. On July 4th, they whizzed into the night sky, burst in mid-air, and spewed a shower of multicolored sparks. Cars lined up on the other side on West Neck Creek and honked as the barrage reached its crescendo.

The adults were never sour. We all got along. Nobody argued. There was never a cloudy morning that didn't turn bright. The days were hot, but never too hot. The water was cold but not enough to make us shiver. After a few minutes we didn't notice. We went to bed exhausted and woke renewed, ready.

On Sundays we drove to Our Lady of the Isle church. In the afternoon the adults drank cocktails and napped. We stole away to the Sunken Garden where we were told not to go, picked raspberries and blackberries, and scored our hands red with scratches. When the adults saw the marks and our berry-colored lips, they pretended to be mad. We knew they weren't.

The mayor visited from the city. There was an adults-only dinner. My father and a boatload of men went fishing on Col. Roe's *Margaret R.* They came back with few fish and bad sunburns. Nobody complained. They enjoyed their day at sea, and the sandwiches and plenty of cold beer.

Babe Ruth spent the day. It was his last summer, shortly before he died. My brother and I were infants. Somebody placed us on his lap. I cried and wet my diaper and the pee came through onto his white duck pants. The Babe laughed good-naturedly, as did everybody else.

I heard the story so many times, I hated it. I welcomed when the time came I could recount my encounter with Mickey Mantle, which made me something more than a mewling, incontinent dwarf.

The summer ended with a huge bonfire. The last night, we threw on scrap wood and dead branches. We got so close, it felt like sunburn. The adults sang and sang. My parents had fine voices. They sang the parodies my father wrote. We stayed up late and slipped into sleep hoping against hope when we woke summer would be just beginning.

Winter came. We re-accustomed ourselves to bricks and shoes and elevators. Slapped back into parochial-school uniforms, burdened with schoolbags filled with pens and textbooks and homework—the load grew heavier as the year went on—we slouched our way to school.

By Christmas, we stopped thinking about summer, until the lengthening days and lingering light told us it was coming, and then it did. We knew the day we'd set foot on Shelter Island was fast approaching.

We returned to Shelter Island but not to the farm. My parents rented a house in the Heights. There were no bitter partings. Time was moving on. People had new priorities and different destinations. We went to a few more clambakes. They were smaller than I remembered. There were no July 4th fireworks. Shelter Island remained part of our lives, but it was never the same.

Those summers are sealed in memory, mythical and wonderful, perfect and untrue, fashioned by time and distance into an unblemished place, unreachable, unreal but real.

I've returned many times, in dreams and daydreams, when I've been anxious and winter-weary and worried about endless things to worry about. So much more fragile than I knew, the moment stays intact in my heart. No summer can ever be as carefree, as gentle, as contented. What did Eve feel when she looked back on Eden?

■■■

Many of the island's permanent residents were descendants of the original settlers. They were plumbers, carpenters, landscapers. They manned the ferries, pumped gas, repaired boats and docks, fished and clammed for income rather than sport.

The islanders were known locally as "hareleggers." The etymology was disputed. Some claimed it grew out of when the island was a nesting ground for long-legged herons; others maintained it was how mainlanders described the islanders' mad dash to catch the last ferry.

Hareleggers shared a special disdain for "summer people," a term synonymous with privileged, arrogant, lazy, seasonally predictable intruders whose lucre was crucial to the island economy and presence a barely tolerable nuisance.

In the '20s, eastern Long Island was a stronghold of the Ku Klux Klan.

During the election of 1928, when Al Smith ran as the first Catholic candidate for president, a flaming cross burned on the bluff overlooking Greenport. The Klan went away. The politics and attitudes of many islanders remained sharply conservative.

Billy Sanwald, a native islander, became a close friend of my brother and me. He was our first Protestant friend. We were probably his first Catholic ones. At the start, he was reticent about spending time with us. In our favor, our older sister married into an island family, which made us less outlanders than we might otherwise have been.

We looked up to Billy as a scout and guide. He took us through woods and marshlands summer people didn't reach. He had a rifle we could touch if his father was present. He carried a knife. He had a pet racoon. He knew the best places to go crabbing and fishing.

Billy was a sweet kid. There was no danger he was going to take us in the woods to turn us into Presbyterians. Our parents were unconcerned. Billy's parents never mentioned it. His grandmother did. Her deeply formed Calvinist conscience recoiled at the thought he was palling around with superstitious, hell-bound "mackerel snappers."

He ventured with us into Our Lady of the Isle church. He walked onto the altar and touched the tabernacle. He gazed at the Stations of the Cross, the statues of Mary and Joseph, and the banks of flickering votive candles. He was thoughtful when he exited. "It's really weird," he said.

We visited the stark, severe interior of the Presbyterian church where his family worshipped. Devoid of candles, statues, or stained glass, it struck me as uninteresting and pedestrian where *church* should suggest the otherworldly. When he asked, I was honest. "It doesn't feel like a church," I said. "It's boring." Throughout our friendship, which church weird and which bland never came up again.

Governor Carey could be prickly and demanding. He was also direct, funny, appreciative, and often encouraging. He trusted I'd provide speeches he could use and never treated me as less than a professional.

He was elected at a moment when the Empire State was in Roman-style decline. The imperial fisc was running on fumes. His predecessor Nelson Rockefeller is alleged to have half-jested, half-confessed, "Poor Hughie. I already spent all the money."

The state's precarious condition was exceeded by New York City's.

Thanks to a declining tax base and out-of-control debt made possible by Ponzi-like gimmickry, the budgetary hole the city dug for itself began to look like a grave. The nation's financial capital was faced by bankruptcy and all its unforeseeable and unpleasant consequences.

Carey started with the premise he wouldn't let it happen. By force of will, he cajoled bank presidents, Wall Street machers, and iron-assed union leaders to the same table. He got them to move beyond their traditional cobra–mongoose relationship. He found ways out of dead ends and circumvented ideological impasses.

Budget cuts fell heaviest on the poor. But he never conjured "welfare queen" or villainized people on public assistance. He did what he could with the resources he could muster to avoid the city's falling into receivership and losing all freedom of action. His objective was to buy enough time to reorder the municipal finances, which is what came to pass.

Others have been credited with engineering the instruments that saved the city from going over the cliff. Hugh Carey made it possible for them to try. He took the political heat. Denunciations from right and left rained down on him. There wouldn't have been a rescue without his indomitableness. He was the indispensable man.

By midpoint of his second term, if the thrill wasn't gone, it was going. The worst of the financial crisis was behind. The annual months-long grind of haggling over the state budget and inhospitable Albany winters took their toll.

There was a brief shining moment at the 1980 Democratic Convention in New York. Ted Kennedy's challenge to President Jimmy Carter sputtered in a series of primary losses. Carter was the clear winner. Hard feelings remained. The party stayed divided.

Carey was part of a group of party leaders who called for an "open convention." The governor had me write an op-ed for the *Times*. The premise was that the only way to bring the party together behind a nominee was for the candidates to release their delegates and throw the choice open to the floor.

There was a ferment of back-room maneuvering and excitement. Who knew what would come to pass? It never got that far. Ted Kennedy gave his memorable "The Dream Shall Never Die" speech. The president was renominated. No elected president had been denied a second term since Herbert Hoover. Jimmy Carter was KO'd by Ronald Reagan.

At a point in our lives—it varies from person to person—it dawns that more of life is behind than ahead. The last chance has arrived to take hold of vanishing abilities and aspirations. It's as if, finding yourself on an elevator with only a down button, you imagine another elevator will take you back up, and you rush out in frantic search of it.

Some try to resolve the so-called midlife crisis with hair implants and BMW silver convertibles, or by going from one martini a night to three (or four), or, more drastically, by abandoning commitments to spouses and children. Hemingway put a shotgun in his mouth.

A former high-ranking member of Congress and a Democratic governor, Carey wanted to do his best to start out on the sunny side of the incoming Republican president. On January 20, 1981, he attended the inauguration of Ronald Reagan.

It came at a delicate moment. A close relationship with a woman he admired had ended. Washington must have generated memories of departed friends and reinforced awareness of a career moving toward dusk. He never stopped missing his wife, Helen.

He met a soi-disant widow from a prominent Midwest real estate family. It resulted in an infatuation that led to a hasty, ill-considered marriage fated to end the way those things predictably do.

First, there was the honeymoon. The governor and his wife decided to go to Greece, where her roots were, and Ireland, his ancestral homeland. He put me in charge of the Irish leg. I left a few days ahead of time to work with the Irish Tourist Board to put together an itinerary and work out details.

Enthused to welcome the Irish governor of New York and a member of the Four Horsemen, the Irish government paid the expenses. It was necessary to sometimes remind them this was a honeymoon, not a diplomatic mission.

The *Times* took editorial exception to the arrangement, which the Irish government ignored, as did the governor.

From the moment the governor stepped off the plane, I could see how at ease he was. He left behind a cage fight between construction unions and environmentalists over construction of a multi-billion-dollar expressway on Manhattan's west side. Ahead was a week of welcomes and open-handed Irish hospitality.

There was a lavish lunch at Iveagh House, a Georgian mansion that housed the Irish foreign ministry, a small VIP dinner at the Shelburne, a reception at the Dail, the Irish parliament. The Taoiseach, the Irish prime minister, played host at the hurling finals at Dublin's Croke Park.

We spent several days touring the countryside. We stayed in high-end hotels, recycled castles of the Anglo-Irish Ascendancy whose thresholds were never crossed by my peat-reeking, forelock-tugging ancestors. We headed to Galway. I sat in front with the driver, the governor and his wife in back. The soft, bright September weather belied the island's reputation for endless rain and mist.

We drove through the bogs and starkly beautiful landscape of Connemara. In the distance were the Bens of the Beanna Beola range, their names like a line of Irish poetry: Benbaun, Bencullagh, Benback, and Muckanaght.

In 1861, Charles Kingsley, eminent Victorian, Regius Professor of Modern History at Cambridge, and tutor to Edward, Prince of Wales, toured this same territory. The population had been greatly reduced by the recent Great Famine. He saw enough of those who didn't fall victim to hunger or typhus or weren't swept away to America to form a distinct impression.

"I am haunted," he wrote, "by the human chimpanzees I saw along those hundred miles of horrible country. I don't believe they are our fault. I believe that there are not only more of them than of old, but that they are happier, better, more comfortably fed and lodged under our rule than they ever were.

"But to see white chimpanzees is dreadful; if they were black, one would not feel it so much, but their skins, except where tanned by exposure, are as white as ours."

Our driver, who enjoyed the governor's company, recommended a pub for lunch. The proprietor twigged to having an important guest but wasn't quite sure who he was. When the driver told him, he acted as if a cousin he hadn't seen or heard from since his long-ago departure for Australia or America had magically reappeared.

Word got around. The pub began to fill. Somebody began to sing. No person I ever met more enjoyed singing than the governor. Lunch lingered into late afternoon. His bride looked part amused, part bewildered, as she had for much of the trip.

Not wanting to spoil the *craic* by attempting a song, I sat in a corner and nursed my pint of Guinness.

My paternal great-grandparents emigrated from Ireland the year before Charles Kingsley's visit. They left a hollowed-out colony in which they knew if they stayed they'd die in the same social and economic station they were born.

I was in a pub with the governor of New York—both of us descendants of those who left but never forgot—in a proud, independent republic rapidly shedding centuries of poverty and inferiority and taking its place in the European community.

There wasn't a chimpanzee in sight.

Peter A. Quinn, employed as a civil engineer on building the IND subway. He attended Fordham Law School at night. (1930)

My father being sworn in as a judge by Mayor William O'Dwyer. I'm at the extreme left in my Aunt Marion's arms. Tom is in my mother's arms. My sisters, Sheila and Kathleen, are in the front row. (1949)

Viola Murphy Quinn, senior year at Mt. St. Vincent's College, where she was a classics major. (1929)

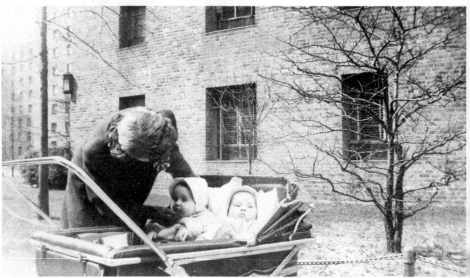

Tom and I being wheeled through Parkchester. (1948)

Introduction to Bronx politics. My father was running for the Municipal Court. (1949)

Putting out fires. Parkchester. (1950)

Westmoreland Farm, Shelter Island. Tom and I were mascots for the Farm's baseball team and had the uniforms to prove it. Col. James Roe, the Farm's proprietor, is between us. (1950)

Westmoreland Farm. Tom and I digging in on the losing side of a tug-of-war. (1951)

Judge Quinn second on the left, Cardinal Spellman on the extreme right. (There was no love lost between them.) Msgr. Thaddeus Tierney, the parish's long-serving, much-beloved pastor, is at the mike. (1951)

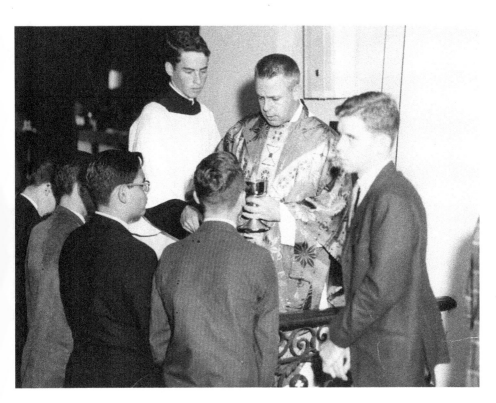

Altar server. Students' Retreat, Manhattan Prep. The Latin Rite was still in use. (1963)

Kansas City, Kansas. VISTA. A year in the heartland. (1971)

Justice Peter A. Quinn, State Supreme Court, 800 Grand Concourse, Bronx. On the wall behind is a copy of Holbein's portrait of St. Thoma More. (1973)

A neophyte speechwriter waiting outside the governor's New York City office, 1350 Avenue of the Americas. (1979)

St. Patrick's Day Parade with Governor Hugh Carey. (March 17, 1980)

After a fourteen-year courtship, Kathy Burbank ("The Girl from Hot Dog Beach") and I wed in the Fordham University church. (October 3, 1982)

The Capitol, Albany. Governor Carey delivers the State of the State address to the legislature. I follow along while a grim-looking Lieutenant Governor Mario Cuomo surveys the room. Two weeks later the Governor announced he wouldn't run for a third term. (1982)

Albany, the Governor's Press Office, with Tim Russert and Steve Schlesinger. (1983)

Albany, with Bill Hanlon, the governor's speechwriters (aka "Pad and Pen"). Behind us is the Wall of Shame featuring that week's finalists for the worst in bureaucratese. (1984)

South Bend, Indiana. Arriving at Notre Dame University for Governor Cuomo's speech. Notre Dame President Fr. Theodore Hesburgh is on the left. Father Richard McBrien, chair of the Theology Department, is in the middle. The plane was struck by lightning on the way there. (1984)

Notre Dame, minutes before the governor went on stage to deliver his speech on "Religious Belief and Public Morality: A Catholic Governor's Perspective." As a quixotic attempt to create a middle ground in the abortion debate, it failed. The inscription reads: "Peter, Thanks for the words . . . and the music. Mario 1985"

At Averill Park, recording an interview with Bill Kennedy. My last full day in Albany. A fitting farewell. (1985)

A NORTHERN LIGHTS EVENT

"BOTH SIDES NOW"

an evening of music and spoken word
celebrating the people of Northern Ireland

starring
PHIL COULTER
AND
JAMES GALWAY

... and friends
GREGORY PECK
EDNA O'BRIEN
FRANK McCOURT
and the
DIFFERENT DRUMS OF IRELAND

Created by
PHIL COULTER AND FRANK PRENDERGAST

Script
PETER QUINN

Produced by
FRANK PRENDERGAST

Hosted by
IRISH ECHO NEWSPAPER

Gold Sponsors
AER LINGUS
MUTUAL OF AMERICA

Program for "Both Sides Now," performed in St. Patrick's Cathedral in celebration of the Good Friday Agreement ending the conflict in Northern Ireland. I wrote the script that was performed by, among others, Gregory Peck and Frank McCourt. (1999)

Ringing the changes: AOL Time Warner co-chief operating officer Bob Pittman, right, and communications director Peter Quinn, centre, applaud after chief executive officer Gerald Levin, left, rang the New York Stock Exchange bell opening the first day of trading in the $105bn merged company yesterday. Regulators out of step on the net, Page 9. AP

A Zelig Moment: NYSE. Ringing the bell with Gerald Levin and Bob Pittman for the first trading day of AOL Time Warner stock. It was all downhill from here. (January 14, 2001)

Outside the White House with Roma Downey and President Bill Clinton. Three days after the performance at St. Patrick's, "Both Sides Now" was performed at an evening ceremony on the White House lawn in honor of Senator George Mitchell. Clinton spent the afternoon at the rehearsal.

Bloomsday, the Irish Consul General's. With the unduplicable McCourt brothers, Frank and Malachy. (2003)

Time Warner, 75 Rockefeller Center. St. Patrick's is in the background. After 9/11, the echo of bagpipes from the funerals of members of the FDNY killed in the collapse of the Twin Towers was constant. (2005)

A mess of a desk. If I didn't know where everything was, my assistant, Helen Ross, did.

East Quogue, Hot Dog Beach. July 24, 2018, the fiftieth anniversary of the day Kathy and I met. "Love is not time's fool."

The Quinn twins turn 70 on safari in the wilds of southern New Jersey. (2017)

The Quinn clan. *Right to left:* Daniel, Peter, Kathy, Sam. Front row: Erica, Genevieve, Lila Viola. (2022)

I suppose a deep thinker like Immanuel Kant could answer whether pure happenstance or an inscrutable cosmic force took me to Albany, not that it matters. Either way, I found myself working in the same city as the girl from Hot Dog Beach.

We had a brief rapprochement two years before, in 1977. She moved from Westhampton to Saratoga Springs. She was studying at SUNY Albany for her masters in rehabilitation counseling. I came up and stayed with her. Saratoga is a wonderful resort town, especially in the summer when the track is in full swing.

She worked as a waitress at the track. In the mornings, I accompanied her when she set up. Binoculars hanging around their necks, an ecumenical minyan of Runyonesque equine devotees studied the daily race sheet with the intensity of Talmudic scholars.

Afternoons, I returned to watch and wager. I discovered I had an uncanny ability to pick also-rans. I was thankful I hadn't acquired a passion for the ponies earlier in life.

Our relationship wasn't rehabilitated. She felt I was pressuring her. Her priority was to start a career as a counselor. I thought I was following a conscientiously applied program of reconciliation and incremental seduction. I told her this time was final. She didn't agree or disagree. We parted for good.

Several months later, I stumbled into my speechwriting job that required I be in Albany several days a week. She moved not far from the Capitol. On my way to and from my monastic cell in a seen-better-days motel near the bus station, I walked past the office building on State Street where she worked as a counselor with the Cerebral Palsy Vocational Program. Sometimes I lingered. Once I spent an entire afternoon.

I contacted her just to say hello and remarked what a funny coincidence we worked a few blocks apart and suggested we meet sometime for a drink or dinner. No pressure, I said. When she had the time. Just an old-friends (I left out former-lovers) kind of thing.

She called a few days later. We met for dinner. I walked her back to her place. She said if I was ever stuck for a place to stay, I should call. The couch was mine. I walked back through Washington Park. It was dark and empty. I howled like a lonesome hound at the starless night, the hidden moon, the slumbering squirrels and silent birds.

The governor was scheduled to speak at the opening of Albany's new

Cerebral Palsy Center. It was the kind of event that required singling out people for recognition. I knew he'd stick to the text. Amid a reaffirmation of the state's obligation to people with disabilities and commitment to the work of the center, I singled out the work of "dedicated counselors." I named her and a close colleague.

She called me, which I expected, even if I told myself I didn't, though I did. She said when her boss came back from the ceremony, she reported some of the higher-ups were miffed that the governor had given the spotlight to two lowly counselors.

We laughed together at the governor's role as unwitting messenger. I said I knew he'd be amused. I had no intention of finding out.

We had another cordial dinner. We reminisced about old times in the Hamptons, friends from the Bronx we kept or lost touch with. I didn't ask if the offer of the couch still stood. It had the feel of a finale. At last, I told myself.

I'd started dating a woman back in the city. She was independent, attractive, funny, and she loved to read. We became seriously involved. I was moving on.

Winter passed slowly. Spring snuck in the way it does upstate, tentatively, at first unnoticed or ignored, as if too good to be true. The state budget was passed. The legislature left town. Albany was slipping into its summer somnolence. The bars were quiet.

In Northern Ireland, the hunger strike by Bobby Sands drew international media coverage. Support among Irish Americans was almost unanimous. After a sixty-six-day fast, Sands was near death. I was in charge of putting out a press release from the governor's office when it happened.

The governor made a personal appeal to Prime Minister Margaret Thatcher. She didn't bother answering. The empire was physically gone but not psychically. An attitude had hardened into a perpetual pretense. Margaret Thatcher incarnated it body and soul.

Sands's death came too late for me to catch the train back to the city. A solitary night in Albany stared me in the face. I decided to stop into Justin McNeely's, a bar on Lark Street, for a glass of Jameson in Sands's memory.

She was sitting by the door with a girlfriend. There was no stranger-across-a-crowded-room moment. We were anything but strangers. The place wasn't enchanted. It was practically deserted. What happened was amutually spontaneous acceptance that what drew us together would always be stronger than what pulled us apart. Her friend left. We went back to her place. I didn't stay on the couch.

There were one or two more bumps, but no ruptures. On October 3, 1982, I married Kathy Burbank, the girl from Hot Dog Beach, at Fordham University Chapel, where my grandmother was baptized 120 years before.

Governor Carey sang "New York, New York" at the reception.

After fourteen years, we made a brand-new start of it.

Is it true we never fully know our parents until they're gone and we take their place? As I moved on in life, married and concerned with making a living as a writer and starting a family, the past took on a prominence it hadn't before. I found myself revisiting moments I'd half-forgotten or hadn't thought worth remembering.

I knew my father. And didn't. We came late into his life. He was happy with his two girls, who spent their time in my mother's care. Age forty-three, nursing the wounds inflicted by his electoral loss, shocked at his unexpected fatherhood, he was unprepared for Tom and me. Near the end of her life, my mother told me, "No man was ever less excited with twin boys."

In the opening days of the postwar era, when a returning army of youthful dads coached and encouraged their ball-playing sons, he was an anomaly. Too old to serve in the war, he preferred homburgs to baseball caps. Instead of spending Saturdays having a catch, he retired to his room to read. On Sundays, after Mass, he tackled the crossword.

He took us to an occasional ballgame at the Polo Grounds, or to the Bronx Zoo, or schlepped us to the Museum of Natural History, where we spent listless hours wandering among stuffed bison and dinosaur bones. Wherever we went, he was half-present, adrift in his own mental orbit, landing in places that made him appear more grieved than distracted.

The month before we were born, his mother, whom he revered, died. "It wasn't unexpected," my mother told me. "But it hit him very hard." He kept a picture of her on his bureau.

Patrick Quinn, his father, died in 1940. My father spoke of him with respect, but with a note of trepidation, never of affection. Pat was a hard, intimidating, demanding man, not given to emotional displays. He emigrated from Tipperary to New York as a small boy with his parents and five siblings.

How much schooling he had is unclear. Minimum is a good guess. He was short, thick, and muscular. My father was slender, almost six feet, a graceful dancer.

"Narrowbacks" was the derisive term immigrants like Pat used for soft, thin-shouldered, second- and third-generations, spared by American birth and mobility from a lifetime of digging and hauling.

Pat was dismissive of my father's aspirations to acting or songwriting. He leaned on him to become a civil engineer and pressured him into politics. The stories my father told about him were fascinating, and sometimes frightening. He was not a man to be ignored.

He rented a rowboat and took my father and uncle along. They were seven and ten. He gave them the oars and told them to row. When they were far from shore, he gasped and doubled over. He said he was having a heart attack and pleaded with them to row as fast as they could.

They pulled desperately. My father cried and begged his father not to die. When they docked, he jumped off the boat and walked away.

He spent a good part of the year traveling as a union organizer. He often took my father along. My grandmother protested he'd fall behind in school. My grandfather said the boy was smart enough that missing school wouldn't make a difference. He was afraid she was turning him into a "mama's boy."

In April 1916, they were in Toronto. It was shortly after the Easter Uprising in Dublin. Thousands of Canadians were overseas fighting with the British Army. Patriotic feelings were running high. At dusk they were crossing a square. The Union Jack was being lowered. A band played "God Save the King."

Men and boys removed their hats. My father went to remove his. My grandfather stopped him. A crowd gathered. They shouted and demanded my grandfather remove his hat. My father was frightened. He went a second time to remove his hat. My grandfather took firm grip of his arm.

In a voice loud enough for all to hear, he said, "That flag stands for empire and aristocracy. We never take off our hats to it. Anyone who thinks we should is welcome to try." When the ceremony was over, they went their way.

My father was six when Pat said it was time he learned to swim. He took him to Coney Island and threw him off a pier. It might have been only a few inches above my father's head. What my father felt at that moment, water rushing in his mouth, closing over his head, how he got back to the pier, whether he saved himself or his father intervened, he never said. It's possible he learned to swim.

We thought the stories were entertaining. Only in retrospect did I understand he was teaching, not entertaining, conveying the message Pat conveyed to him: The world will crush you unless you stand up to it, fight back, refuse to be intimidated. People who don't learn how to stand on their own wind up on their knees.

I know almost nothing about Pat's parents beyond their names. The truth is, I never asked. Except for his sister Kate and brother John, I'm unclear what happened to his other three siblings.

Pat and his brother left New York and went west. He paid their fare by working as a boxer in impromptu matches in stockyards and the backrooms of saloons. After a stint as a coal stoker on the Union Pacific, disillusioned perhaps with the opportunities he sought and didn't find on the frontier, he returned east.

He got his start as a labor militant when he traveled to Chicago to participate in the massive 1894 strike against the Pullman Company that was broken with the help of Federal troops. He was mugged by Pinkerton detectives hired to intimidate "radicals and outside agitators."

Back in New York, he married. Shortly afterward, his wife died in childbirth. He left his infant daughter, Gertie, with his sister Kate and went off to Cuba, whether to hunt for gold or join the insurrectionists is unclear. Maybe both.

Returned once more to New York, he wed my grandmother, Margaret Manning. He was forty, she was thirty-nine. They had two boys, my father the younger. Somewhere along the line he became a skilled coppersmith, rose to head the New York chapter of the American Federation of Labor (AFL), and served as president of the Central Federated Union. In 1904, he led New York's Labor Day parade. I have the sash he wore.

He ran a saloon on the corner of Dry Dock and 11th Street. My father was born over it in 1904. (The block was long ago demolished and replaced by public housing.) A decade later, either because he lacked a business sense or at my grandmother's insistence that "No honest dollar was made across a bar," he sold it and moved the family to the Bronx.

He waited until he was on his deathbed to reveal his first marriage to my father, admonishing him that just because Gertie was his half-sister, he shouldn't use his wiles as a lawyer to cheat her out of what was coming to her.

He never said much to my father about Tipperary. He was silent about his childhood. In Pat's world of post-famine immigrants, the notion of Romantic Ireland was a stillborn fantasy.

A particular pleasure of working in the Capitol was the chance to talk with Governor Carey's choice for lieutenant governor, Mario Cuomo. My office in the Capitol wasn't far from his. Everything seemed to interest him—theology, history, philosophy, sports.

Under the best of circumstances, the office of lieutenant governor requires the skill set of a mannequin. Cuomo had a lot of time for conversation.

Cuomo first came to public attention defending a group of mostly Italian-American homeowners in Corona from the city's intent to raze their houses and build a school. His reputation as a negotiator grew when the city proposed to build public housing in solidly middle-class Forest Hills, an experience he chronicled in his book *Forest Hills Diary*.

In an interview I did with Governor Carey a few years before he died, he told me that when he launched his 1974 long-shot campaign for the Democratic nomination for governor, he asked Cuomo to join his ticket as lieutenant governor. Cuomo accepted.

Then Cuomo got the same invitation from Howard Samuels, the sure-bet winner, and switched horses, literally. Samuels, a multi-millionaire industrialist, former Secretary of Commerce, and Chairman of the New York City Off-Track Betting Corporation, was best known as "Howie the Horse."

Carey replaced Cuomo on the ticket with upstate state senator Mary Anne Krupsak. A shrewd and relentless campaigner, and a veteran of tough re-elections in a swing district, Carey hired David Garth, one of the country's savviest operators in the burgeoning political consulting industry. Carey pulled off an upset in the primary.

Aided by the Republican disgrace in the wake of Watergate and the public's weariness with sixteen years of Republican governors, he ran away with the general election.

If all wasn't forgiven between Carey and Cuomo, it was temporarily forgotten. Carey recognized Cuomo's appeal to the party's liberal wing and appointed him New York's Secretary of State. Despite its weighty-sounding title, it involved no heavy lifting. Among his responsibilities was supervising the licensing of cosmetologists, barbers, and private eyes.

New York's financial crisis entered a critical phase. Carey was determined to get rid of the incumbent mayor, whom he regarded as feckless and hopelessly out of touch. He convinced Cuomo to run in the primary and promised to stick with him to the finish.

The entry of Manhattan Congressman Ed Koch made it a three-way race. Koch won the first round but not by enough to avoid a run-off. Koch accused Cuomo of starting a whispering campaign alleging he was gay. ("Vote for Cuomo, not the homo.")

Cuomo vigorously denied it. A nasty campaign got nastier. Their mutual contempt was the kind that brought Aaron Burr and Alexander Hamilton to a fatal confrontation on the Heights of Weehawken, a method of conflict resolution no longer available.

Carey campaigned hard for Cuomo. Koch won a convincing victory in the second round. Cuomo stayed in the race on the Liberal ticket. Carey cut him loose and endorsed Koch, who beat Cuomo for the third time.

In 1978, when re-election time rolled around for Carey, his chances didn't look good. The state's economy was still struggling. The hard choices he'd made in the fiscal crisis pissed off important constituencies. His adamant opposition to the death penalty was widely unpopular.

Accusing him of not giving her anything to do—given the nature of the office, it was like an Eskimo complaining about snow—Lieutenant Governor Krupsak mounted a primary challenge. Carey won the primary. He faced a well-financed, widely known Republican opponent. One poll showed him getting thumped by a margin of 28 percent.

Cuomo remained popular with the liberal wing of the party. Carey convinced him to join the ticket as lieutenant governor. He promised a real role. Cuomo was glad to be back in the play. When Carey carried the election, Cuomo quickly discovered his role had dropped from understudy to usher. He felt duped.

From the beginning, the Carey–Cuomo combination was a match made in purgatory. Their cool relationship turned polar. The governor made it plain he thought Cuomo best suited to be an assistant professor of sociology at a junior college.

Cuomo went to Bob M., the secretary to the governor. The highest-ranking appointed official in the Executive Chamber, the secretary oversaw the day-to-day operations of state government. When Cuomo asked to see the most recent draft of the State of the State, he was told there was no need. The important points had been decided. I was told that if he asked for a copy, I was to inform him the governor was keeping the text to himself.

When Cuomo came to my office seeking a copy, I put the speech on my desk and left the room. When I came back, he said the speech was a jumble of programs and promises aimed to satisfy the narrow demands of various interest groups and without a central organizing theme. That's what made it a State of the State, I said. He'd eventually find that out on his own.

In *Diaries of Mario Cuomo: The Campaign for Governor*, Cuomo reported that, "The Governor reached out at the last minute to sit down with me, but we were cities apart and it didn't work out." The secretary's derisive nickname for him was "cackle head." His version was when Cuomo came on his own initiative to talk to the governor, he was told there was nothing to talk about. The speech wasn't going to change.

###

When Governor Carey announced in January 1982 he wasn't interested in a third term, I began my job search. At a corporate recruiter's behest, I flew to Detroit to interview for the top speechwriting job at Chrysler. I was whisked past Lee Iacocca, the company's celebrity chairman, who was in the middle of turning the company around. He briefly inquired about Hugh Carey. It was obvious I wasn't the make and model he was shopping for.

A headhunter approached me about interviewing at GE. I knew CEO Jack Welch's reputation as one of the country's toughest bosses, a standout among the bullying, soul-crushing executives who, as one commentator put it, "inflict pain by messing with your mind as well." Making a living was one thing, putting myself in the hands of Hannibal Lecter another.

I had a pleasant interview at IBM. The company didn't need superstars, I was told. It needed team players. I was never any good on teams. After college I became a serious runner because I could be by myself. I thought of speechwriting as a job for people who liked to play solitaire.

It was clear, although he put off a formal announcement, that Cuomo was running. A slew of other potential candidates explored entering. The rumor that Ed Koch was considering a run sent them scurrying to the sidelines.

In his Mephistophelean desire to play kingmaker—an apotheosis realized with Fox News's 24/7 pimping of the forty-fifth president—Rupert Murdoch used the *New York Post* to trumpet a "Let's Draft Ed Koch" movement. Koch did nothing to quell it. Confronted with his statement "Life in

Albany would be worse than death," he snapped, "Everybody's got to die sometime."

The night Koch announced his candidacy, there was a dinner at the Governor's Mansion for those who worked on the state budget. I oversaw writing the script. It rivaled the State of the State in dreadfulness but was shorter.

Cuomo showed up late. While he was in hearing distance, nobody brought up Ed Koch. They didn't have to. It hung over the room like a haze of cigar smoke. As hard as it must have been, Cuomo was cordial and upbeat. Carey extemporized a few remarks. He was brief and funny and avoided mention of Koch, Cuomo, or the election.

I met Cuomo on the way out. Polls showed that if Koch was his opponent, he'd be trounced. I said I was sorry about the day's developments. Cuomo was momentarily silent. I was afraid I had insulted him. "There's nothing to be sorry about," he said. "Koch has cleared the field. Now it's just me and him. This time I'll win." He sounded convinced. Even if I didn't share his faith, I admired it.

In the oldest and most predictable of political traditions, he quickly discovered that many of those who loudly proclaimed their to-the-death support had their Road-to-Damascus moment. Blinded by the light, they switched loyalties and supported Koch. Cuomo took it in stride. He asked me if I'd be willing to help.

I said I was getting married. My wife and I were going to settle in the city. I couldn't afford to leave my job. I didn't say that, as much as I admired his idealism and intellect, I wasn't about to climb atop a funeral pyre. I offered to help where I could from behind the scenes.

Bill H., his campaign manager, sent me several assignments involving state matters in which I acquired enough of a not-entirely-superficial expertise to write something useful. I did what I could do on the QT.

Koch's chief speechwriter called. He asked if I'd fill him in on the details of what it was like to function out of both Albany and New York. He was surprised I was the only speechwriter. He thought there should be a staff. He didn't offer me a job, so I didn't have to decline. He proposed we meet right after the election. I agreed.

The last shovel of dirt was thrown atop the grave of the Cuomo campaign when Carey endorsed Koch. John Jude Francis Cassidy, a classically trained habitué of the Saratoga track and longtime sparkplug in Albany's smoothly functioning political machine, told me Cuomo was about to earn the Latin honorific *"victus diebus quattor"*—four-time loser.

The day of the election I was in the office of the governor's advance team. There was a dispute over whether to schedule a brief drop-in to the loser's headquarters. Should the governor go before or after congratulating the winner? It came to an end when one of the participants bellowed, "Fuck Cuomo."

That night, Kathy and I were at a restaurant on Waverly Place making final arrangements for our wedding reception. When we got home, I turned on the radio to hear the weather. I was stunned by news that Cuomo had pulled off a Dewey-Defeats-Truman upset.

Overjoyed for him, I was ambivalent for myself. I knew I missed the opportunity to write for him. The pay in private industry was two to three times what I made with the state. There'd be stock options and an expense account. The prospect of writing speeches and annual reports about sales volume and profit margins struck me as about as exciting as working in a rug factory.

Kathy and I left on a month-long honeymoon in Ireland and Scotland. We wouldn't be back until after the general election. I welcomed the prospect of not suffering another Siberian Albany winter. At the same time, I wondered whether at some point I'd kick myself for missing the chance to write for a different kind of politician like Mario Cuomo.

Returned from my honeymoon, I had a second interview with the executive at IBM who ran the "speechwriting operation." We ate lunch at an exclusive Midtown restaurant. He didn't write speeches. He supervised "the team" that did.

His hair was gray, so was his suit, so was the job he described. He talked about "the IBM way." He said, "The focus must always be on 'the customer and the product.'" He spoke with the understated conceit of an executive in the world's most profitable industrial company.

I met a friend for a drink. He was still working on his Ph.D. I considered returning to finish mine. In the sober light of dawn, I came to my senses. I thought about getting into publishing. Working with manuscripts and writers might pay less, but instead of a morning shot of mental Novocain awaiting at places like IBM, it would be exciting and absorbing.

I got in touch with a headhunter who I was told had contacts in the industry. He said I was a little old and had no experience. "Your worth is as a speechwriter," he said. I didn't think one speechwriting gig should define my career. I wasn't in a position to argue.

I sent Cuomo a note congratulating him on his electoral win over Lew Lehrman, his well-financed opponent. He wrote back and asked me to come to his office. He had something to talk over. He included our meeting on Thursday, November 18, 1982, in his book *Diaries of Mario Cuomo: The Campaign for Governor.*

"I talked about this later in the day with Peter Quinn," he wrote, "who I hope will be a speech writer—it's obvious I can't write all the speeches I'll need to give." He went on to make some highly complimentary remarks (if you're interested, p. 365) that I sent to my mother as soon as the book was published.

It was obvious I couldn't write them all either. This was going to be speechwriting on another level. We agreed I could seek out a writer who he'd be comfortable with. I approached Bill Hanlon.

I was introduced to Bill at the outset of my days as a speechwriter. He wrote and edited speeches, articles, and books for a high state official who advertised himself as sole author of his own material. On one occasion Bill wrote an op-ed for his boss, who decided to share the byline with the governor.

When it received a good deal of positive attention, his boss had second thoughts. "I don't know why I shared credit," he groused, "when I wrote every goddamn word myself."

Bill went through the pre–Vatican II traditional course of study to be a Jesuit. He had the sharpest mind I ever encountered. His stainless-steel intellect and disciplined thinking showed in his writing. He told you what he thought without your having to ask.

He took a hand in seeing that I was hired. In those early days of my speechwriting career when everything was daunting and brand-new, I went to Bill with my fears and doubts. He was my father confessor.

Bill proved the iron man of the speechwriting operation. He stayed on through Cuomo's first two terms and brought a degree of stability and consistency it would have otherwise lacked.

Tim Russert was the new press secretary. He took the more expansive title "Counselor to the Governor." It gave him a wider brief. Russert, who won repute as a shrewd political operator while chief of staff for Senator Daniel Patrick Moynihan, was a high-powered hire who hinted at the governor's intent to be heard outside the Empire State.

We went to lunch. Russert brought up that Carey and Cuomo were very different in their styles. Was I confident I could switch from writing in "Carey's voice to Cuomo's?" I was honest. I never tried to write in any one's voice. I wrote the best I could. If it sounded like it was in someone else's voice, I was happy.

It was only weeks until the State of the State. The governor was preoccupied with putting a new administration together. Many of the Democratic appointees under Carey who thought the new Democratic governor would keep them on quickly discovered he wouldn't. At times the situation was chaotic.

He asked me to draft his inaugural. When I sent it to him, he shot back the inaugural he'd already written. His version was moving and deeply personal. I made a few edits and additions and sent it back. It drew wide attention and praise. Richard Nixon heard it on the radio and sent a note expressing his admiration.

I was bewildered why he asked me to write a speech he didn't need and wasn't going to use. Over time I learned he thrived on uncertainty and confusion, especially when it was self-created. He liked his people to deal with the unexpected. He was comfortable with all parts in motion, and him the calm center. "Life," he said on more than one occasion, "is motion, not joy."

Bill and I missed the inaugural and the reception afterward because we were racing to finish the State of the State. Beyond instructing that he wanted it "forward looking," the governor didn't offer any guidance. Finally, on Sunday night, two nights before the speech, he sat down with us.

In his *Diaries*, he wrote, "I haven't liked it from the first draft [this was the first draft he paid attention to], mostly because it's not well organized. It's not the fault of the people who are working on it with me: we should have begun working on it earlier."

Bill and I were clued in for the first time on a pivotal fact somehow left out of previous discussions: The state faced a billion-dollar budget gap, the largest in its history. Before there was any looking forward, the fiscal guillotine looming directly ahead had to be faced.

We began redrafting. The governor circulated the new versions. Nothing was satisfactory. The speech was too dour. It was too rosy. It needed "to speak to the future." It was "too future oriented."

We worked through the night. Dawn broke. I lay my head on the table. Bill taped the speech to the wall. He had the ability to revisit a text for the umpteenth time and see it with fresh eyes. I didn't. He moved paragraphs like the faces on a Rubik's Cube. He rescued it.

The chaos the speech came out of didn't show. "Mario Cuomo, the man," a *Times* reporter wrote, "really lifted his voice."

The next day, seemingly out of the blue, Jimmy Breslin, among the most gifted, iconoclastic, and irascible journalists in the history of the profession, used his column in the *Daily News* to launch a blistering attack on speechwriting and speechwriters.

It was a job for hacks, he wrote, second-rate writers who couldn't make it on their own, lapdogs who licked their master's hand, a tool of the weak-minded, the lazy, the inept. Mario Cuomo was a stand-alone politician who never resorted to them.

The governor's speechwriting operation consisted of his "pad and pen." Bill and I were stunned. We had no idea where it came from.

I met Breslin once when Mike P., Carey's press secretary and the former labor editor at the *Daily News*, introduced us. Mike and I became close friends. He was my Vergil through the demimonde of the press's after-hours haunts.

Mike took me to a bar around the corner from the *Daily News* where Breslin was holding court. When he found out I was Hugh Carey's speech-writer, he went off on "Society Carey," a moniker he'd conferred to mock his nighttime socializing in exclusive New York watering holes.

I told him that Carey wasn't a graduate of the Cotton Mather School of Public Service. If his days were absorbed by state business, I didn't see anything wrong with the bachelor governor's enjoying the nighttime perks of office. He accused me of making excuses for the governor to hide behind. "But that's what speechwriters are paid for, isn't it?" he said.

Tim Russert explained that my name came up the day before when Breslin called the Mansion to speak with Cuomo. Matilda Cuomo, the governor's wife, informed him that he was over at the Capitol "working with his speechwriters."

I knew from people acquainted with him that along with his talent and prowess as a journalist, Breslin had the Irish ability to nurse his grudges and play the bully. Still, I found it hard to believe our spat was the reason for his all-out attack. Wasn't I too small a blip—our encounter too brief—to provoke such a gratuitously nasty assault?

Whatever the reason, his surprise attack was a brutal mugging. Bill and I had no way to hit back. I complained to the governor. He told me it was no big deal, "just Breslin being Breslin," which was a little rich coming from a man who spent untold hours browbeating reporters over the phone for their supposed misreporting and perceived slights.

Breslin set in concrete the image of the one-of-a-kind politician, a philosopher-king who could write and rule and compose his own speeches. Bill and I were removed from the list of those who were delivered a daily compilation of news clippings. We disappeared from the office phone listings. We went from speechwriter, the title I held under Carey, to "commu-nications specialist." It made it sound like we were telephone repairmen.

Bill resigned and returned to his old job in the Health Department.

Kathy urged me to leave. I wasn't ready to quit. Friends had congratulated me on being asked to stay on in a new administration. I turned down other jobs. I was intrigued and enthused to write for Cuomo. I wanted to believe we could still make it work. Skulking out of this job was a blow to my ego I wasn't prepared to take.

My earliest impression of the governor was that he was transparent, uncomplicated, easy-to-get-to-know. That's how he was on the surface. The longer I worked for him, the more I perceived that beneath was a complex, impenetrable opaqueness.

If some politicians played checkers, Cuomo's game was three-dimensional chess. You could never be sure what level he was playing. Did he tell me this because he thought it was important for me to know or because I'd tell Joe who'd pass it on to Jane who'd tell Jack who'd share it with Jim who'd react in a way that revealed his true intentions?

A politician with a shrewd sense of human nature, he possessed the finesse of a skilled cross-examiner. His penchant for introspection, endlessly weighing competing possibilities, and conducting public debates with himself earned him the title "Hamlet on the Hudson."

The press speculated about his "dark side." Mostly, this reflected the contrast between the reasoned, equipoised public figure and the angry, aggrieved, behind-the-scenes rumbles he had with reporters or commentators he judged unfairly critical, which didn't take much.

The first time I saw that side was not long after the inauguration. We were discussing an upcoming speech when he took an incoming phone call. Listening to his side of the call, I could tell he was discussing a person from the campaign who was pressing his case for a significant position in the administration.

The longer it went on, the more irate the governor became. He rapped the desk so hard with his college ring it reverberated like a gunshot. He exploded in a singeing stream of expletives that the job seeker was the press's prime source for stories about the governor's caliginous nastiness. Not only would he never get a job in Albany, he'd be lucky to leave town with his genitals intact.

I didn't rate the governor's dark side darker than a lot of other people's. He had a temper. He could be brusque and often enough was hard on people around him. I never saw him take wanton pleasure in humiliating subordinates. Fierce competitiveness was sometimes mistaken for cruelty.

At Time Inc., I became friendly with Ed McCarrick, a fellow Manhattan College graduate who went on to become the publisher of *TIME*. His father had been a professional baseball scout for the Dodgers. Ed sent me a copy of a 1952 report his father sent Branch Rickey on players for the Brunswick Pirates, a minor league farm team.

The longest profile was of centerfielder Mario Cuomo. McCarrick made some astute observations. "Potentially, the best prospect on the club he could go all the way," he wrote. "He is intelligent and a straight A student at St. John's . . . He is not an easy chap to get close to but is very well-liked by those who succeed in penetrating the exterior wall . . . He is another who will run over you if you get in his way."

When I was hired it was agreed I had to be in Albany only one or two days a week, when the legislature was in session. The rest of the time I could work out of my office on the 57th floor of Two World Trade Center. One or two days turned into three or four—or more. Cuomo took up full-time residence in the Governor's Mansion, which Carey hadn't.

I got used to the governor's hours. When our phone rang at 5:30 A.M., Kathy and I knew who it was. There was no use letting it ring. He waited as long as it took. He started talking right away. He presumed you were writing it down. One boiling summer night, I went to bed naked. I jumped out of bed when the phone rang.

I didn't have a pad or pen handy. I asked him to wait. He kept talking. I stood pen-less, pad-less and pants-less for the next fifteen minutes as we discussed his upcoming speech to the AFL-CIO convention at Kiamesha Lake.

After the State of the State came the budget. Nobody expected rhetorical flourishes. The effects of recession lingered. New York's recovery lagged. The days of wine and roses were little more than, as the song has it, "a passing breeze filled with memories." Budget Director Mike Finnerty, a helicopter pilot in Vietnam and fellow Manhattan College graduate, went out of his way to make it easy for me to get the messaging right.

The selling of the budget package went into high gear. The governor inserted in every speech a reference to "the family of New York, bearing one another's burdens, sharing one another's blessings." It was a theme he introduced in his inaugural. Mickey Carroll, a streetwise, sardonic reporter, pulled me aside. "If New York is a family," he said, "it's the Addams family."

Cuomo was filled with the enthusiasm of a new governor, with undented ambitions and unlimited energy. But the rules stayed the same. It was—and remains—a familiar routine since Al Smith put the executive budget in place.

The governor presented his budget. Legislators objected, dissented, and offered plans of their own. The governor traveled the state to stir up public support and pressure the legislature. No one budged until up against the deadline for approving the budget and a compromise was reached.

I prepared a boilerplate speech adaptable to different venues. It began with a joke he insisted on using so many times the reporters traveling with him groaned. I told him it was time to get a new one. He kept it because, he said, the audience loved it and it annoyed the press, which he enjoyed.

He sent me tapes of remarks he thought were particularly effective for transcription. Easy as it might sound to turn a tape into a coherent text, it wasn't. The leaps and gaps—occasional lapses into stream-of-consciousness—became glaringly obvious. The narrative wandered, the logic lagged, the metaphors mixed and collided. As a rule, it's not good when the speaker lacks a text and time constraints.

The governor started as a fan of events in the Red Room, the Capitol's ornate chamber used for ceremonial occasions. They required a written text that was referred to as "remarks" rather than a speech. Shorter than speeches, they often took longer to write.

It was increasingly difficult to keep pace. Tim Russert told me he reached out on the governor's behalf to Steve Schlesinger, an accomplished writer and journalist. "Meanwhile," he said, "the governor says to write faster." Russert was joking. I wasn't sure about the governor.

One morning, Steve appeared at my office. He tried for weeks to find out about the speechwriting position but couldn't get an answer. I told him to sit in the empty office next to mine and let the office manager know. She said she didn't know anything about a second speechwriter and needed to check. She called a few minutes later. The governor, she said, "was surprised Steve finally made up his mind."

As the scion of one of the country's premier intellectual families, and co-author of an admired book on the CIA coup in Guatemala, he wasn't destined long as a speechwriter (i.e., communications specialist). In a sign the governor was looking beyond next year's budget, he was quickly elevated to advisor on national and international affairs.

Cuomo laid out a bread-and-water diet for the state. The Executive Chamber would get the crumbs. Salaries were frozen. Staffing was minimal. Overwork was the order of the day. A sole off-the-radar writer/communications specialist fit the profile.

Late afternoons, the governor and I talked in his office about upcoming speeches. Maybe he was probing to see if I had put Breslin's assault behind. He never brought it up. He quickly went off-topic. We talked about books. He was an autodidact who read with the intensity of an insomniac. He didn't have much time for novels but greatly admired Bill Kennedy's Albany saga. He grazed anthologies, encyclopedias, general histories.

He had a special affection for the Jesuit paleontologist/theologian Teilhard de Chardin, whose theories on spiritual evolution were suppressed by keepers of church dogma until after Vatican II. For many, he became a touchstone of reform and renewal. I found him dense.

Cuomo often went back to Reagan's success. President Carter had created FEMA in 1979 to be first on the scene to let disaster victims know the federal government was there to help. It was popular from the start. Cuomo found it incredible Reagan was able to turn "I'm from the government and I'm here to help you" into a gag line.

It seemed to us both that, in one way or another, the whole of modern America was built on government help. We both grew up in a culture where public-sector employees weren't seen as useless, counterproductive bureaucrats but as civil servants—teachers, sanitation workers, court clerks, cops, housing and food inspectors, firefighters, parkies, et al.—people whose work made communities safer, cleaner, more civilized.

The New Deal was rooted in New York. In the wake of the 1911 Triangle Shirtwaist Factory fire, which left scores of immigrant working girls dead, state legislative leaders (and future governor and U.S. senator, respectively) Al Smith and Robert Wagner introduced an unprecedented program of progressive legislation.

Workmen's compensation was instituted, workplace safety standards set, child labor regulated and curtailed, health codes made stricter and expanded.

Government fostered the growth of organized labor. Unions lifted people's wages, achieved a measure of job security, and protected against the abuses of arbitrary management. For immigrant families, government wasn't a threat to their independence and livelihoods but protector and ally.

We both saw firsthand, in our own families, how Social Security revolutionized life for older Americans. Medicare—which Reagan predicted would "invade every area of freedom as we've known it"—made possible a level of health care the elderly had never enjoyed before.

The G.I. Bill allowed a generation to go to college. It was a foundation of middle-class success. The Interstate Highway System, proposed by President Eisenhower, altered every aspect of how Americans traveled and lived.

Federal loans for homeownership, higher education, and small businesses expanded the opportunities for millions to lead better lives. The FDIC stabilized the country's banking system. The Civil Rights Act struck at the apparatus of American apartheid. The EPA protected the country's water resources.

The SEC gave stockholders protections they never had before. The FDA guarded against medical quackery and toxic food. The National Park Service maintained a magnificent system of unspoiled landscapes and open spaces for every American to enjoy. Government paved the way for millions to join the middle class. It was hard to think of an area where government didn't help.

What Reagan had going for him, I suggested, weren't facts but a story. He co-opted the Hollywood saga of how the West was won, the lone hero, Shane riding into the sunset, John Wayne framed in the doorway in the last scene of *The Searchers*, Gary Cooper alone in *High Noon* facing down murderous thugs.

Photographed on horseback, wearing a wry smile and a worn cowboy hat, Reagan galloped across the high chaparral, ready to ride with the wild stallions of the free market.

He fought back against "welfare queens" (bandits), wild-eyed leftists (Indians), and socialists (misfits) to free a nation of rugged individuals to make their own way, seek their own fortunes. He was driving off fusty bureaucrats and effete paper pushers to unleash the forces of free enterprise and harness the energy of America's new pioneers.

"When the legend becomes fact," says the newspaper editor in *The Man Who Shot Liberty Valance*, "print the legend." Reagan upgraded the legend into a national media blitz.

You don't beat a story with better facts. You beat it with a better story. I felt that Cuomo had a powerful, countervailing narrative. The country's success wasn't built by solitary men in search of the next horizon. The families who piled all they had into covered wagons, carried the weak as well as the strong, and overcame every hardship to build a better life for their children—they were the heroes.

The Homestead Act of 1862 granted farmers 160 acres. It fueled settlement of the western lands. The government subsidized the building of the transcontinental railroad, which spurred economic growth in the East as well as in the West. Pioneers built towns, raised barns together, and saw one another through hard times.

The survival and success of generations of immigrants didn't depend on libertarian loners but on government largesse, on its ability to tame the savage excesses of *laissez-faire* capitalism, and open new opportunities for settlers and immigrants.

It wasn't the ethic of Wall Street gunslingers that made America a fairer, better place. It was families that built neighborhoods and communities and, at their best, acted together, through and with government, to lift up the country.

A rising tide lifted all boats, except those stranded without one. The market wasn't going to care for all those who couldn't care for themselves. It couldn't maintain the country's educational network, or care for the millions who couldn't care for themselves.

The private sector couldn't make the immense investments in building and maintaining the country's infrastructure that government alone could do.

The governor and I had had different childhoods with large similarities. We went to similar schools. We shared the religious and political loyalties of outer-borough ethnic Catholics. The Church's social teaching has long been strongly pro-union and in favor of workers' rights.

I'm not sure if it's correct to label what Cuomo and I shared as a "New Deal attitude," but that's the way I think of it.

Steve Schlesinger picked up on something when he observed to the *Times* that, when it came to speechwriting, Cuomo would only develop "a close relationship with someone of mainly the identical background."

The governor traveled to Washington to speak to the Democratic National Committee. It was his first venture to address the party's elite. He told me he wanted a speech that called the party to be true to its beliefs and not try to turn itself into a watered-down version of Reaganism.

Russert reported that it got an enthusiastic response. The governor sent me the text. Scrawled across the top was "Let's figure out what we did right and keep doing it!"

He was scheduled to speak to a convention of educators in California. It was the July 4th weekend. I gave him a draft several days ahead of time. I didn't hear back. Kathy and I took a bus to Cape Cod for the weekend. I always left a number where I could be reached.

Saturday night I got a call that the governor wanted to see me in Albany.

He liked parts of the speech, especially the wagon-train imagery, but wasn't happy overall. In the pre-digital age, there was no way to e-mail versions. It took two buses and half the day to get to Albany.

When I arrived there was a note at the hotel desk telling me to call the mansion. I did. There were no preliminaries. The personal could never take precedence over work. We went back and forth well into the night.

At summer's end, Kathy and I took a week's vacation ferry-hopping from Block Island to Martha's Vineyard and Nantucket. When I got back, the list of upcoming speeches had multiplied. I was immediately swamped. I barely got speeches to the governor before he delivered them.

He complained to Steve M., a *supermensch* and assistant press secretary, about my tardiness. He and I were among the few Carey appointees whom Cuomo retained. Steve spoke up in my defense, "Peter's problem is he has too much work." Cuomo replied, "Peter's problem is he took a vacation."

I went to the governor's office. I was blunt. As much as I wanted to stay, either I got help or was gone. He asked if I had anyone in mind. "I want to bring back Bill Hanlon," I said.

Chemistry was a big part of speechwriting. I knew the governor admired Bill's writing, valued his intellect, and found him easy to work with. "Go ahead and try," he said.

###

I was approaching my fifth year as a speechwriter. The anonymity of speechwriting weighed on me. The nature of the job was that everything I wrote belonged to someone else. Except that I intended to make a career as a writer, I'd no idea of what job I'd look for next. Career planning was never one of my strengths.

When I first arrived in Albany, I tasted its nighttime delights. The legislature was in session, the after-work shenanigans gave the city the feel of a college town, with graduates from twenty years ago balder, stouter than in their student days but their instincts for away-from-home frolicking still intact.

I was approached by an attractive woman in the Stone Grounds Pub. I discerned her services were for hire. She asked if I was a member of the legislature. I admitted I wasn't. She quickly vanished.

Late on winter nights in frozen Albany, I stalked the Capitol's corridors as the north wind echoed the haunted voices of the anonymous, long-departed scribes who labored in service of the famous and celebrated, Teddy Roosevelt, Al Smith, FDR, Tom Dewey, Nelson Rockefeller.

I knew my fate was the fate of all but a famous few. Ahead was entombment with the night-shift cleaning crew.

I sought refuge in the state library. I researched speeches and searched for something I couldn't name. I retreated to my hotel room. I read novels I never got around to in college. Thomas Mann's *Magic Mountain*. D. H. Lawrence's *Women in Love*.

For some reason, maybe because it looked imposing enough to fill nights spent in solitary confinement, I bought a used copy of Thomas Carlyle's *The French Revolution: A History*. Part James Joyce, part Thomas Babington Macaulay, it was a joyride, the past offered up with the verve of a novel, history that blazed with the present tense of fiction. It transformed my cinder-block cell into the streets of revolutionary Paris.

Carlyle's narrative sweep, his impassioned depiction of the Revolution, his calling to life the crowds of vengeful sans-culottes started me thinking of the people on the periphery who suffered history rather than made it, the faceless, nameless mob, the complexity and individuality of women and men gathered under the pronouns *they* and *them*.

Studying history and possessed of only a few fragments of the story of my own family, I was aware that 99.9 percent of human beings leave barely a trace. Their inner lives, the dense and restless passion of what it means to be human, were utterly lost.

Even with exhaustive biographies, the deepest feelings are beyond reach. What was it like to be alive on a certain day in a certain place? When the door opened suddenly, who was the unexpected stranger standing there? What was it like when what we take for granted as history was the hidden, unknowable future?

Where the historian must stick to the Sgt. Joe Friday dictum, "Just the facts, ma'am," the historical novelist has an open field of play. He's the closest anyone can come to penetrating the past, conjuring moments of intense privacy, whispered intimacies, the unconfessed and the inconfessable.

It was Carlyle, a historian, who woke me to the vastness of history's untold stories, unrecorded lives, unremembered voices. Alone with him in my hotel room, I knew for the first time that I wanted to enter the worlds where honest historians cannot go. I wanted to write novels. I didn't know how. Or where I'd find the time. But I knew I had to.

I read books on how to write a novel. I never got very far before I felt I was learning how somebody else wrote a novel. I took a night course on fiction writing at the New School with Hayes Jacobs, who was renowned for his blunt and astute teaching methods. I submitted random pieces. He was encouraging. I didn't have the time to go back.

If I was going to learn how to write novels, I decided, it would be the same way I learned to be a speechwriter: I had to teach myself. I read novels with an eye to understanding what made them work. What brought a character alive? What was the best way to work in flashbacks? Was there a secret to plotting a story?

Instead of one-size-fits-all methods, I discovered an endless variety of styles, slants, acrobatics, divinations, prestidigitations. Bill Kennedy told me in an interview I did with him, "I don't aspire to imitations." Neither did I. Every writer does it his or her way, or they shouldn't bother.

I studied Tom Flanagan's National Book Award–winning *Year of the French*, a brilliant fictional account of the bloody 1798 uprising in Ireland from the perspectives of those who participated and those who observed. I dabbled with writing a novel set in Ireland during the famine. I didn't get much beyond page three before I sank up to my knees in the wet, pliant peatlands of the Bog of Allen.

Genevieve Corcoran, the wife of my mother's brother Jay, lived across the street from us in Parkchester. She was the secretary to the chairman of ESSO. As small kids, we visited her in the executive office. It was high in the Chrysler Building, a space of *Citizen Kane* dimensions, in a setting worthy of Ming the Merciless's sky palace.

She was a distant descendant of General Michael Corcoran, who headed the 69th New York Militia. In 1860, when the Prince of Wales became the first British royal to visit the United States, Corcoran refused to march his mostly Irish regiment in honor of the "Famine Prince." He was court-martialed for leading the only ethnic mutiny in America history, and released to fight in the Civil War, in which he died.

I asked her about him. Did she have any stories? She didn't know any and wasn't really interested, which in a way was better because with a child's fecund imagination, I could create my own heroic Civil War fantasies and peddle them to friends as if she had told them to me.

Confederates by Tom Kenneally, who later wrote *Schlindler's List*, reignited the interest in the Civil War that started in my early childhood when I was given an American history coloring book.

Set during the buildup to the Battle of Antietam, Kenneally's book scrubbed history clean of abstractions, clogged your mouth with the dust of dry summer roads, parched your throat with the acrid smoke of cannon fire, and made real the bowel-churning terror of soldiers facing imminent death or mutilation.

I doubted myself. I should stick to a straight historical narrative of events I already knew. I published both of my graduate seminar papers. They had a total of nearly 200 footnotes.

The most difficult thing about being a novelist, at least for me, was to start. The second was to stay with it in the hope of seeing it published. An Irish writer friend who published one critically acclaimed novel and couldn't get anything else in print, told me I was wrong. She said a novelist writes her book. It's out of her hands whether it's published or not.

There are great books that have suffocated for years in attics and desk drawers. Think of Melville, she said. He died a literary nonentity. *Billy Budd* wasn't published until after he was dead. I thought of Melville and the indignities writers suffer. I thought, who wants to be discovered after they're dead?

I regularly received catalogues from university presses. I ordered *Armies of the Streets*, by Adrian Cook, from the University of Kentucky Press, a study of the New York City Draft Riots of 1863. A combination race riot/urban insurrection, they remain the largest, most destructive such disturbance in American history.

What I knew about the Riots wasn't much. I saw estimates that 1,200 died during the week they raged. Doing what no historian had done before, Cook went through the morgue records. He reached a death toll closer to 120.

Skimming the list of names, one immediately stopped me: "Peter Quinn, of 264 West 37th Street, shot at the corner of Ninth Avenue and 44 Street, July 14." With that spare entry, devoid of age, occupation, marital status, with no indication if he was a rioter or a bystander, the abstractions of history turned flesh and blood.

It struck me that while even the smallest Civil War engagements had their chroniclers, Cook's was one of the few to delve into the details of an explosion that tore apart New York. It was a conflict Civil War re-enactors never went near.

New York had notable reminders of the Civil War. Grant's Tomb. The Soldiers and Sailors Monument. General Sherman's gilded likeness. Brooklyn's Grand Army Plaza. There wasn't even a plaque to mark the Colored Orphan Asylum, at the corner of 43rd and Fifth, where on July 13, the first day of the Riots, the 200 African-American children were barely evacuated when a mob looted and burned the building.

The Riots, it seemed to me, were the Civil War battle that never ended. The conflict that raged on the streets of New York, the toxic mix of race and class, the feral antagonisms between nativists and immigrants, the viral resentment of African Americans, is as real now as in the summer of 1863. It didn't need period-dressed re-enactors.

I wasn't interested in a social history or an analysis of the Riots' effects and implications. I wanted to know the people whose lives were changed by that week—Irish, African Americans, maids and stockbrokers, the well-off, the brokenhearted and down-and-out. I wanted to live the Riots with them.

I needed time more than anything. I had a job that involved endless deadlines. The longer I was there, the more assignments came my way. We had our first child. Nights and weekends were taken up. I whined to a novelist friend of mine about the squeeze I was in, with no time to do my own writing.

He responded tersely, "Make the time." I resented his utter lack of sympathy until I realized he was right. Never much of a morning person, I started getting up at 5:30 A.M. and arrived at my desk before seven. I did it five days a week. I never wrote on weekends. They were reserved for family time.

I worked for two hours before turning to my day job. Neither snow, nor rain, nor heat could stay me from my desk. Over the years, I wrote down scenes that came to mind. It was a random process. I thought up characters, then discarded them.

I loved the research, reading old newspapers, poking around the State Library. It carried me back to my happy stint as a graduate student. I slipped off when I could to the 42nd Street library to consult texts and check facts. I studied the building of the Croton water works (fittingly enough, the library occupied the space that once held the collecting reservoir) and the revolution in sanitation it brought about. I found an instruction manual for female domestics.

I was sitting in the library's old newspaper division on 43rd Street and 11th Avenue. It was a steamy August evening, closing time. The air conditioning was broken. Kathy and the kids were on Shelter Island. I was considering other areas for research when I realized I was using research as an excuse not to write. I'd either write the novel or I wouldn't.

I had no outline, no foreordained ending, only a half-realized cast of characters, people thrown together in the cauldron of a seething metropolis. I gathered them together under the title *Banished Children of Eve*. It was a phrase borrowed from the *Salve Regina*, a prayer I learned as a child.

I had no agent, no book contract. I started with no idea where I'd end. I listened to a conversation between two men in a saloon on the Lower East Side.

It was a wet morning in April 1863. "A fine morning on the River Styx," one said to the other. I was in charge. Nobody would know their story unless I told it. But they had to tell it to me first.

The governor was a national figure. As the year wore on and the 1984 presidential election approached, there was speculation he might enter the race. He batted it away. He had the job he wanted.

Candidate or not, he was a rising star. People wanted to hear from him. Invitations poured in. Except to speak to Jewish groups in Las Vegas and Miami, he never left the state. He made it a practice to never stay away overnight.

The primary season was directly ahead. Seven candidates were getting ready to run, including John Glenn, Jesse Jackson, Walter Mondale, and Gary Hart. Depending on whom you talked to, they were either the "seven beauties" or the "seven dwarfs."

Cuomo privately loathed Hart's "new ideas" and "new politics," with its rejection of the party's traditional emphasis on social legislation to aid the working and middle classes in favor of generic techno-speak innovations and airy, unspecified "new directions."

Although Cuomo wasn't running, it was clear that his endorsement carried weight. He was assiduously courted by all except Hart.

In November 1983, the governor accepted an invitation to speak at St. John the Divine Cathedral on the Sunday after Thanksgiving on "The Stewardship of Political Power." For whatever reason, he had a proclivity for accepting invitations around holidays.

It was the type of self-reflective, theological theme most politicians avoided. Since the arguments around JFK's Catholic faith in the 1960 election, there was little serious debate over the tension between politics and religious values.

Jimmy Carter commented about committing "adultery in my heart," drew attention. The quiet, sincere transparency of his faith made it short-lived. In the main, public discussion of religion stuck close to Eisenhower-era, pan-Protestant bromides.

The civil rights movement and the Vietnam War generated political activism by moderate as well as radical elements within the religious communities. The rise of the gay rights movement and the Supreme Court decision in *Roe v. Wade* put the role of religion in shaping public policy center stage.

Cuomo left it up to Bill and me to produce a draft. There was no reason to expect media attention. The subject wasn't the type reporters would run to cover, especially at the bottom of the long Thanksgiving weekend.

Cuomo had recently issued an executive order banning discrimination against homosexuals in state government. At the beginning of the 1980s, hostility toward and suspicion of gays as medical as well as moral subversives were fed by the growing specter of the AIDS epidemic.

He asked me to sit in on a private meeting in his World Trade Center office with a group of rabbis, Black ministers, and a Catholic *monsignor* opposed to his order. It didn't go well. The clergymen were clear that, as they saw it, Cuomo was putting the state seal of approval on behavior antithetical to the most basic tenets of Judeo-Christian morality. They intended to campaign as hard as they could for the ban's reversal.

In his speech, Cuomo cited a letter he'd received. The writer asked, "How can you claim to be a Christian when you go out of your way to proclaim the right of people to be an abomination in the sight of God?" The letter will not be found in the governor's papers. It was my condensed, toned-down summary of his recent meeting.

Cuomo began by making clear "I'm not a theologian." He evoked the immigrant, pre–Vatican II church of his childhood, with its view of the human condition as "the poor banished children of eve mourning and weeping in this vale of tears." He said Teilhard de Chardin, the Jesuit theologian and paleontologist, changed his perspective. He "reoriented our theology and rewrote its language."

The Constitution created common ground, he said, where religious values weren't abandoned but where believers, nonbelievers and the not-quite-sure could work "to promote the general welfare." The country's history was involved in including those left out—slaves, women, Catholics—not in finding reasons for exclusion.

He wondered how a country as religious as ours, in which a significant majority expressed a belief in God, could increasingly follow the Social Darwin gospel of "survival of the fittest."

The speech built on themes set out in the inaugural and speeches to the Democratic National Committee and National Education Association as well as anticipated the keynote at the convention. It made no mention of abortion, an issue which had yet to take the prominence it would in the upcoming presidential election.

The next day, when I arrived in Albany, Bill held up a copy of the *New York Times*. Maureen Dowd had attended the speech. It was on the front page under the headline CUOMO, IN PULPIT, TALKS OF ETHICS AND RELIGION. The speech, she wrote, "mixed politics, ethics and personal religious experience."

The press office was already inundated with requests for copies.

Soon after, a letter arrived from Father Richard McBrien, chair of the Department of Theology at Notre Dame. He read the speech and invited the governor to come to South Bend and expand on it. The governor and McBrien agreed to revisit the possibility later in the year. There was no hint of the national attention it would draw.

Directly ahead was another State of the State. If Cuomo regarded it as important, the press was sufficiently jaundiced to entertain no great expectations. The business of the speech was the business of the state, and the parochial business of New York, no matter the spin, was specific and prosaic. The business of the speechwriters was to do no harm.

In essence, the State of the State is the hometown version of the president's State of the Union. Until Woodrow Wilson, it was a written document the president sent Congress.

Wilson was a professor. He enjoyed lecturing. He made the unfortunate decision to deliver it in person. State governors made the unfortunate decision to follow his example.

Ronald Reagan stripped away the occasion's solemnity, about the only thing it had going for it, and turned it into a prime-time variety show. He filled the gallery with assorted heroes and celebrities he could salute and be assured of applause from both sides of the aisle. His Democratic and Republican successors kept it up.

It reached its nadir—at least up until now—when President Trump used the occasion to present the Presidential Medal of Freedom to the huffing and Montecristo-puffing king of far-right talk radio, Rush Limbaugh.

The governor's address is more boring than the president's—hard as that might seem—because New York doesn't have its own armed forces and doesn't fight foreign wars (except for its role as the staging area for the ill-fated invasion of Canada during the War of 1812).

Faced with the worst fiscal crisis in the state's history, Governor Carey delivered the State of the State's one and only memorable line: "The days of wine and roses are over." I wish I'd thought of it. It was before my time.

My brother, who followed me as a gubernatorial speechwriter, described the process of writing the State of the State as the "stations of the cross." The first station was the promise that this year's address would be different. This year it'd be "in the governor's voice," direct and inspiring, free of the slumberous recitation of programs and policies.

Several weeks and several dozen drafts later, this year's speech ended up as bad as the one delivered the year before, and the one delivered the year before that, all the way back to Woodrow Wilson. As we processed the flow of agency prose, Bill said we should think of ourselves as "a sewerage treatment plant."

Whichever metaphor you prefer, stations of the cross or sewerage treatment, the bottom was scraped the night before, with the rehearsal in the well of the legislature. A peanut gallery of Executive Chamber honchos and assistants, who'd plotz at the thought of having to write it, weighed in with suggestions and additions (subtractions were rare) and random observations (usually unhelpful).

They went home to bed. Bill and I worked until dawn reshaping and deodorizing the pile of elephant dung (another appropriate metaphor) into something that didn't look and smell like elephant dung.

The last station was transferring the speech to a teleprompter. These were the days before word processors and laptops. The technology dated back to Woodrow Wilson.

Using an outsized typewriter that looked like a prop from *Honey, I Shrunk the Kids*, a technician put the speech on duplicate rolls of yellow paper, one for the right side, one for the left, that he moved along in sync with the governor's delivery. When changes were made, the tape was cut and the new sections Scotch-taped in.

The comeuppance came when it was so loaded with tape, it got stuck and the governor had to deliver the speech to the Republicans' side of the Chamber. They must have wondered at the attention he paid. The press didn't notice. No harm was done.

Primary season loomed large. The quadrennial slugfest among Democratic contenders for the nomination quickly became a two-way match. In one corner was steady-as-he-goes Walter Mondale, a stalwart fighter for the traditional values of the Democratic Party.

In the other was Gary Hart. His JFK-like good looks and attacks on "the failed policies of the past"—he was never very specific about which policies or what he'd replace them with—won him a loyal fan base among younger Democrats.

Cuomo went public with his preference for trying to keep together the New Deal coalition and endorsed Mondale. He let slip that Mondale resembled *polenta*, an Italian dish of cornmeal mush. When the press jumped on it, he claimed it was his mother's description and, besides, *polenta* was healthy for you.

Hart pulled off an upset in the New Hampshire primary. Mondale hit back. He invoked the line "Where's the beef?" from a Wendy's commercial to attack the nebulousness of Hart's "new ideas." They battled it out through the spring. By June, Mondale had enough delegates to cinch the nomination.

Mondale obviously faced tough odds in seeking to unseat Ronald Reagan, whose growing popularity was driven by an economic recovery and his inroads among the ethnic vote. Mondale's selection of Geraldine Ferraro, a three-term Italian-American congresswoman, as his running mate made her the first woman nominated by a major party for vice president and spiced up the *polenta*.

The convention was scheduled for July 16–19 in San Francisco. Mondale asked Cuomo to deliver the keynote address. It was an honor he was ambivalent about accepting. Given the raucous nature of conventions, it wasn't difficult to lose the attention of the audience and end up stranded on the podium atop a swirling sea of inattentive, aimlessly wandering delegates.

Bill and I met with the governor to watch tapes of keynotes going back to 1956. The general impression was horrifying. Most performances were underwhelming, a few disastrous. A short while into John Glenn's keynote at the 1976 convention in Madison Square Garden, he lost the audience. His speech wasn't the only problem. His delivery made it worse.

The governor asked for a draft, which I sent him. I hadn't gotten it back when he announced to the press he was writing the speech by himself. I suspected he sent me on the same fool's mission as when he had me write an inaugural he'd already written. Bill took him at his word and left on vacation.

I stuck around waiting to see if the governor would bother sending back the draft. When it came back, he'd recast what I wrote, melding his version into mine. He summoned me to his office. We went back and forth with changes.

I'm not sure I can trust my memory on how long it went on. It could've been two days or two weeks. I slashed and added. He added and slashed. The long litany of "we believe" flowed out of the Credo that we repeated countless times at Mass. Exhausted, I lay on the floor of my office and stared into the cloud-empty sky above the World Trade Center.

At times, it felt like the governor, his longtime assistant Mary Tragale, Helen Ross, and I were the only ones in the building. The deadline drew near. We went through more rewrites before gathering with Andrew Cuomo, Tim Russert, and the governor's secretary, Michael Del Giudice. Andrew said the speech needed to be tested on an audience.

A small group of office workers and staff was gathered in the press-conference room. The lights were turned off. The governor stood spot-lighted at the lectern. His delivery was flat. The audience response was tepid. We went back to his office. Tim Russert suggested that the middle section, in which the governor spoke directly to the president, be moved to the front. It was an important change.

The audience regathered. Some were new, some had heard the previous version. It seemed to go well, but the finale fizzled. Al Cifone, the plain-spoken head of the mailroom, put it simply, "I like the *Tale of Two Cities* stuff a lot but the ending sucks."

Andrew pulled me aside. He asked me to fix it. I said I'd try. I went to my office. I'd been over the speech so many times, I could hardly see it. I started going through my notebooks. I consulted the quotes and anecdotes I'd amassed. Nothing seemed right.

I picked up my copy of his *Campaign Diaries* and flipped through several pages. I stopped on page 9. The words jumped out: "Poppa had calluses on both hands. I saw him once literally bleed from the bottom of his feet."

I had the hook I needed. Here was no lonesome cowboy. Here was a family man, a father, part of an immigrant community, who like millions of others worked to give his children the life he could only dream. His son's political beliefs were rooted in his immigrant father's sacrifices, not liberal abstractions. This is how it came out in the speech:

That struggle to live with dignity is the real story of the shining city. And it's a story, ladies and gentlemen, that I didn't read in a book, or learn in a classroom. I saw it and lived it, like many of you. I watched a small man with thick calluses on both his hands work 15 and 16 hours a day. I saw him once literally bleed from the bottoms of his feet, a man who came here uneducated, alone, unable to speak the language, who taught me all I needed to know about faith and hard work by the simple eloquence of his example.

The governor left the next morning. He was a seasoned speech giver, but this was the first time he would address a national audience. A lot was riding on it for the party as well as for him. He joked to me, I could watch on TV as he *"merda me stesso"*—"shit myself."

I watched it at the apartment of Sandy Teller, a veteran comedy writer and close friend, who gathered a group of enthusiastic Democrats. John Chancellor of NBC prefaced the speech by noting the governor was perhaps the only politician who wrote all his own speeches. My prime-time fear was that all our stitching and unstitching and restitching would be immediately apparent.

It was clear from the keynotes we'd watched that it took only a very short time for attention to wane and the audience to grow restive. The governor had only a small window in which to focus attention. The lights were turned off before the governor spoke. A short film was shown. When the lights came back on, all eyes were on the lectern.

The speech began with his challenge to Reagan's image of America as "a shining city on a hill." The problem was, he said, that there was another city that the president couldn't see "from the portico of the White House and the veranda of his ranch"; the places he didn't visit "where some people can't pay their mortgages, and most young people can't afford one"; where students can't afford the education they need, and middle-class parents watch the dreams they hold for their children evaporate.

"In fact, Mr. President, this is a nation—Mr. President, you ought to know that this is more a 'Tale of Two Cities' than it is just a 'Shining City on a Hill.'"

I held my breath, listened to the overly familiar words, and watched as he pulled it off. The crowd was with him from the start. As the speech went on, the bond grew stronger. Mario Cuomo was a physically impressive man. He had large hands, a workingman's hands, that he moved gracefully.

Watching him deliver the speech, I thought of Yeats's line "Who's to tell the dancer from the dance?" Cuomo wasn't just giving the speech. He was the speech. By the end he could have Pied Pipered the crowd into San Francisco Bay.

By this point I knew the lines by heart. As we listened, I spoke them before he did, which annoyed Kathy. Everybody else was entertained. They congratulated me for my part in making it work. I had too much to drink. I was already nervous about the press poking around to find out what role I had. I wouldn't say anything until I talked to the governor.

Cuomo flew home the morning after the speech. That afternoon, he called me to his office in the Trade Center. He looked exhausted. He had none of the exhilaration that might be expected of a man who had just electrified the country. I talked about how thrilling it was to watch on television. He said he was grateful for all the advice he'd received. He listed people who had nothing to do with the speech. He barely looked at me.

I gazed at the portrait of St. Thomas More on the wall beside his desk. My father had the exact same reproduction of Holbein's portrait on the wall of his chambers. More had a paper folded in his hand. Maybe it was a speech.

I wandered back to my office. I was confused. And I wasn't. The news was full of praise for the speech and Cuomo's achievement in writing it himself. In one account, he wrote it alone in the Mansion in a single five-hour period.

A few days later, I waited outside the governor's office. I casually flipped through a pile of papers lying atop a small table. It contained drafts of the convention speech, all written or marked up in the governor's hand. Pad and pen had done their work.

An assistant came out of his office and said he was ready to see me. I asked about the drafts. "The Smithsonian has requested them," she said.

When the legend becomes fact, print the legend.

⁞⁞⁞

Bill Hanlon and I occupied an office in the Capitol down the hall and around the corner from the governor's office. It was a weird, windowless space, with a twenty-foot ceiling. A Capitol old-timer told me it was originally used for hangings. He was kidding, I think.

I gave up cigarettes when my father died of lung cancer. When I entered the pressure cooker of the Executive Chamber, I made up for lost time. Bill and I filled coffee mugs with butts. Smoke hung thick in the air.

We kept a large corkboard that we called "the wall of shame." We posted the most hideous samples of twisted, incomprehensible prose that flowed from state agencies and offices across our desks. At week's end, we chose the very worst. It was never easy.

I thought about leaving. Kathy was enthusiastic. It was hard to entertain starting a family when I was spending long hours either in the office or in Albany.

In a display case in the nearby Capitol Rotunda was the blood-stained tunic of Col. Elmer Ellsworth, the first Union officer killed in the Civil War. Sometimes I stared at it for a long time. I contemplated the unfinished novel I was trying to write.

I dreaded looking for another job as well as finding one churning out terminally dull corporatese. There was something more. Though I often felt like a mill horse, pulling the grindstone in endless circles, I thought what Bill and I were doing was important. I believed in the political cause Cuomo represented. I believed his words mattered.

Frank Lynn, a veteran *Times* reporter I got to know when I arrived in Albany, advised me, "Politicians can seduce you into believing you're a friend. Don't be fooled. You're as expendable as a mismatched sock. It's nothing personal. For them, it's a matter of survival. They're in the business of getting re-elected, not amassing old acquaintances."

I knew the validity of Frank's advice. He witnessed politicians toss supposed friends overboard to save the ship from capsizing. Still, I was sure Cuomo and I had something deeper than an employer–employee relationship that I wasn't ready to turn my back on.

There wasn't much time for mulling over the future before the post-convention riptide pulled me back in. The invitation Father McBrien sent after the St. John the Divine speech the previous November to give a talk at Notre Dame assumed an importance neither could have anticipated.

As a congresswoman, Geraldine Ferraro was an outspoken champion of a woman's right to an abortion. In her heightened role as Mondale's choice for vice president, her public identification as a Catholic drew the fire of New York's Archbishop John O'Connor, who declared it was impossible to support a pro-choice position and claim to be a Catholic.

The Republican Party had been split on abortion. George H.W. Bush had changed his position from pro-choice to pro-life. As governor, Ronald Reagan signed into law the California Therapeutic Abortion Act of 1967. As a presidential candidate, he endorsed a constitutional amendment to ban abortions.

Abortion had been legal in New York since 1970. Republican Governor

Nelson Rockefeller signed into law the nation's most liberal abortion law. He vetoed an attempt to repeal it. The liberal eastern pro-choice wing of the Republican Party Rockefeller embodied was fast sinking into oblivion. Pro-life Evangelicals were a rising force in the party.

The Democrats' pro-choice position hardened to the point where the pro-life faction was effectively shown the door. The debate over abortion had divided along party lines.

O'Connor's public scolding of Ferraro put the issue of abortion at the center of the presidential election. Cuomo's position was the same as his predecessor Hugh Carey's, whose thirteen children fireproofed him to a degree against being perceived as a proponent of abortion. He held that though personally opposed to abortion, the Supreme Court made a woman's right to choose the law of the land, which he was sworn to uphold.

Carey had a personal relationship with Terence Cooke, the Cardinal Archbishop of New York. He called into question Carey's countenancing of the state's Medicaid funding of abortion, but he didn't call down the heavens.

O'Connor wasn't Cooke. He was appointed head of the New York Archdiocese by Pope John Paul II in January 1983 as part of his determination to weed out what he deemed the dangerous laxity in Catholic teaching and practice that followed the Second Vatican Council. John Paul closed down the debate on married priests and the ordination of women.

Though Cuomo and O'Connor agreed on issues like the rights of organized labor and society's obligation to the poor—O'Connor was a strong supporter—there was no personal chemistry between them. If there was, it was the explosive, nitro-plus-glycerin kind. Speeches like the one Cuomo gave at St. John the Divine, where he identified as a Catholic and endorsed gay rights, didn't endear him to His Eminence.

The tension between the two burst into public view when O'Connor hosted a televised press conference. In light of Cuomo's refusal to veto state Medicaid funding for abortion, the same stance as his predecessor's, a reporter from a far-right Catholic publication raised the example of St. Ambrose, a fourth-century bishop, who excommunicated Emperor Theodosius for the massacre of 7,000 innocent civilians.

Would the archbishop excommunicate Cuomo, he asked, for signing legislation funding abortions for Medicaid recipients that would result in ending the lives of thousands of the innocent unborn?

Cuomo was watching along with his wife. He expected O'Connor to dismiss the comparison. (Technically, Cuomo lived in the Brooklyn diocese and was outside O'Connor's authority, but the point was made.) When instead of offering a firm rejection O'Connor hemmed and hawed, Cuomo was furious.

As the abortion debate moved to center stage in the presidential election, the press focused on Cuomo's upcoming speech at Notre Dame. The buzz around it continued to grow. In view of the changed circumstances, McBrien came to Albany to discuss the speech.

McBrien had an international reputation as a theologian. Despite reservations expressed by the Catholic Bishops Committee on Dogma (or maybe because of them), his immensely popular two-volume *Catholicism*, a guide to the history of the Church and its doctrines, sold 150,000 copies.

The governor invited Bill and me to lunch with McBrien at the Mansion. He reported that some alumni as well as faculty strenuously objected to giving a venue to a pro-choice politician.

Father Theodore Hesburgh, the high-profile university president, didn't back down. He thought it entirely appropriate. It would be years before Notre Dame became more closely identified with conservative Catholic thought.

Cuomo wasn't facing an election. He could round up the usual bromides, and duck and cover. But he didn't. He wanted to lay out the complexities and explain why he took the position he did. Marty Steadman, the governor's press secretary, a hardboiled pressman out of *The Front Page*, said to me, "I don't get it. The idea is to flee a fire, not jump in."

The lunch with Father McBrien went on late into the afternoon. Afterward, Bill and I went over with the governor the notes we took. He made clear he didn't want to sound like a theologian. He was a lawyer and politician seeking to balance the role of religion in the public sphere with the limits placed on it.

For Bill and me the speech was as much an attempt to articulate our views as the governor's. We were both raised in devout families. We were educated—from kindergarten through graduate school—in Catholic institutions and came of age during Vatican II. Bill had spent eleven years studying to be a Jesuit. We were practicing Catholics and married laymen.

Bill and his wife had four children. My wife and I were on the verge of starting a family. Like me, she was the product of Catholic grammar and high schools, and a Catholic college. She's always been the deeper thinker. I valued her opinion above all others'.

She'd never choose an abortion herself, she said. But given the individual circumstances of other women, she wouldn't support denying their right to make decisions about the most intimate parts of their lives.

Bill and I struggled with the draft. We volleyed and served, argued, and edited. The governor frequently called to check on our progress. He laughingly referred to what we were doing as the "Quinn–Hanlon speech." When we were both satisfied—or as satisfied as we could be—we gave him the draft.

In *More Than Words*, the book of speeches he published several years later, the governor wrote that after going over what he wanted to say "with Peter Quinn and Bill Hanlon of my staff, two bright, clever, gifted thinkers and writers, both of them profoundly Catholic and just as troubled as I was by the task of agonizing over the powerful, almost paralyzing issues raised by the abortion question . . . We wrote, discussed, debated, and finally decided . . . There was left the last task: finding the right words."

The words—at least most of them—had already been found and were on paper. The governor made additions, some that Bill and I argued against. Revisions and deletions were made.

When the speech was finished, we sent it to George Hunt, S.J., the editor of *America*, and Father McBrien. They both had points to make. In general, they thought the speech was effective. The governor shared it with Peter Steinfels, editor of *Commonweal*, who offered some helpful comments.

I was under the impression that he asked Joseph Sullivan, the auxiliary bishop of Brooklyn, for his opinion. Like other members of the clergy who were consulted, he preferred to stay anonymous.

In my experience, Cuomo wasn't pretending to believe something he didn't. He was a sincere Catholic attempting to tackle a widening chasm in the Democratic Party that endangered its ability to achieve its traditional progressive agenda.

The composition of the Democratic Party began to change during the Vietnam War. Though LBJ waged it, the bulk of the party turned against it. The anti-war advocates became the leading voices, which led to a rift in the ranks. Blue-collar Democrats remained mostly in support. By 1968, the intraparty dispute helped elect Richard Nixon.

The 1972 reforms within the Democratic Party demoted its traditional constituencies and gave greater influence to those who in the past had had a marginal voice, mainly women, Blacks, and young people.

The nomination of liberal anti-war standard-bearer George McGovern aggravated the tensions. The Republicans labeled the Democrats as the party of "acid, amnesty and abortion." *Roe v. Wade*, handed down the next year, provided a new source of division.

Hailed or at least accepted by a majority in the liberal wing of the party, it was especially opposed by many blue-collar Catholics who saw it as an assault on their cultural values.

The *coup de grâce* was Ronald Reagan's election in 1980. Economically, his championing of anti-union, pro–free market policies went against the best interests of the working class. But his red-meat patriotism and opposition to abortion and affirmative action led to the emergence of the "Reagan Democrats."

Cuomo felt Mondale's embodiment of "family values" and his record in support of the party's traditional pro-working-class stance was unassailable.

In writing the speech, we had no illusions. It was impossible to make both sides happy. The hope was that if abortion could be framed as a nuanced issue that raised complex questions politicians couldn't easily solve, maybe the opposing sides could be moved away from their scorched-earth positions.

There were equally important issues affecting the dignity and worth of human life to be considered in supporting or opposing a political candidate—racism, discrimination, an all-consuming arms race, homelessness, poverty, hunger, rampant and worsening inequality.

Along with a paucity of social programs to support mothers and children, the United States' disgracefully high levels of infant mortality set it apart among industrial nations.

We pointed out to the governor that the speech was going to be broadcast. It wasn't going to be entertaining. We didn't see how it could be much longer than fifteen minutes, the station-break interval at which viewer attention waned and channel surfing began. He said he didn't care how long it was. He wanted to say what he thought had to be said.

I flew with the governor, Mrs. Cuomo, and a plane full of reporters to South Bend. The plane was hit by lightning. The cabin momentarily filled with an eerie fluorescent glow. A reporter jokingly asked Marty Steadman if he thought God was sending a message. Steadman said, "Yeah. Don't fly into electrical storms."

Before he spoke, I handed Cuomo my father's rosary. When my mother gave it to me, I told her I was never any good at saying it. "Then carry it." she replied. "It can't hurt." It didn't, though I've never mastered the art of praying it.

Cuomo gave the speech in the middle of a presidential campaign. Unlike today's debates, which have stopped being debates and become slugfests of recriminations and interruptions, he made no denunciations or personal attacks. He did his best to avoid indicting anyone's motives. He didn't avoid tackling complexities.

He read it deliberately, with none of the theatrics of the keynote. He spoke to the audience in the hall. He ignored the television cameras.

We were barely back on the plane when the reactions began rumbling in. Papers across the country ran editorials. The *Daily News*'s next-day headline summed up the speech as Cuomo saying, "Keep God Out of Politics."

In fact, what he said was "God doesn't demand political neutrality." Believers have every right to base their political views on their faith. What they still must do is convince those who don't share their faith that what they propose serves a valid public purpose.

In the wake of Notre Dame, if the debate over abortion didn't disappear, it faded for the time being into the background. No politician wanted to tread where Cuomo had and deal point-by-point with the issues he raised. In their debate, Mondale and Reagan moved quickly past their fixed positions.

When vice-presidential candidates Ferraro and Bush debated, she restated her stand that it was a woman's right to decide what to do with her body. She wouldn't impose her religious beliefs on those who didn't share them.

Bush replied that he respected her position. (Although they kept it to themselves at the time, Barbara Bush as well as Nancy Reagan also shared her position.) As it turned out, the election was decided on the economy. Abortion played a negligible role.

The deluge of correspondence that followed the speech was either laudatory or denunciatory. (There was more of the latter than the former, much of it vicious ad hominen attacks.)

Kathy and I went out to dinner with friends who identified with the Catholic charismatic movement. They wasted no time in lambasting me for my role in the speech. Any attempt to engage in the particulars of the speech or change the subject was useless.

I was invited by a classmate to a Fordham fundraising dinner. When a woman at the table learned I was a speechwriter for the governor, she launched into a tirade that forced me to leave.

Cuomo's speech remains a point of reference and contention. Depending on where you stand, the speech was a rank betrayal of the Church, an eloquent statement of the liberal Catholic position, masterful, disgraceful, fatuous, an indigestible porridge of clichés, a brilliant examination of the Catholic conscience. Quoting from it extensively in a *Times* article in September 2021—thirty-seven years after it was delivered—Linda Greenhouse described it as "a remarkable performance."

Ethicists, academics, clergy, social scientists, and moral theologians continue to discuss it. It was invoked in the debate among Catholic bishops whether to deny communion to pro-choice politicians like President Joe Biden, a step Cardinal O'Connor never took and that Pope Francis has rejected.

No politician has substantially added to it. In the almost four decades since, the debate has grown only more bitter, each side more intent on demonizing the other.

The governor said he wanted to make a follow-up address to answer his critics and expand on points he felt were underexamined at Notre Dame. Bill and I argued that he had made his case. Another speech would only invite another flood of epistolary invective.

Cuomo came to public attention achieving a compromise between two sides bitterly divided over the placing of public housing. That was part of his take on the abortion question. The object was to lay out a middle road, not spring surprises. The problem was—and remains—there's not much interest in finding any. At least Cuomo had the courage to try.

The Notre Dame speech raised the governor's profile even further. A cresting wave of speaking invitations turned into a *tsunami*. Following Mondale's flattening at the polls, Cuomo's star ascended still higher. Some hailed him as the party's best hope in '88.

The fall turned out less overwhelming than feared. Cuomo wisely refrained from overexposure and giving the impression of running for president while the corpse of the Democratic Party was still warm.

The State of the State slouched round again. I don't remember much except the routine revisions, the same-as-always competition among program associates and deputy commissioners to include their pet projects, and the predictable chaotic finale, all ending in a speech forgotten before it was finished being delivered.

In pursuit of a mental break, I sometimes retreated to the State Museum, where I was sure not to encounter anyone from the Executive Chamber, a place where interest in the past didn't extend beyond yesterday afternoon.

One day I came upon an exhibit on public transportation. Along with an Albany trolley was a vintage New York City bus of the kind Ralph

Kramden drove. Stranded and forlorn, it looked like a relict dinosaur from the Late Cretaceous period.

The signage on the front identified it as a Bx 40, the bus I took for eight years to high school and college. There are moments when an event or memory wakes us to the press of time's accumulated weight. Here was a first ring of the alarm clock. I firmly resolved to avoid the near occasion of another year in Albany.

Aching to get away, I was aware how much Albany had changed my life. Over six-and-a-half years and two administrations, I gained a trade, reconnected with the woman I'd marry, worked in tandem with Bill and true professionals who became close friends, enjoyed and endured the inner workings of politics—the sausage-making Bismarck said was better unseen—and learned what I couldn't as an academic.

Despite scorning the prose powers of state workers, I developed respect for the career civil servants who carried out the difficult, complex, day-to-day responsibilities of government. Their work went mostly unappreciated and unnoticed, except when things went wrong and the press jumped all over them.

If a whaleship was Ishmael's Harvard and Yale, Albany was mine.

Cuomo accepted an invitation to deliver the Chubb Lecture at Yale. It was his first major speech since Notre Dame and the drubbing of the Democratic ticket in a defeat of historic proportions. The press was primed.

There was already a growing chorus in the party calling for a reassessment of the core beliefs—the creed of the New Deal—that had driven and defined the party for a half-century.

In the eyes of these "Third Way Democrats" (which often looked suspiciously like the Republican way), instead of an inspiration, the New Deal's emphasis on economic intervention and income redistribution was an impediment to ever taking power again. History had moved on. The party could follow or resign itself to impotence.

The New Democratic Party would be "market-oriented." Wall Street was to be cultivated, not regulated. Financial controls needed to be reduced or removed. Stumbling blocks instead of boons to productivity, unions needed to adjust to the competitive realities of free trade and global competition. The social safety net was an entangling web of helplessness and dependency. It must be dramatically pared.

Cuomo would have none of it. If the party pulled up its roots every time it lost an election, what would it be but "a reed swayed by the wind"?

I remembered the apocryphal tale about how Galileo, rising from his knees after the Inquisition forced him to recant his assertion that, contrary to Scripture, Earth revolves around the sun, he whispered, "E pur si move." *But still it moves.* It was the perfect hook.

For the fourth time since his inauguration, a speech by the governor was featured on the front page of the *Times*: "Cuomo at Yale Urges Democrats to Remain with Their Tested Principles." Inside were extensive excerpts as well as a requisite photo of him at his desk, in solitary labor with pad and pen.

He carefully crafted the speech, the article reported, "aware that whatever his own protestations, it would be looked upon by some as another in a series of speeches he began at the Democratic National Convention. . . ." Beginning with his inaugural, through his speeches at St. John the Divine, the convention, Notre Dame, and Yale, Cuomo laid out a philosophy of liberal activism that he never strayed far from.

Cuomo's warnings were prophetic. The economic decoupling between classes came to pass. Executives' pay soared. Ordinary wages stagnated. The share of wealth that went to the richest 1 percent doubled. Unions shrank in numbers and influence. The net worth of the bottom half fell to near zero. The best of times for a few proved the worst for far more.

The Great Recession unmasked the failed magic of self-regulating markets, the epic irresponsibility of supposedly astute financial wizards, and the cluelessness of fiscal gurus and monetary masterminds who unleashed a storm that came close to capsizing the ship.

The collapse that Fed chief and economic mastermind Alan Greenspan—winner of the award for Distinguished Public Service given by high-flying, fraud-ridden Enron—assured the country couldn't happen again, happened. The cocksure captains of high finance and masters of Brobdingnagian banks, contemptuous of government regulation, were panicked and helpless. "We are perishing," they cried, "government must save us!"

Washington provided the trillion-dollar life preservers. None of the culprits drowned or went to jail. Most enjoyed the comforts of severance pay, deferred compensation, and superabundant pensions. The most brazen returned to argue against the regulations that would have prevented the crisis in the first place.

With the crash, capitalism could no longer be worshipped as a cure-all. Free markets, the world's greatest system for wealth creation, couldn't regulate themselves or see to an equitable distribution of rewards. Free of government, the Tale of Two Cities grows more dire.

As summer approached, the number of invitations that flooded in to deliver college commencements was almost laughable. The governor promised to be selective. Bill and I learned his elastic interpretation of selective when he accepted thirteen. He told the press he didn't intend to recycle any.

If he wanted to squelch talk about his national ambitions, this was a strange way to go about it. Bill and I protested that what he wanted was impossible. "We'll do our best," the governor said. Bill and I did do our best to make the speeches different, but it turned out not to matter. The audience was glad to have him there. They had no idea what he said elsewhere, and didn't care. The press didn't bother keeping tabs.

A way out finally presented itself. I was contacted by Bob R., head speechwriter at Time Inc. Bob was Senator Ed Muskie's speechwriter in the days when he enjoyed the inside track on the 1972 presidential nomination. He worked at the White House as part of President Jimmy Carter's speechwriting team.

A native Floridian, Bob was laid back, cordial, easy to get to know, the way you expect southerners to be, although once you get past the surface, they're often not. He saw a passing reference to me in the press as a member of the governor's staff "who helped with speeches." He guessed there was more to it.

He asked me to lunch. One lunch turned into several. He and his wife, he told me, wanted to slow down and go back to Tallahassee and have more time with their three young children. With his expenses reduced, he could make a comfortable living freelancing.

If I was interested, he said, he'd put my name in the mix as a possible replacement. Desperate was more like it. No longer the rock-solid conservative bastion it had been under founder Henry Luce, Time Inc. retained its place in the top ranks of American media.

Few companies took themselves as seriously. The three-volume company history covered sixty-five years. Edward Gibbon took six volumes to cover the centuries-long decline and fall of the Roman Empire. The perks and benefits it offered its employees led some to dub it "Paradise publishing."

Time Inc. made a difference in the quality of mainstream journalism and entertainment. Its magazines dominated the industry. HBO was the ruling power in cable TV and had no close competitor. With Time-Life Books; Little, Brown; and Book of the Month Club, it had a significant presence in book publishing. It was exactly the kind of enterprise I fantasized joining.

PART THREE

Killing Time

IN VETERAN JOURNALIST Dick Clurman's account of the merger of Time and Warner, *To the End of Time*, he described Time Inc.'s preference for hiring those who fit the "Time type."

"The personnel department," he wrote, "was still using that old rejection code scrawled across the top of interview forms, 'NFT,' not for Time—one step away from the dowagers' codeword admonition 'NOCD,' not of our class, dear."

I went through a series of interviews before meeting my prospective employer, CEO Dick Munro. Unlike the borderline sociopaths often found in the corner office, Munro had a reputation as accessible and unpretentious, a leader by example, which he proved to be.

A man of singularly simple tastes, he rode a commuter train to work each morning with the same seatmates, none of whom were high-placed executives. He ate in the company cafeteria, never lauded his own abilities, or acted the tyrant, or treated employees as disposable assets. He was unfailingly collegial, accessible, and the last of a breed.

A staunch Democrat amid a lion's den of Republicans, he wasn't afraid to speak out on issues like arms control and racial justice. For many CEOs, stepping down—especially the loss of the corporate jet—involves a jarring loss of prestige and perks. When his time came, what was one giant step for some CEOs was one small step for Munro.

Munro embodied the unwritten postwar compact that tamed the worst excesses of capitalism and corporations. It recognized corporations' community obligations, valued loyalty and job security, and avoided excessive avariciousness.

The so-called organizational man spent his career at the same company, worked his way up to CEO, and emphasized consensus. He was well paid but not extravagantly enriched. (Sloan Wilson's 1955 novel *The Man in the Gray Flannel Suit* captured some of the era's zeitgeist. Wilson was a part-time speechwriter and worked at Time Inc.)

By the mid-1980s, international competition and deregulation had upended the era of economic equilibrium. Business went from an arcane concern of bankers and investors to a cynosure of public attention. Deemed quaint and irrelevant, the ethos of the generation that came of age amid the Depression and World War II passed into history. Mammon was God, and Milton Friedman its prophet.

My last interview was with the chairman, Ralph Davidson. A handsome westerner, with a craggy, tanned, outdoors face—Gary Cooper meets Robert Redford—he was a graduate of Stanford and the CIA. His rise from salesman to publisher of *Time* had been frictionless.

Davidson slipped easily from the hand-on-the-shoulder bonhomie of a salesman to the gravitas of the chairman of a storied American media corporation. Never a journalist, he enjoyed being mistaken for one. He was the company's public face. CEO Dick Munro ran it.

Davidson shared that he got good reports from the succession of executives I interviewed with. Writing for Mario Cuomo, he said, was qualification enough to be a speechwriter. He gestured to the unopened envelope on his desk with the speeches I sent. He confessed he hadn't read them yet. He was sure he'd find them "more than acceptable."

He had an expansive way of sitting back with his hands behind his head. On the table behind him was a Frederick Remington bronze. "Besides," he added, "nobody can bullshit better than the Irish."

Davidson's throwaway line wasn't the first time I heard the suggestion of a singular genetic connection between Irishness and linguistic ability. While it's true Irish Americans have had a significant presence as journalists, actors, songwriters, and entertainers, they're far from unique. America's ethno-racial mix brims with verbal acrobats of every stripe. Where would Broadway and comedy be without Jews? Who's added more than African Americans to the rhythms and beat of American music? Walt Whitman would've loved rap.

When I die, I plan to be cremated and my ashes scattered around the Bronx. If I change my mind and opt for a tombstone, I've directed it be inscribed: "Nobody Was a Better Bullshitter. (But Not Because He Was Irish.)"

A week went by after my interview with Ralph Davidson. I heard nothing. I succumbed to my native pessimism and wallowed in the miserable certainty I'd been judged NFT.

The call finally came. All the candidates had been interviewed. The job was mine if I wanted it. I shocked myself by hesitating. I was never any good at transitions. I was attached to Bill and the people I worked with. I asked for a day before I gave my answer.

They upped the offer. I was embarrassed that they thought I was playing hard to get. I called Kathy. She said to pull myself together, call them back immediately, and accept the job, which I did.

I knew that informing the governor I was leaving would be awkward. He was still talking to me about upcoming speeches and had no idea of my job search. When I told him I was in touch with executives at Time Inc. who had made an offer in the category of irrefusable, he bristled. "Who the hell is Munro to go behind my back and pull a stunt like this?" he said.

"It's no stunt," I answered. Since one of his favorite tropes was "the family of New York," I explained that Kathy and I were trying to start a family, which was made difficult by my spending half my time in Albany. (I didn't add that the other half was stress and sleep deprivation.)

He said he could arrange for me to spend most of my time in the city. I knew there was no chance it would work that way. He did too. I didn't say anything. He let it go.

Not long after I departed Albany, a package arrived with a framed photo of the governor and me minutes before his speech at Notre Dame. He's drinking a glass of water. I have my arms folded so tightly, it's as if I'm trying to hold myself together, which I was.

It was inscribed, "To Peter, Thanks for the words . . . and the music."

My first day on the job, I lingered in the lobby of the Time & Life Building. It had the feel of a place where important things were done. I was wracked with doubt. I went to a small Catholic college in the Bronx. I wrote political speeches. I knew next to nothing about how corporations worked. No one in my immediate family had ever worked for one.

I was assigned an office on the thirty-fourth floor, next door to Dick Munro. Most corporations have a thirty-fourth floor, shorthand for the company's executive roost—as in "If you want to cover your ass, you better run it past thirty-four." I wasn't an executive, just somebody whom Dick wanted close at hand.

My one condition when I went to Time Inc. was that Helen Ross, my assistant at the governor's office, come with me. The only African American on the floor, Helen sat in a spacious alcove outside my office.

To give her privacy, Dick saw to it that a wall was put up. I could tell she was upset. "They don't want a Black person on public display," she said. I went to Dick and told him his good intentions had backfired. By that afternoon, the wall was gone.

Helen came to love working there. She interrupted me when she thought I was too long on the phone with a friend. She questioned entries on my expense account. She warned me not to do anything to put our jobs in danger.

Helen was an intensely private person. I rarely saw her outside the office. In all the years we worked together, she never accepted my invitation to join Kathy and me for Thanksgiving or Christmas. She rarely went to lunch with me, never to dinner. She socialized with a small group of female friends but traveled alone to Asia and Europe.

Just before he retired as Time Inc. CEO, Dick told me how impressed he was that his speeches were free of typos and misspellings. I told him the pages would have been clotted with them if it hadn't been for Helen.

I shared with Helen that if we lived in a world where race and gender didn't matter, the odds were I'd be working for her. She thought I was kidding. I wasn't.

The first names of the thirty-fourth floor's residents were a clue to its ethnic makeup: Winston, Thayer, and Kelso. I said to Helen that it sounded like a row of battleships. There was office politics—the slow-motion kind, not the immediate bullet-in-the-back-of-the-head type beloved in Albany. That would come later.

There was a British style to how executives dressed, a loyalty to tradition and decorum, and a penchant for secretaries (all female) with English accents. The benefits went beyond liberal to beneficent. One legendary executive, known for expense-account lunches and dinners at the 21 Club, earned the nickname "Old 42."

Employees were cultivated rather than treated like interchangeable parts. Once they demonstrated they had the requisite skills, it was presumed they'd spend their careers. There were no mass layoffs or firings intended to drive up the stock price.

Don Wilson, the head of corporate communications, was a Time type par excellence. A graduate of Deerfield Academy and classmate of George H.W. Bush's at Yale, he wrote for the *Yale Daily News* and served on bombing missions over Nazi Germany. Fresh out of the service, he was hired by Time Inc. and served as *Life*'s Far East bureau chief.

He left to join JFK's presidential campaign. He was Ed Murrow's deputy at the United States Information Agency. When Murrow died, Wilson became acting director. He went back to Time Inc. and took a second leave to work on Bobby Kennedy's 1968 campaign. He was with Kennedy in the kitchen of the Ambassador Hotel when he was shot.

When I'd interviewed with him, he'd done his best to put me at ease. He was very interested in my experiences with Cuomo. A part of him missed politics, he said. A bigger part was grateful to be at Time Inc. He reached into the cabinet behind his desk and asked if I'd be interested in a drink. I didn't pretend I wasn't.

He poured us each a dram of Scotch, enough for a toast. "I think you'll like it here," he said. We threw back our drinks. He turned out to be a true gentleman and a great boss.

Famous people came in and out of the Time & Life Building. The custom was to pretend you didn't notice. One day, I met the great photographer Alfred Eisenstaedt in the elevator. Almost ninety, he came most days to the *Life* magazine offices. A Jewish World War I veteran of the German army, he was forced to flee by the Nazis. He was short and shy.

Since we worked for the same company and were the only two in the elevator, I felt emboldened to break the rule. I told him how much I admired his photography. I didn't bring up his photos of Parkchester's plentitude of baby carriages.

I mentioned the iconic print on my office wall of the sailor planting a V-J Day kiss on the nurse's lips in Times Square, and how it reminded me of Ulysses returning to Penelope. He smiled and nodded but didn't say anything. It was clear that he didn't value attention.

Time Inc. was filled with talented, intriguing, accomplished people on the business as well as on the journalistic side. It was a wonderful place to work in every way. In the industry, its reputation for excellence was taken for granted.

Allowing for a degree of Time Inc. hubris, a former editor-in-chief wrote, "To spend your days among people of thoughtfulness and honor, and at the same time people of real intellectual force and professional dedication—that is not necessarily the usual experience out there in the corporate and institutional world."

A staffer put it more succinctly: "Time Inc. is like having sex. When it's great it's fabulous. When it's not so good, it's still okay."

The happiest period of my working life was as Dick Munro's speech-writer. The schedule was full but not unreasonable, pay and benefits admirable. Munro, who as well as remaining CEO succeeded Davidson as chairman, was hard-driving when he had to be and easygoing most of the time. If I had to create an ideal boss from scratch, he would come out looking a lot like him. After the salt mines of Albany, I sucked in fresh air and bathed in sunshine.

***

Three months into my job at Time Inc., Kathy became pregnant. When Genevieve was born, all the clichés of newly minted fatherhood—amazement, gratitude, sheer delight—applied. The delivery-room nurse rested her, fresh from her mother's womb, in my arms. She instantly stopped crying and lay still. I wept with happiness and awe. Life is joy, not motion.

She was only a few months old when my life was upended by back pain so excruciating it threatened my ability to work. I was diagnosed with a herniated disc and told it required surgery. Seeking an alternative, I spoke with a friend who recommended a program run by Dr. John Sarno at NYU's Rusk Institute that treated most back pain as a symptom of psychological distress. He prescribed a program of psychotherapy and massage.

I thought it far-fetched at first. I knew little about the relationship between psychic and physical pain and feared the stigma of mental instability. Instead of the quick fix of surgery, there was no way to predict how effective therapy would be or how long it could take. Hesitant as I was, I sensed the root of my trouble was more profound than a disc.

I began working with a wise and caring therapist. She pushed me on my relationship with my father. She patiently helped me face my unspoken fear at replicating with my daughter my unhappy experience with him. My back pain gradually subsided.

When my son, Daniel, was born, I felt the same emotional thrill I had with Genevieve. Then the back pain returned with a vengeance. I wavered in my confidence that psychotherapy could bring permanent relief. I toyed with back surgery before I went back to my therapist.

We dug deeper this time. Progress was slower. She returned to my interactions—or lack of them—with my father. "When you talk about your father," she said, "you seem to know everything and feel nothing." I spoke about his childhood, his own difficult relationship with his father. "As a child," she said, "you couldn't know any of that. All you knew was what was in front of you."

After I circled around various memories, she asked, "What crime did you commit?" I was taken aback. Whatever my misdeeds, they never rose to the level of criminal. It took a while before I put what she said in the context of my religious upbringing and substituted sin for crime.

Instead of following the biblical commandment to honor my father, I'd been possessed by silent resentment and rage, and the guilt that followed. It was only after I allowed myself to feel and articulate the full measure of those emotions that I could confront the lode of sadness and regret that I'd done my best to leave unearthed.

Except for the occasional twinge, I was never again bothered by back pain. I joined Kathy in the ordinary and extraordinary work of raising Genevieve and Daniel. In the beginning, I acted from sheer determination to avoid my father's mistakes.

I knew I'd make mistakes of my own. I wouldn't repeat his. I quickly discovered that along with the tribulations and frustrations, fatherhood brought intense joy and satisfaction in the love openly given and freely reciprocated. I understood that in the gulf between my father and me, his loss was greater than mine.

I've passed the age he was when he died. I find myself often reflecting on my memories of him. I remember the sighs drawn from a place burrowed within, as though he were exhausted from wrestling with ghosts he left unnamed.

I recall how as a small boy I walked beside him on a pitch-black summer's night. Gripped by the fear of showing fear, a double fear, another disappointment, a wordless whimpering at the dark and its imaginary terrors, I bit my lip until it bled.

Once, on a rare excursion, he took my brother and me fishing. Far from land, bathed in sea-sparkled air, he sang lightheartedly, as if delighted with our company. Sometimes I ache with all that went unsaid.

When he died, fellow judge Tom Hughes offered a moving and eloquent tribute. In part he said, "Possessed of a clear, incisive mind and a scholar's bent, the Honorable Peter Anthony Quinn, Justice of the Supreme Court, Appellate Division, kept a tray on his desk inscribed with this quote from Socrates: 'Four things belong to a judge: to hear courteously, to answer wisely, to consider soberly, and to decide impartially.' Judge Quinn honored those words every day of the 25 years he presided from the bench."

Years later, my brother was bartending at McFeeley's on 23rd Street. Two lawyers were in deep discussion about the judges they argued cases before. He politely interrupted to mention his father had been a judge. When he told them who he was, one said, "He was the most compassionate judge I ever appeared before."

As well as reconcile as best I could to my father's limitations, I came to appreciate his goodness. He gave away so much of his earnings to religious and charitable organizations, he sometimes alarmed my mother. His life savings came to a few thousand dollars.

His intellect and integrity earned him the high regard of colleagues and peers. None of that can change what did or didn't take place between us. It's useless to wish otherwise.

Facing my own mortality, all I can do is reach across time and say that I love him.

Among the many perks of Time Inc. were the corporate retreats. They were nothing like the compulsory stays at secluded, austere retreat houses that were an annual routine at Manhattan Prep. Time Inc. preferred the sybaritic over the ascetic.

These secular retreats were moveable feasts. We went to a luxurious Bermuda resort for a "strategy session" on the future of the company's book business, exclusive Lyford Cay for a conference on expanding Time Inc.'s video business, a posh, waterside hotel in Charleston for a conference on I forget what.

Business was never allowed to get in the way of swimming, tennis, golf, lunch, dinner, and the cocktail hour that stretched well beyond.

As good as things seemed, I was often subject to the lament of "You should have been here when paradise publishing was really paradise." Maybe so, I told myself, but Proust was right: All paradises are lost ones, and lost or not, I was privileged to be part of this one.

Dick Munro conveyed a proposition from the head of the magazine group who thought it'd be a good idea if those who wrote speeches for the publishers and other executives reported to me. I'd manage their schedules, edit their work, and make sure "the company's messaging is consistent." I'd be promoted, given a new title and a commensurate raise.

I told Dick it was a good idea for somebody else. Management was a full-time job, one I had no interest in. In my experience, writers were loners by nature. They didn't take criticism well. They were congenital kvetchers. They weren't good managers. I'd be one of the worst. I wanted to stick with words.

If it was a take-it-or-leave-it deal, I'd show myself out. The matter was dropped. Given the chaos that soon followed, I took special satisfaction in my decision.

As time went on, there was increasing anxiety over the company's indecision and lack of direction. The media world was in flux. Roy Larson, a classmate of Luce's, was among the original Time Incers. When he retired in the 1970s, he was asked what was the biggest change in publishing in his lifetime. "Air conditioning," he responded.

Now air conditioning was about the only thing that wasn't changing. The Digital Age was coming to birth. Half of Time Inc.'s revenue now came from video. HBO was the driver of the company's growth.

The Reagan Revolution, deregulation, and the velocity of technological change were toppling old landmarks and unleashing financial buccaneering unseen in generations. Upstart Capital Cities swallowed much-larger ABC television network. GE took over RCA and its NBC network. Ted Turner made a run at CBS, which fell into the arms of Laurence Tisch's Loew's Corporation, a conglomerate of, among other things, hotels and cigarettes.

Overseas powerhouses like Bertelsmann, SONY, Hachette, and superpredator Rupert the Ripper Murdoch were stalking attractive prey.

It became obvious Time Inc. couldn't stand on its own much longer. Size and synergy were the watchwords. Companies either bought or merged with enterprises with assets and operations that complemented their own, and made them too big to acquire, or found themselves on the auction block.

Munro made clear that he wouldn't stay past sixty. He was a man of his word. The campaign to be his successor went into full swing. It came down to his two protégés, Jerry Levin and Nick Nicholas. Their rivalry was set in motion when the video group ran into trouble and Nicholas, Time Inc. COO, was sent to replace Jerry.

Nicholas was practical and operational, the nuts-and-bolts numbers guy. The more cerebral Levin headed the strategy group. "The trouble was there was no group," Dick Clurman wrote, "and no strategy." Munro named Nicholas as his heir apparent. He was made president and COO and promptly removed Jerry from the board, a slight that was reversed before long, but neither forgiven nor forgotten.

Soon after, the company was absorbed by the contest between two seasoned journalists to be Time Inc.'s new editor-in-chief. The guarantor of journalistic excellence and the wall Luce put between business and journalism—the company's "church-and-state" arrangement—the editor-in-chief served as pope, formidable if not infallible. There were only three in the company's history.

There were hushed conversations on the thirty-fourth floor, never any shouting. That wasn't the Time Inc. way. (Come Warner, there'd be a lot of it.) The winner fired the loser. Though it wasn't obvious at the time, the fight was a last hurrah.

The position of Time Inc. editor-in-chief, once one of the most influential positions in American journalism, would soon be a tarnished trophy stuck in a dusty display case in the back of the gym. The glow around Luce's legacy was the twilight, not the dawn.

I was now Nicholas's speechwriter as well as Dick Munro's. Nicholas, a graduate of Princeton and Harvard Business School, had a reputation as "Nick the Knife" that came from his blade-sharp management style and his purported skill in eliminating rivals. As one Time Incer said to me, "Nick could cut your balls off so expertly, you wouldn't know it until you got them in the mail."

Working one-on-one, I never saw that side of him. He was thoughtful and considerate, high in his expectations and generous in his appreciation. He had a sharp intellect, a clear idea where he wanted to take the company, and the resolve to do it. I think at least part of his fearsome reputation came from envy.

Mine was the only office in the corridor between Nick's and Dick's. It was the summer of 1989. Not a lot of people were around. I knew from the traffic between the two and accidental (mostly) eavesdropping that negotiations were advancing with a potential partner. Which one, I didn't know.

When Don Wilson confided in me that talks were underway with Warner Communications, I doubted they'd come to anything. Time Inc.'s button-down, collegiate way of doing business was antithetical to the high-flying Hollywood swagger and questionable reputation of Warner supreme leader and benevolent despot, Steve Ross.

I was vaguely acquainted with Ross from news accounts of the collapse of Atari, its video game business, which almost brought the company down, and his questionable involvement with the mobbed-up Westchester Dinner Theater.

I was in his presence once, at the Governor's Mansion, at a post–State of the State reception. (He wisely skipped the speech.) Governor Carey and he were Brooklyn boys who made good. He was a generous donor to the governor's re-election. They traveled in the same circles (and at one point dated roommates).

Ross was tall, with carefully coifed silver hair, a wide smile, and teeth that testified to the artistry of American dentistry. His suit and shoes were bespoke. He had a suave Hollywood air. Bob M., the governor's all-powerful secretary who before long would become CEO of Warner Music, guided him around the room to meet the legislators and commissioners it was important he meet.

From his start in the funeral business and parking garages, Ross had gone on to put together a media powerhouse that included Warner Bros. Studio, Warner Home Video, DC Comics, Warner Records, and cable franchises. Though referred to as the founder, Ross was an accumulator. He bought businesses rather than started them.

One morning, I went to see Nick in his office. He looked bedraggled and deflated. I thought it was from walking through the heat of a dog day in August from his Central Park West apartment to the office. He filled me in on the negotiations with Warner. They broke down, he said. It was a missed opportunity that might never come again.

I did my best to hide my glee at what seemed a happy result. When the *Times* reported the story of the clandestine negotiations, most Time Incers were shocked that the company had entertained merging with a shady, wheeling-dealing *arriviste* like Ross.

"He lied on his résumé," one horrified editor said. Résumés were sacrosanct at Time Inc. They told you about a person's social background, professional qualifications, and, most important, schooling.

To a kid from Brooklyn like Ross, who went to a two-year college and graduated from funeral homes and parking lots to high-powered, multi-million-dollar business deals, a résumé was aspirational rather than factual, more a menu than an accurate account of educational and professional achievements. Items could be added or deleted—or embellished—at the chef's direction.

I cared less about who was merging with Time Inc. than that the company I knew was coming to an end. I wanted Time Inc. to stay as it was, an independent publishing company with a truly unique culture and a high regard for its employees, a place where I could spend a career writing for executives interested in speaking on issues of public policy.

Scrubbing the talks with Warner seemed to ensure that, for now at least, Time Inc. would stay what it was. It didn't for long. The talks were back on track. In March 1990, they ended in an agreement that left no doubt who came out on top.

In Time Inc.'s desperation to expand, it elevated Ross into the ranks of the uber-wealthy. He kept his $14 million salary, one of the highest of any executive in the country.

He was far from alone. Executive compensation ballooned across the board.

In the heyday of postwar capitalism, with the memory of the Depression still fresh, the distance between executive salaries and those of managers and other employees was not that great.

The wave of acquisitions and mergers lifted executive compensation to unheard-of heights until, no longer in the same ballpark as that of other employees, it was no longer on the same planet. The trend grew stronger. Between 1980 and 2020 the average CEO pay ballooned by 940 percent; the average worker by 12 percent.

Time Inc. would make good in cash Ross's $125 million in accumulated stock and benefits. He'd be chairman and co-CEO with Nick Nicholas, who'd also serve as president. The CFO, general counsel, and board secretary were all to come from Warner.

After five years Ross would step down as co-CEO (don't hold your breath) but remain chairman for five more. Thanks to the premium Time Inc. was paying to acquire Warner stock, Warner would end up holding 62 percent of the stock in the new company.

It was a "mutually advantageous agreement," one Time Inc. lawyer told me, "in the way the Japanese reached a mutually advantageous agreement with General MacArthur on the deck of the *U.S.S. Missouri*."

Once the deal was announced, Time Inc. put itself "in play," opening the way for other companies to attempt a hostile takeover. Rupert Murdoch,

Coca-Cola, Salomon Brothers as well as Donald Trump (his interest was posturing rather than real) were rumored to be considering a run at the company. None proved true. The necessary government agencies gave their approvals. The deal seemed ready to close.

I was invited to attend a *Fortune* conference in Venice. Kathy hated corporate events and rarely came along. But Venice was a city we'd always wanted to visit. It was too good to turn down.

When I raised it with Dick Munro, he said to go ahead and enjoy ourselves. The phone call from Martin Davis, the notoriously abrasive CEO of Paramount (recently Gulf + Western/a.k.a. Engulf + Devour), came immediately after. He was making a bid to acquire Time Inc. stock at 40 percent above its current price, for a total of $10.7 billion.

Dick called me into his office. Time Inc. would not go gentle into the arms of Paramount. He wanted a reply to Davis that would "fire a rocket up his ass." I followed his instructions. Dick Clurman wrote, "Munro's letter of reply to Davis was right in his face. By comparison, it made George Bush's later ultimatum to Saddam Hussein read like a valentine."

There'd be no trip to Venice. The prospect of a restful, peaceful summer blew away in the hurricane that followed. The thirty-fourth floor went into lockdown. It was immediately clear that whatever contingency plans were in place, there was no plan for this. It felt like naval headquarters the morning after Pearl Harbor.

Time Inc.'s stock shot up. Dick expected Time Inc'ers to be loyal to the company and not cash in. He was wrong. The old Time Inc. was going away, and employee loyalty with it.

The floor flooded with lawyers and bankers. A catering operation was set up in the hallway. Dick took me along as a notetaker to a conference room filled with high-priced legal gunslingers from some of the city's most prestigious firms. There were extended monologues and heated shouting matches.

I tried taking notes but at times the financial talk was so complicated and convoluted I was lost. Dick signaled for us to leave. Outside, he said with exasperation, "I can't stop thinking of all the mega-mansions we're helping build in the Hamptons."

I sat in a windowless room with Lou Slovinsky, vice president for public relations, and Bruce Wasserstein, high-powered investment banker and advisor (for which he was paid $13 million). Wasserstein explained to Lou and me—or attempted to—the deal's complex financial framework. He ate a plate of cookies while he talked. He left behind a lot of crumbs and a lot of confusion.

By the time it was over, Time Inc. would foot nearly $500 million in fees to bankers and lawyers. The houses in the Hamptons would be sumptuous, with well-stocked wine cellars.

Paramount's tender offer torpedoed the planned cashless, debt-free Time-Warner stock swap. In its place, Time Inc. acquired Warner for $14.5 billion in borrowed funding, making the combined companies too expensive to devour.

Warner stockholders got a pot of gold. Time Inc. stockholders were left with the pot—deflated shares and a company in which publishing went from center to periphery. By way of solace, Bruce Wasserstein predicted a high for the company's stock of $400 per share. In the three decades of Time Warner's existence, it never came close.

Paramount's run at Time Inc. hit a wall in the Delaware Chancery Court where, for legal reasons, many companies are incorporated.

The court pushed aside Time Inc.'s decision to avoid a shareholder vote on the Paramount bid by buying Warner. It held that, given Time Inc.'s unique journalistic culture, "to protect that 'culture' [was] the first, and central requirement." The merger could go forward.

(Quipped one critic of the merger, "Journalistic independence allows the editors of the *Sports Illustrated* swimsuit issue to decide for themselves exactly how skimpy the bikinis will be.")

Champagne was popped on the thirty-fourth floor. Among shareholders, including some Time Inc. retirees and employees with accumulated stock, the reaction was consternation.

Synergy was *le mot de jour*. As it turned out, apathy and hostility proved closer to reality. The joining of the cable companies, which was the original premise of merger discussions, was a strategic plus. Except for a few executive passes to the Oscars, the studio had nothing to give the magazine division, and vice versa.

The merger of the book divisions was a rounding error in terms of the larger company. The music division was careful to guard its prerogatives and stick to the strum of its own guitar.

Although it was touted as a marriage made in Hollywood heaven, Warner Bros. and HBO never made it to the altar. The outsized egos in charge weren't about to go out of their way to add to the profit and glory of the other. If HBO wanted to feature Warner movies, it was going to pay full price. Warner had a better chance of lunch at Spago with sasquatch than landing a special deal with HBO. The stilettos came out and stayed out.

░░░

My initial dealing with Steve Ross involved writing the letter to shareholders from Dick and him. Dick signed off right away. I had to wait several days for Steve's reaction. Printed in oversized letters across the top was, "WHERE'S STEVE'S TRADEMARK PIZZAZZ? WHERE'S THE OOMPH?"

Pizzazz and *oomph* were not words that I was accustomed to seeing in Time Inc. corporate documents. I showed the page to Dick. He laughed. He told me to toss in some adjectives and superlatives, which I did. It came back loaded with a new supply of superlatives that Dick immediately struck out. It went on like this for a day or two.

Dick was no longer laughing. He called Steve and told him that the letter was done and, no matter how lacking in oomph, pizzazz, and superlatives, was going to the printer.

The headquarters of the new Time Warner was in the Warner building at 75 Rock, across the avenue and around the corner from Time & Life. Since I'd be writing speeches and editing corporate material, I was among the first to take the leap. My colleagues regarded me like a lamb about to be turned into lamb chops.

I was quickly made to feel at home. The vibe was more Brooklyn than Brooks Brothers, a blend of New York Jewish bluntness and withering wit that I remembered from the Bronx. It wasn't a sin to raise your voice. People went out of their way to help me get settled. One of the first people I met was Joan N., head of investor relations.

She was funny and earthy. She guided me through the company's financials. Anything involving a number over 10, I ran past her. She patiently explained accounting arcana like the difference between EBITA and EBIDA (don't ask), even when it was for the fourth or fifth time.

Steve loathed firing people. It was said one way to get rich was to be terminated by him. He provided a severance package that soothed his conscience and made you rich. Some executives lost their jobs but were allowed to stick around. One former division head, let go several years before, left his office once a day for lunch in the executive dining room.

It was sometimes unclear what certain people did. The lines of reporting often seemed fuzzy. Some people seemed to have the same job. Everything revolved around Steve. He was the Sun King, the source of power and light, Warner his Versailles.

Each day when he arrived, his bodyguard scouted the lobby and secured an elevator. He went up to the barber directly above the executive floor to make sure his silver combover was convincing.

The executive suite was more apartment than office. Steve's quarters were tastefully opulent. The halls were decorated with original Impressionist paintings. There were several meeting rooms and, if I remember correctly, a full kitchen. Secretaries abounded.

The first conference I attended Steve greeted everyone warmly, as if we were all old friends, a skill, I supposed, dating to his days in the funeral business. He assumed his place at the head of the table. I sat several coffin lengths away.

He discussed the history of Time's and Warner's cable businesses. Warner ran QUBE, an experimental interactive system in Columbus, Ohio. The technology was clumsy and not transferable to other systems. But interactivity was the shape of things to come. He went on about the potential benefits.

A pessimistic syllable never passed his lips. The superlatives were superlative, the fantastics fantastic. I looked around. I was the only one taking notes.

It was an impressive presentation that I'd hear word-for-word several times over the next few months. The same was true of other presentations. Steve had the ability to store mental tape recordings in his head. When called on, he pressed the start button and the tape began to run. I understood why I was the only one taking notes.

Steve was always the gentleman but, when it came to speeches or shareholder letters, an incurable fussbudget. I never saw him pick up a pen and write himself. He sketched out deals, scratched down numbers, and drew connecting lines. He picked over everything put in front of him. One minute, the phrasing was right, the next "a disaster." It could go on for hours.

Once a group of us labored with him far into the night trying to get a press release just right. When we stepped out of the room there was a duffel bag for each of us stuffed with expensive Warner Bros. paraphernalia. Steve was always making gestures like that, small and grand, to actors, musicians, directors, people he wanted to cultivate, those he wanted to thank, those he wanted to like him.

Underneath the veneer of good feelings was a thick layer of corporate intrigue. Nick and Steve were predestined to having a falling out. The idea of co-CEOs was a near-certain guarantee of fratricide. Nature abhors a vacuum. Power abhors division. For someone like Steve, accustomed to divine right, the notion of sharing the glory or taking direction from anyone but himself was abhorrent.

Steve was cavalier about the company's enormous debt. He floated a rights offering that touted "strategic partnerships" with international media companies. The annual report was published in six languages—English, German, French, Italian, Japanese, Spanish—a nightmare that required endless calls and meetings clarifying meanings and English idioms.

He pushed ahead with acquisitions, convinced that the trick was to grow, not cut, your way out of debt. Nick believed a balance sheet should be filled with numbers, not superlatives. He looked for places to pare and consolidate. He did the unthinkable and proposed selling parts of businesses.

Nick thought hype could carry you only so far. Steve believed it could carry you far enough until you figured out something else or fate intervened.

The magazine division suffered special problems. Corporate headquarters deserted the Time & Life building for the Warner building at 75 Rock. Time Inc. was no longer the heart of the company but one division among several.

Symbolically, Time was the first word in the company's title. Realistically, Time Inc. was the least dynamic of all the company's businesses. The editor-in-chief was no longer an ex-officio member of the board. The oomph belonged to the video side. The rank and file felt the demotion.

Outside and inside the company, there were rumors about the likelihood of Steve Ross's tossing aside the notion of church and state and pressuring magazines like *Time, People,* and the newly launched *Entertainment Weekly* to skew its reviews in favor of Warner Bros. films.

There was no truth to it. The Studio's management was too sophisticated to do something so dumb. Reviews in Time Inc. magazines weren't going to ruin or redeem any film and, most important, unless he was on the cover, Steve wasn't much interested in magazines.

To calm any fears, he agreed to speak at an event held by the American Magazine Association. Steve was laid up with a "bad back." I was sent with Dick Stolley and Marilyn H. to his apartment to brief him on what was expected and collect his own ideas.

A star in American journalism, Dick was a longtime writer and editor for *Life.* He pulled off the coup of snagging the Zapruder film, the stunning, live-action recording of JFK's assassination. *Life* reprinted the most dramatic frames. Dick went on to become the founding editor of *People*, the industry's number-one moneymaker.

Marilyn, who came to Warner from *60 Minutes*, was savvy and smart. She had a core of iron. Her corporate career was hindered by her blunt insistence on telling the truth no matter who was in the room.

We took the elevator to Steve's apartment. It opened into an elegant foyer. A maid took our coats. She said Mr. Ross wasn't ready for us yet and showed us into the library. On the fireplace mantle was the Best Picture Oscar for Warner Bros.' *The Jazz Singer*, the world's first talkie. We declined the offer of drinks.

After a short wait, we were shown up a wide staircase to Steve's bedroom. He was sitting up in an emperor-sized bed. His sky-blue pajamas were covered in a blue-silk robe, his initials monogramed on the pocket, a white handkerchief flowing out of it.

Carmen F., his trusted longtime assistant, sat on the edge of the bed, a phone beside her. At the bottom of the bed, three chairs were arranged in a row. Without having to be told, we took our places.

Dick told Steve how pleased the editors at Time Inc. were with his decision to address the AMA. The phone rang. Carmen answered. "Yes," she said, "he's expecting your call." Steve apologized for the interruption. He was waiting for this call all day.

The phone conversation went on for a quarter of an hour. When it ended, I got in a few words about the importance of church and state, and the need to reinforce it as an inviolable part of Time Warner's identity. Carmen interrupted with another call that couldn't be missed. A long conversation ensued. Marilyn speculated later it was the only type of call he got.

The meeting broke up. Steve thanked us for coming. We showed ourselves out. As we stood at the elevator, Dick leaned over to me and whispered the last word of the protagonist in Orson Welles's *Citizen Kane*—the key to the dying press baron's innermost longings: "Rosebud." If Steve had a rosebud of his own, he kept it to himself.

Steve delivered his speech to the AMA. He stuck to the text. It was the last time I heard him express any interest in the publishing business.

I kept in touch with the governor. I arranged a lucrative opportunity for him to address the Time Inc. board of directors' dinner. I wrote a speech he delivered at a luncheon hosted by *Time* magazine and ghosted an article for *Life*. We spoke on the phone occasionally. But I kept my distance. I knew there was no half-in, half-out.

Rumors he was ready to enter the 1992 presidential race grew stronger. There was talk that he was putting together a campaign staff. The governor called. We had what felt like an aimless conversation. Before he hung up, he asked if I was still happy at my job. "Very," I said.

He referenced the time we worked together. He believed "our words" made a difference. Would I consider doing it again? He didn't say when or why or under what circumstances. He didn't have to. I swallowed my uncertainty. "Yes," I said.

My ego was big enough to grab the chance to be the president's speechwriter. It was a way to dot the *i* in my family's quasi-religious identification as Democrats. Then there was the reality of the gerbil wheel, the life I was so desperate to leave behind. Relentless deadlines. Endless revisions. Countless hours.

I talked over joining the campaign with Kathy. We had two small children. I'd take a big pay cut. She told me she'd support whatever decision I made. I discussed it with Dick Munro, who stepped down as CEO but was still on the board. He remained a close friend. He said the governor might wash out in the primaries. He was sure Time Inc. would welcome me back no matter.

The day set for the announcement that Cuomo was entering the New Hampshire primary, I spoke to Brad Johnson, head of the state's Washington office. It was all set. A chartered plane was on the tarmac at Albany airport to take the governor to Concord, where he'd formally enter the Democratic primary. I informed my colleagues of my intent. They were thrilled for me.

That afternoon, the governor announced he wasn't running. I went numb. I couldn't get up from my desk. My colleagues came by. They didn't laugh in my face. They were decent enough to wait until they got back to their offices.

Dick Munro was consoling. "There are a lot worse things in life," he said. He knew what he was talking about. As a young Marine, he was awarded three Purple Hearts in Korea. I refrained from telling him I felt as if a hand grenade had gone off in my face.

Every morning I got up at 5:30 to work on my novel. The next day, I called the governor just after six. I knew he had probably been awake for an hour and a half. I was angry and upset. My life had been turned upside down for no reason. I looked like an idiot in front of my co-workers. I blurted, "Governor, pardon me, but what the fuck was that all about?"

He took no offense. "I had no choice," he said. "I couldn't leave Ralph Marino with the state budget."

Marino was the colorless, odorless Republican majority leader of the state Senate. The odds this was the real reason is a number below zero. It was the only one I got.

Over the years, I was approached by those who imagined I had inside information that I didn't about why Cuomo didn't run. Some had theories of their own. Cuomo knew he couldn't win. He hated fundraising.

Rumor-mongers abounded. Several shared a theory vociferously advanced by a charmless, inveterate know-it-all who claimed a relationship with the Cuomos she didn't have. It involved whispered ties between an in-law and the Mafia.

Gennifer Flowers, Bill Clinton's secret squeeze, recorded a conversation in which she remarked that she'd be surprised if Cuomo didn't have "some Mafioso major connections." Replied Bill, a man of impeachable habits, "Well, he acts like one."

Whatever his faults as a politician, in his personal life Mario Cuomo was a man of unimpeachable moral integrity. The imputations were a raw wound. They were made behind his back and to his face. When it comes to the mob, innuendo is an Italian name.

I never shared with the governor my suspicions about my father. At one point, he was pushed to run for statewide office by Walter Lynch, chairman of the New York State Democratic Committee. A friend and fellow Fordham Law School graduate, and former candidate for governor, Lynch thought my father's career as engineer, lawyer, assemblyman, congressman, and judge made him an ideal candidate.

My father dismissed the idea. He loved being a judge. Declaiming from atop a bench was as close as he could get to fulfilling the aspirations to the stage that his father leaned on him to abandon. I can't help thinking he suspected, the higher he went, the meaner the election, some opponent would dredge up brother-in-law Bill Brady's murder and the mob connection.

It was guilt by egregious association, which doesn't mean it's not an effective political tactic. My father was fierce enough an advocate to bat it away. But there was no way he'd risk reopening wounds as hurtful as those Bill Brady's murder inflicted on my mother's family. He stayed where he was, in the same Parkchester apartment, contentedly, until he died.

Was the fear of having his family smeared in a national political campaign sufficient to cow Cuomo from running for president? If it was, the shame is the country's, not his.

The doomed duopoly of Steve and Nick slouched toward its inevitable denouement. After the reconfiguring of the executive floor, their offices were only a few yards apart. I was writing a memo that would come from them both. I showed it to Steve, then Nick. He asked me what Steve was thinking. I realized they were no longer talking.

Nick called several of us to his office. He closed the door. Steve's bad back had turned out to be a recurrence of prostate cancer. He was terminal. It was only a matter of time.

Steve died the week before Christmas. I wrote an appropriately heartfelt statement from Nick, who took no obvious satisfaction in Steve's death. But the company he worked so hard to bring together was now his. He couldn't pretend not to be pleased.

Most Time Incers were relieved. Despite all Steve's protestations, they couldn't be sure whether or not his irrepressible deal-making instincts would lead to a spin-off or sale. Nick was a known quantity and a surer bet. He began making plans. He intended big changes.

On the Thursday before the Presidents Day weekend, I flew with Nick on the company plane to the Corcoran Gallery, in D.C., for the launch party of *Songs of My People*, a record of African-American life through the eyes of fifty prominent Black photographers. Time's subsidiary Little, Brown, was the publisher. The company picked up the tab for the festivities.

On the return flight, Nick told me he was leaving for Vail the next day. He said that as soon as he got back he wanted to sit down with me. He was counting on me to help, he said, "to articulate my vision for the company." That Saturday, he got a call from New York. There'd be no articulating or envisioning. The board had fired him.

I met him on his return, but not to talk about what was ahead for Time Warner. Abandoned by board members he considered friends, he was given no chance to speak for himself. His face was red and puffy, as if he'd been punched. He railed against Jerry, the lead conspirator behind the board coup, with a barrage of scatological superlatives. Up to the end, he said, Jerry had talked as if they were partners.

Nick's secretary was already packing up his files. The movers were setting up. Corporate politics was beginning to resemble Albany's.

Jerry's drive-by takeout of Nick took everyone by surprise. Steve loyalists were thrilled. They regarded Nick as a bean counter, not a builder, incapable of dreaming Steve's big dreams or conjuring the deals he did to take Warner from bottom of the pile to top of the heap.

Time Incers were shaken by the coup but reassured that Jerry, a well-known, much-respected company executive, was his successor.

Jerry had a deceptively mild-mannered demeanor. He dressed neatly, with an accountant's lack of flair. He never wore carefully tailored suits or two-tone, French-cuff shirts. He was intellectual and introspective. Alone among company executives he sported facial hair, a neatly trimmed mustache. His skill as a ruthless political infighter came as news.

That skill was soon on display again when he got rid of the co-conspirators on the board who'd helped bring down Nick. How could the emperor trust someone who had already conspired to depose an emperor? It was a lesson as old as imperial Rome.

As time went on, it became apparent that the most dangerous situation for any executive was to be perceived as Jerry's successor. Those who imagined themselves immune were soon disabused.

Bronx-born Fred W., the head lawyer for Warner Music, was endowed with a brilliant mind—he graduated from Bronx High School of Science at sixteen—and graced with a generosity of spirit that led to his being known as "Brother Teresa."

It was agreed he was the funniest person in the company. He tagged Jerry with a nickname that stuck: Caligula.

Jerry exulted in his new role. Without saying so, he left no doubt that he credited his rise to the top to destiny, not treachery. He sometimes spoke as if he'd been anointed by Henry Luce.

Immediately after the coup, he went to the Grammy Awards. Newly hatched admirers, who knew all along he was the only one with the brains and balls to carry on Steve Ross's legacy, flocked around. Jerry wasn't taken in by their praise, which doesn't mean he wasn't pleased.

He could appear humble and act that way, but he wouldn't be treated that way. It wasn't hard to get on the wrong side of his ego. I strayed there several times.

I published an op-ed piece in the *Times* under my own name. Jerry didn't say anything to me but remarked to a colleague, "Maybe Peter should think about looking for another job." When my novel was published by Viking Penguin, he skipped the book party that my colleagues at Time Warner hosted for me. He never uttered a word of congratulations or acknowledged the novel.

Irish musician Phil Coulter asked me to put together the script for

"Both Sides Now." A combination of music and narrative, it celebrated the Good Friday Agreement that had been negotiated by Senator George Mitchell and ended the violent conflict in Northern Ireland. It was performed in St. Patrick's Cathedral and read by Frank McCourt, Gregory Peck, and Anjelica Huston.

Two days later, on St. Patrick's Day, "Both Sides Now" was staged at an evening performance on the White House lawn at which President Clinton presented Mitchell with the Presidential Medal of Freedom. Roma Downey and Aidan Quinn narrated.

On a preternaturally warm March afternoon, Clinton came out in a Banlon shirt and mingled with the musicians and performers. It was barely a month since his impeachment trial in the Senate. He appeared to be relaxed and enjoying himself. Hillary was nowhere in sight.

The next morning, I went to Jerry's office eager to share the details. I knew he was an enthusiastic Clinton supporter. I barely got started when he interrupted. "This needs work," he said, handing me the draft of a speech I'd sent him.

I was featured as a talking head in Ric Burns's film *New York: A Documentary Film*. I was standing next to Jerry at the opening of the short-lived Warner Bros. Fifth Avenue store. A friend came over and said how much he enjoyed the series. He asked Jerry if he'd watched it. Jerry shrugged. "Parts," he said as he walked away.

Jerry didn't always need the spotlight. He was capable of shunning it, as long as everyone was clear that it was where he belonged, and nobody try to step in while he was outside.

Whatever honeymoon Jerry enjoyed after taking over as CEO was short-lived. He toured the different divisions, shook hands, offered encouraging words. At a meeting of the film division, he brought up the notion of *agape*, truly selfless love. He wrote about it in his college thesis. He saw it as a bridge between Christian and Jewish moral teaching.

The essence of Time Warner, he said, had to be in the willingness to work together, to act with a degree of selflessness and look out for one another. There was more to success than individual ambition. I thought he might have just gotten off the phone with Mario Cuomo.

There were as many people in the room interested in *agape* as there were mourners at Jeffrey Epstein's funeral. He had to know it was the wrong message. Sometimes what he said sounded directed at himself. He switched tracks and went on to speak about the Studio's financials. He was a master of fiscal and operational details. He regained the audience.

The high purpose he spelled out for the company was soon put to the test. Warner Music Group brought out a CD by rapper Ice-T entitled "Cop Killer." The jacket was a body bag. The Rodney King riots that tore L.A. apart were still fresh in people's memories.

Police unions were up in arms. Editorialists and columnists swarmed in. Advertisers threatened to go elsewhere. Politicians did what politicians do. Executives within the company were indignant. They regarded the record business as run by bomb-throwing, drug-abusing, sex-crazed leftovers from the '60s (they were wrong about the bomb throwing) who didn't care what harm they inflicted.

Rap was already in the crosshairs. Conservatives as well as women's groups were in a fever over its crude, sexist, misogynistic lyrics. Tipper Gore, the vice president's wife, was leading a crusade to force the use of labels that would warn against offensive content.

The pressure mounted. Jerry called a meeting in his office of lawyers, music executives, and public relations people. Tod H., a veteran of the White House and vice president for communications, warned that doing nothing wasn't an option. Withdraw the CD or stand by it. The alternative was death by a thousand cuts.

Bob M., formerly Governor Carey's secretary and now head of the Music Division, made clear that if the CD were withdrawn, he'd face a mass mutiny of recording artists who wouldn't abide censorship of any kind.

Peter H., Time Warner's head lawyer, said if the company gave in it was inviting an endless campaign by pressure groups left and right against movies, books, and articles they found offensive or politically incorrect.

The consensus was that Time Warner wouldn't call back the CD. We needed to explain that the issue was larger than any one division but involved the First Amendment's guarantee of freedom of expression. The place to begin, Jerry said, was inside the company, in a memo to employees that explained why the company was putting itself in this position and why they had a stake in it.

Once everyone else left the room, I was left alone with Jerry. His last words were that the memo had to go out first thing the next morning. I returned to my office. It was around 2:00 P.M.

I wrote and rewrote until 3:00 A.M. I started with the premise that the

First Amendment argument was inadequate. The company's right to produce "Cop Killer" wasn't in question.

The issue was why the company used that right to produce music that was patently offensive and a potential incitement to violence against the police. Was it the case, as some accused, of a witless desire to exploit racial tensions in pursuit of substantial profit?

Rap was born in a Bronx housing project. Hate it or love it, it arose as an authentic voice of a generation of ghetto dwellers that eventually won over white contemporaries and graduated into a musical genre with global reach. Neither a fan nor part of the intended audience, I recognized what it came out of.

Throughout American history, the energy of popular culture emanated from the margins, from African Americans, immigrants, sexual outcasts. The vibrant musical tradition of working-class protest, anti-war movements, and social discontent went back to the earliest days of the Republic. The respectable classes rarely liked what they heard.

The margins in this case were the ghettos spread across the country, from South Central L.A. to the South Bronx. Rap was a consequence of social disaffection, not an incitement. It pulsed with pent-up rage at centuries-old policies of discrimination and deprivation.

Bitter and disturbing, music like Ice-T's "Cop Killer" voiced the explosive, unresolved resentment that periodically erupted in American cities.

Stifling it would have no effect on Time Warner's bottom line. It would allow the industry to avoid controversy. It would also reinforce the country's obliviousness to a message it needed to hear and encourage the simmering anger to find other outlets.

I had a draft ready in the morning. There was pushback against going beyond the First Amendment. The majority thought the message was right. After more tinkering, the memo went out. There was an enthusiastically positive response. The decision was made to submit an edited version to the *Wall Street Journal*, which published it the next day.

I made a feeble protest that bringing in the *Journal* would feed the controversy and remove any chance it would burn itself out on its own. I was overruled. The *Journal* made edits of its own. The furor grew. Opposing op-eds spread. Letters poured in. Immediately ahead was the annual meeting scheduled in L.A., in the ballroom of the Beverly Wilshire.

I loved staying at the Wilshire, with its spa and stately bar room, amenities, and meals on the company dime. Not this time. This time felt more like an execution than a luxury excursion.

The ballroom was SRO. A picket line of protesters was outside. Jerry offered a perfunctory report on the company's performance and prospects for the year ahead, then made a defense of the decision not to withdraw "Cop Killer." There was a weak smattering of applause. He invited questions.

Screeds rather than inquiries followed. The few defenders were overwhelmed by an angry parade of police departments, some far from L.A., that came to the mike. Charlton Heston descended from the heights of the Hollywood Hills to denounce Time Warner with outrage worthy of Moses's takedown of the Golden Calf–worshipping Israelites.

It went on for five hours. Ice-T didn't help matters by driving by in a Bentley and flipping the bird at the protesters.

All the nightly news shows reported the meeting. The next day's papers were filled with it. Advertisers kept up the pressure. Police groups threatened a boycott.

Two weeks later, Bob M. had his Appomattox moment, waved the white flag, and announced that the CD was being withdrawn. There was no mutiny. Ice-T went on to star, *mirabile dictu*, as an undercover cop in a TV crime show.

Before long, rap went from cutting edge to mainstream. A reckoning with issues of racial inequality and law-enforcement accountability was postponed rather than confronted. The culture wars decamped to other battlefields.

Through the *Sturm und Drang* of the merger and assorted controversies, I never stopped working on my novel. We were living in Park Slope. I got up weekdays at 5:30. I took the D train to work, which stopped in Rockefeller Center, right beneath the Time & Life Building.

In the beginning, I left my door open. I learned the hard way that other early arrivals took it as an invitation to wander in and kibitz about matters I had no interest in.

I locked the door. In the winter, I turned on a single desk light. Every minute of the next two hours was precious to me. Some mornings, I barely churned out a single paragraph; some, I produced a page or two that I re-read the next morning and tossed out or felt satisfied with; some, I gave up on after a sentence or two and spent the time reading.

There was no Internet to do research on, but Time Inc. had perhaps the country's best corporate library. The librarians could get practically any book you wanted on inter-library loan. If they wondered why the CEO's speechwriter needed a book on nineteenth-century plumbing, they never asked.

If I hit a dead end, I backtracked and tried another route. I spent a month pursuing two characters through a love affair only to realize I had to know what it told me about the characters. What the reader needed to know I summed up in a few sentences.

The story unfolded as I wrote. Characters, real and fictional, came in different ways. Some were born out of my imagination. Others were historical characters. I found out that Stephen Foster, the author of classics like "Camptown Races," "Jeanie with the Light Brown Hair," and "Hard Times Come Again No More," was living on the Bowery at the time.

His early music, like the audience it appealed to, was unabashedly racist. He stopped using the N-word early on. Songs like "My Dark Virginny Bride" didn't mock the slave but found the pathos in the love of one slave for another and treated it as tragedy, not comedy.

He enjoyed spectacular success. The largest sale of his sheet music before "O! Susanna" was around 5,000. His "Susanna" sold 100,000. The telegraph—the world's first Internet—carried it coast to coast.

He lost it all, drank too much, was trusting and easily swindled. He became the music industry's first has-been. He lived out his last days in a hotel on the Bowery. He died poor and alone in an attic room, his throat cut by an accidental fall or his own hand.

I rarely visited sites I included in my story. In many cases they had long since disappeared. The city I inhabited was the imaginary one in my head. I knew it from old maps, drawings, and photographs. It was often more real than the city in which I lived and worked.

The building where Foster died was still there. I presume it's there today, although in New York, you never know. I stood in front. Every novelist, I think, has his or her psychotic moments, listening to voices of the long dead and the never-were, phantoms as close as the flesh-and-blood beings around us.

I didn't hear Foster's voice. But in that moment I thought I came to know him. There was something special in Foster, an underlying melancholy. I thought he had a secret. I thought I knew what it was.

The time I spent in a world of my own making, as frustrating as it could be, belonged to me alone. I felt freed to sacrifice the rest of the day on the altar of Time Warner. The speeches and texts I wrote could be criticized, revised, rejected. What couldn't be touched was the manuscript in my desk drawer. My employers were welcome to the rest.

My plan was to not stop until the conclusion. Two-thirds through, I saw what the first third lacked or needed. I went back and rewrote it. The last third flowed naturally.

After six years of wandering and researching, and three-and-a-half of writing, I finished. At times, I told myself that would be enough. Even if it were never published, I had the satisfaction of telling the story I wanted to tell. I knew I was lying to myself. What mattered was that it be published, that the characters not be stillborn, that they come alive in readers' heads.

The finished manuscript was 800 pages. I approached a writer friend and asked if he'd read it. He said he wouldn't until I cut 200 pages. No matter how much I resented his cavalier suggestion, I went ahead and tried. He proved right. The paring was easier than I anticipated. The story grew stronger. Subtractions added to the clarity of the plot.

He read the revision. He found himself drawn in. He told me the manuscript was "eminently publishable." What I needed was the right agent. His wasn't taking on new clients.

Traditionally, without an agent a writer has as much chance of being published as being struck by lightning at the bottom of a coal mine. That might have changed with the Internet and the growing popularity of self-publishing, but that's a world I know nothing about.

I turned to Tom Flanagan, the award-winning novelist whom I'd been lucky to get to know. We were on the board together of the American Irish Historical Society. I mentioned that I'd finished the novel I'd discussed with him several years before. Without my asking, he volunteered to read it.

He read it quickly and wrote an endorsement beyond what I expected or even hoped. He told me to send it to his agent, Robin Straus, who became mine too and a quarter-century later still is. A faithful, forceful advocate for her authors, she banged on a lot of doors. Three opened. We chose Viking Penguin.

My editor was Al Silverman. We crossed paths briefly when he was CEO of Book of the Month Club, a Time Inc. subsidiary. I knew his reputation as sage, thoughtful, astute, and kind. A writer himself, he proceeded as if, no matter how outwardly blustery and self-confident, most writers' egos were as fragile as porcelain teacups.

My single greatest experience as a writer was having Al as editor of my first book. We read the manuscript together. He made it clear the changes he suggested were mine to accept or reject. "You're the one who'll answer to critics and readers," he said.

When we were done, I felt fulfilled with the result. "A novel," wrote Randall Jarrell, "is a prose narrative of some length that has something wrong with it." I knew the faults and imperfections would be brought home by critics. I'd be the one to answer to readers. I'd done my best.

I kept wandering into bookstores in anticipation of my book's being deployed on the shelves. One day, in the spring of 1993, I found on prominent display *More Than Words: The Collected Speeches of Mario Cuomo*. I stood in amazement. I had no idea it was coming.

I browsed through it. I recognized speeches he didn't write or had substantial help with. Besides the brief mention of Bill Hanlon and me in relation to the Notre Dame speech, there was no mention of Tom and others who wrote and drafted speeches, important speeches. It was all pad and pen, all the time.

The words belonged to him in the sense that he delivered them, which made a difference in the way that Hamlet played by Sylvester Stallone or Laurence Olivier would evoke divergent responses. This struck me as a step beyond the illusion of performance. It wasn't acted on a stage. It was printed in a book. It felt like Breslin redux, this time a rubout instead of a mugging.

My initial anger sobered into acceptance. My therapist pointed out that my relationship with Cuomo was a shadow of that with my father. Both self-made men, they worked themselves up from working-class beginnings to success as public speakers, lawyers, politicians. They both had the same picture of Thomas More on their office walls. Their approval was out of reach.

After I left, Cuomo was quoted in the *Times* as saying that "the only writer to approach being 'my Ted Sorenson' is Peter Quinn." Now I was free of being taken as a simulacrum of someone else. My book was mine. Every word. I'd rise or fall on that.

The public relations department at Viking asked if the governor would host a book reception in Albany. I told her I was sure he would. I took it back. I wanted no mention of my speechwriting in the short bio on the cover flap. There'd be no book-tour stop in the capital. Shortly after, when Cuomo lost his bid for a fourth term, it became a moot point.

It would be twenty years before I talked to the governor again.

###

I sent my mother a galley of the novel. I didn't hear back. I suspected what was up. For some Irish Americans, "lace curtain" had the derogatory connation of middle-class wannabes lusting after respectability. My mother saw nothing wrong in respectability, or in striving for it.

Catherine Riordan, her mother, got her first pair of shoes when she made her First Communion at age seven. She emigrated in 1888, at age sixteen, but claimed to be eighteen so she could join her sister as a maid in New York—an occupation so filled with Irish girls that (white) domestics were labeled with the generic name "Bridget." They sent half of what they made back to Ireland as passage money for their siblings.

The arrival of masses of Jewish and Italian immigrants made the Irish less threatening than they once were. But the prejudice hadn't gone away. Soon after Catherine landed, the Rev. Charles Parkhurst, the city's foremost crusader for moral reform, thundered a widely shared view when he declared that if the country "rid itself of rum and the Irish, it could close three-quarters of its poorhouses and tear down half its prisons."

Catherine Riordan served wealthy New Yorkers for a decade until an unspecified "incident"—perhaps sexual—caused her to quit. She married my grandfather James Murphy, a native Irish speaker from Macroom in County Cork. They had six children. My mother, born in 1907, was the youngest.

They lived on the top floor of a tenement on 149th Street in the Bronx, where my mother was born, until a co-worker of my grandfather got divorced, which was unusual at the time, and sold him his house in Edgewater, New Jersey, at a steep discount. It was a short commute by ferry and trolley to my grandfather's job in Manhattan.

When they moved in, the house was surrounded by fields. The bucolic setting gradually gave way to industrialization. A barrel factory opened across the street. The interior of the house reflected the style of living my grandmother had learned in the homes of the well-to-do.

The tasteful furniture was purchased piece by piece. The Oriental rugs were second-hand but showed no sign of wear. The immaculate lace curtains, delicate enough to let in the sunlight but opaque enough to blur the changes outside, were pronouncements of respectability.

My mother, the youngest of the six, fulfilled her parents' immigrant aspirations. Unlike her mother, whose short, stocky frame reflected her impoverished childhood and years of physical labor, my mother was tall and thin, attractive enough to consider a career as a model. She was a college graduate, a modern American girl, genteel, lovely, respectable in every way.

She was in her eighties when *Banished Children of Eve* was published. When her reaction finally came, it was hostile. "It's a terrible disappointment," she said, "to reach my age and realize you've a son with a pornographic imagination."

She was hurt and horrified by the disreputable Irish I resurrected, thugs, thieves, drunks, prostitutes. "We never knew people like this," she said. "What will my friends think?"

I didn't argue. I didn't point out only three friends were still alive, and one was her sister. I knew where she was coming from and respected her sensitivity. I let it go. In a short time, so did she.

I burned to one day walk into a bookstore and see something with my name—my name alone—on it. The day it happened I went to Scribner's, on Fifth Avenue, to see if my novel was available. I was on my lunch hour. The book was on a shelf by the door.

I was afraid if I moved, it would disappear and I'd wake up back at my desk laboring on the State of the State or the annual letter to shareholders. I stood a long time waiting for somebody to buy it. Nobody did.

Another time in another store, a woman was in front of me on the checkout line. She was holding my book. I was so delighted I tapped her shoulder. "That's my book," I said. "I'm sorry," she replied apologetically. "I didn't know this was yours." She raced to put it back on the shelf.

I shared with a friend my thrill at seeing my novel in bookstores. "That's nice," she said, "but isn't the object to get it out of the stores?"

It's said that the happiest time in a writer's life is the night before her first book is published. It wasn't quite that for me. The Irish part of me was attuned to what the wizened patron of a pub in Galway once advised: "Always expect the worst. You'll rarely be disappointed."

When *Banished Children* was published in March 1994, I was expectant but anxious, a little like before the birth of my kids. It was out of my hands now. I'd done all I could. I felt all my ducks were in a row.

The first quacks from the critics were all I hoped for and more. One or two were unfavorable. The worst approached evisceration. The problem was with the timing, not the critics. My book debuted at the same time as Tom Flanagan's latest historical novel, *The End of the Hunt*, E. L. Doctorow's *Waterworks,* and Caleb Carr's blockbuster historical thriller, *The Alienist*, the latter two both set in nineteenth-century New York.

As they took flight, mine struggled to get off the ground. I did a book tour that included Boston, Chicago, Minneapolis, L.A., San Francisco, and Austin. There are writers who say they hate book tours. I rejoiced in the chance to escape my office and read my own stuff in front of an attentive audience. The reactions varied, sometimes wildly.

The book reporter for the *L.A. Times* attended the reading and did a long, highly favorable piece. At a reading in a bookstore in Philadelphia, a man in the audience got up and denounced the book as "making excuses for racist violence," "using deeply offensive racist language," and "expropriating Black history."

I answered as best I could that I wrote a novel, not a historical text. It wasn't possible to write about the Draft Riots and ignore the use of offensive racial and ethnic terms. I tried to lay out the backgrounds of my characters, not expropriate anyone's culture. My answers didn't mollify him. He got up and left.

At the invitation of the late Danny Cassidy, scholar, songwriter, and author of *How the Irish Invented Slang*, I did a reading at the New College in San Francisco. Danny brought along the eminent African-American writer and iconoclast Ishmael Reed. Reed was insistent on his Irish and Cherokee as well as Black roots. Danny and he had an ongoing dialogue about Irish–Black relations.

Not long after, the Before Columbus Foundation, which Reed founded to promote "contemporary American multicultural literature," awarded *Banished Children* a 1994 American Book Award.

I was hosted at a luncheon by an Irish-American veterans' group. Almost to a man, they told me how much they hated the book. One attendee asked, "Why did you leave out the thousands of Irish who served so bravely on the battlefields of the Civil War? You're a true example," he told me, "of a self-hating Irishman."

As a matter of fact, I said, I did include Irish who served in the war and acted to put down the riot. People are free to write their own novels, create their own heroes and villains, and focus on anything they wish. My main interest was in the people who suffer history rather than write it.

Touring with my book was a hugely satisfying experience. I cared less about what people liked or detested than that they read it, took it seriously, and reacted. The alternative—to be ignored—was the worst fate of all.

The day came when the touring stopped. I was always in touch with my office. There were assignments I couldn't avoid, no matter where I was. But now, like in a bad dream, I was stuck in scheduling meetings, analyst briefings, department pow-wows, strategy sessions, the gamut of corporate gatherings, including the aptly named "brain dumps."

In the buildup to publication, I conceived my OAF plan—Out at Fifty. I calculated that the success of the book, the advance it would bring for the next book plus the stock I'd accumulated, and my 401(k) would liberate me to be a full-time novelist. With that scenario scrapped, I came up with a new plan, SAS—Sayonara at Sixty. It seemed a long way off.

On occasion, executives and division heads asked Jerry if they could "borrow" me to work on a speech. I toyed with pointing out that the 13th Amendment effectively banned borrowing or lending people. I was too well paid to invoke its protections.

The newest CEO of HBO was the son of the former owner of the Concourse Plaza Hotel. Funny, cocky, demanding, and unabashedly ambitious, he turned HBO into a programming juggernaut. I admired him from afar, which is the best way to admire a lot of people.

I was unhappy to learn he wanted to borrow me for a speech he was scheduled to give at the prestigious Edinburgh Television Festival. I was even unhappier at Jerry's instant agreement to lend me.

I met him in his corner office overlooking Bryant Park. He was friendly the way a *maître d'* is to a newly hired waiter. He asked what ideas I had for the speech. Since I didn't, I said I'd know better when he gave me a general idea of what he wanted to say.

"I want to be forward-looking," he said, "winners verses losers, what the industry will be like in ten years."

I'd attended enough shape-of-things-to-come conferences to be wary of clairvoyancy. At an opulent, day-long conference Goldman Sachs held at the Pierre Hotel, a lineup of industry tarot card dealers and astrologists laid out the road ahead.

As it turned out, the future followed a road less traveled. In a short time, little or nothing of what was said was of any value. On the positive side, the lunch was extravagant, as was the cocktail hour(s) that capped the day.

I found that the trouble with these crystal ball–gazing confabs was they ended up sounding like those near-death experiences in which the newly departed passed through a tunnel of white light into bright-shining bliss.

I wondered why there were no accounts of traveling down a pitch-dark tunnel that ended in a vat of boiling oil.

When I offered a mild version of my caveat, he was dismissive. "If I'm right," he said, "I'll be a genius. If I'm wrong, nobody will remember I gave a speech." I couldn't argue with the logic. Whatever he said, I knew, at day's end a sufficiently bibulous cocktail hour would wrap it in a forgiving mist.

He sketched out his thoughts. They were provocative and perceptive. I took notes as fast as I could. I had a lot of holes to fill in. My reservations about working with him ebbed. He said to FedEx a draft to his place in the Hamptons by the weekend. We'd meet Monday, at 7:00 A.M. I was happy with the job I did. A friend at HBO read it and was complimentary.

I was there at seven. He got in at eight-thirty. He didn't say whether he liked what I'd written. "I didn't have time to read it," he yawned. "Tell me what's in it." I had the top-of-the-rollercoaster sensation just before you pitch into the descent. I started to tell him.

About thirty seconds in, he objected, "That doesn't sound like the direction I want to go." He repeated his objection several times. I knew it was back to the future. He gave me new provocative and perceptive renditions of things to come.

He was leaving at the end of the week. He wanted to see a re-draft ASAP. I thought he might be under the impression I was a fast writer and speechwriting second nature. I'm not. It isn't. Most likely he didn't care.

I had better luck on the second try. His assistant called. He had good news. His boss liked the speech. Better yet, he wanted me to travel with him to Edinburgh. "You'd be like George Stephanopoulos traveling with Bill Clinton," the assistant said.

George Stephanopoulos strikes me as a decent person. Turning into his doppelgänger has never been an ambition of mine. I forget what excuse I used: I was scheduled for a colonoscopy, my son was graduating from nursery school, my passport was expired, maybe all three.

Whatever it was, his assistant didn't question it. He regretted I was missing the opportunity. "I'm sure they'll be others down the road," he said. I swallowed hard and stayed silent.

I heard second-hand that the speech went well. He'd seen the future, and it worked. I guess it didn't work as he foresaw since nobody remembers if he ever gave the speech. He continued what looked like an inexorable rise to the thirty-fourth floor. I began to look for a place to hide.

As he neared the top, he fell victim to a signature Time Warner "Et tu, Brute?" moment. Within a short time, people were trying to remember whether he'd worked at Warner Bros. or HBO.

I think of him whenever I pass the Concourse Plaza. Formerly a welfare hotel, it's now a nursing home. *Sic transit in gloria mundi.*

Neither Kathy nor I ever lived in the suburbs. Except for stints in Kansas City and Yonkers, I never lived outside the city. Even among the crime and chaos of the '70s, there was never a time I didn't think of it as home. When our ancestors had nowhere else to go, my father was fond of pointing out, New York took us in.

In 1986, when our daughter, Genevieve, was born, we moved from a one-bedroom walk-up in Manhattan to a two-bedroom co-op apartment in rapidly gentrifying Park Slope.

Squeezed between inadequate supply and excessive demand, we didn't consider ourselves gentry. To those forced out by rising rents, what was being done to them had been done to the city's natives since the Dutch ruled Nieuw Amsterdam.

Park Slope is an easy place to fall in love with. Bordered by the green expanse of Prospect Park, its streets lined with rows of nineteenth-century brownstones, with a plenitude of stores, bars, and restaurants, the Slope (as it's commonly referred to) is a quintessential urban neighborhood. My commute on the D train was a twenty-five-minute ride directly to the Time & Life Building.

As Genevieve and Daniel grew older, the need for a third bedroom became pressing. We thought about buying a house in Park Slope. The soaring rise in real estate prices meant taking out a mortgage approaching the size of the national debt.

My brother, Tom, and his wife, Debbie, had moved from the Bronx to Hastings-on-Hudson. A thirty-minute train ride from Grand Central Terminal on the Metro-North express, Hastings is the first of the four River-towns—Dobbs Ferry, Irvington, and Tarrytown—that went from small manufacturing centers to suburbs.

At one time, Hastings was home to the Zinsser Chemical Company, which produced mustard gas during World War I, and Anaconda Wire and Cable, a main supplier of telephone wire for the Northeast. The factories that made their contributions to befouling the river were gone. A process of remediation was underway. In the way of small towns, the argument over what to replace them with will outlast many residents.

Hastings had the advantage of being eminently walkable. Tom walked to and from the train. His kids walked to school. Running directly through it is the Old Croton Aqueduct. Built in the 1840s by Irish laborers to provide the city with a desperately needed supply of clean water, it was turned into a state park, a miles-long ribbon of trees and greenery. Though it grew wealthier as new arrivals replaced old, Hastings retained a modest feel.

From the bluff above the train station, the view down the Hudson is of the city skyline, which rises Oz-like at the river's mouth, an appropriate image since Hastings was home to both Frank Morgan, the wizard in the MGM classic, and Billie Burke, a.k.a. Glinda, the Good Witch.

We rented for a year, then bought a house. The walk down the hill to the train is nine minutes, the uphill return trip eleven. The train ride beside the Hudson is one of the most beautiful I know.

It was a short walk from Grand Central to Rockefeller Center, where my office was. I wasn't in a car all week. An apartment brat, I never acquired homeowner skills. An apartment brat herself, as in most things she took charge. She handled the maintenance and acted as general contractor.

Our house is a block from Tom's. He and I have remained close all our lives. We both wrote for a living. Tom freelanced for the *Daily News Sunday Magazine, Newsday, Esquire,* and other publications. He followed me as a speechwriter for Cuomo. "I thought about where I could find another Peter Quinn," the governor told me, "then I remembered you're a twin."

Tom was the head writer at the Ford Foundation for eighteen years. For more than a decade, he edited *Waterkeeper* magazine, part of Robert F. Kennedy Jr.'s effort to save the planet's supply of clean water.

Tom often reads over my work and offers suggestions and comments. I've done the same for him. The only time we worked together was on the script for "McSorley's New York," which won a 1987 New York Area Emmy Award for Outstanding Arts/Cultural/Historical Programming.

Our politics, largely inherited from our father, are the same. We constantly talk about books. Our tastes are the same in writers. We attend Mass together each Sunday. Our kids think we're obsessed with things Irish.

Raised a block apart, they're siblings as much as cousins. Our wives are best friends and fellow Bronxites who, attuned to their mates' peculiarities, encouraged rather than discouraged their co-conspiring.

Tom and I spent a lot of time in different places, but we've never been far apart. We're two-egg, two-sperm twins, not identical physically, but in a psycho-spiritual-existential, call-it-what-you-will sense, identical down to deep heart's core.

If the country was no longer in a malaise, Time Warner was. The stratospheric expectations fueled by go-for-broke bankers like Wasserstein Perella proved futuristic fantasies. The world waited to see the "transforming power" of the Time Warner merger to transform anything.

An analysts' meeting was held in the nearby auditorium of the Prudential Building on 7th Avenue. The division heads came armed with charts, videos, and PowerPoint presentations for a full-frontal assault to drive home the unique strengths of their businesses, how each was poised for "double-digit growth," and how the company's share price would soar.

At the lavish lunch that followed, Jerry strayed from his text to pile on paragraphs purple with high-flying promises. The opportunities were limitless. Time Warner was "uniquely equipped to ride the coming wave of global revolutionary technological change." Steve would've been proud.

In the preceding decades, under the rubric of "enhancing shareholder value," the lone measure of a company's performance and success was the price of its stock. If it didn't move up, those in charge feared being moved out. The analysts stayed long enough for the cocktail reception and to collect goodie bags of videos, CDs, and Looney Tune t-shirts. They gradually drifted out. The stock stayed put.

Time Warner Cable spent two years developing the Full Service Network (FSN). The innovative network of coaxial cable and traditional copper wire was in many ways a breakthrough in the introduction of interactivity.

The FSN was rolled out in December 1994, in Orlando, Florida, Time Warner's second largest cable system. I spent days holed up with colleagues in a hotel next to a sulfurous swamp preparing for the rollout.

I asked a cable division executive what the FSN cost. He shook his head. "You don't want to know." I did. But he stayed mute. Whatever the price tag, it didn't change Time Warner's fortunes. The emergence of the

Internet and the digital technologies spawned by Silicon Valley soon made it obsolete. It was shut down three years later. It's as bad to be too far ahead of the curve as behind.

From a personal perspective, it wasn't a total loss. It was nice to spend time in Florida in wintertime. I met Kathy and the kids for a vacation at Disney World.

Jerry kept up a speaking schedule to push the potential of Time Warner and his vision of what was to come for the industry. His credibility as a prophet was low. In its coverage of the 1995 annual meeting, the *Hollywood Reporter* observed, "The stock of Time Warner remains depressed, and the stockholders remain anxious." Many were also frustrated and angry.

When possible, I'd kept to my policy of not attending speeches I wrote, a practice I began with Hugh Carey. Curious about the reception Jerry would get from fledging masters of the universe, I made an exception and accompanied him to the Harvard Business School.

He was treated respectfully, though there was an undercurrent of condescension and a soupçon of contempt. They wanted to know about shareholder value. How could a CEO do so little with so much?

If you can't build it, then acquire it was a part of Steve Ross's philosophy. Time Warner began climbing out of the post-merger pit with the 1996 acquisition of Turner Broadcasting. Years before, despite its considerable news-gathering operations, Time Inc. rejected the idea of trying to start a twenty-four-hour cable news network as unfeasible. Ted Turner ran with it and launched CNN.

Outrageous and in-your-face, Ted was recognized and valued for his genius in building brands like CNN, TBS, TNT, and the Cartoon Network. Jerry told the press Ted was the most important acquisition of all. His $1 billion gift to the UN added to his global celebrity.

No one mentioned Ted's needing a speechwriter. The "Mouth of the South" suffered from dyslexia and attention deficit disorder. Turning transcripts of his snarled and tangled ad hoc remarks into intelligible prose was like hacking through the densest thickets of *Finnegans Wake.*

Jerry wanted Ted out front as a public face of the company. It was decided to feature an interview with him as a prominent part of the annual report. I was assigned to tape and edit it. He'd have the questions ahead of time. I'd work over his responses to make sure they were brief, to the point, and coherent. No small assignment.

When I came into the boardroom to do the interview, he was already there. He boomed, "I know why you're here." I replied, "For the interview."

"Interview, my ass," he said. "You want to justify your job."

I didn't disagree. The interview continued along those lines. He paid no attention to the questions. He was uncensored, profane, outrageous, honest, and all over the place. "Jerry keeps telling people I'm his best friend," he said. "I've never even been to his goddamn apartment."

I did my best to pluck insights from the jumble on the tape and fashion an interview that sounded like him, not standard-issue corporate mush. I showed it to Jerry, who said, "It captures Ted's voice."

Ted went on a rampage when it reached him. He bellowed it made him sound like a "goddamn redneck retard." He wanted whoever wrote it fired. I warmed up some mush, rewrote the interview, and did my best to avoid being seen by him again.

⠇⠇

I wrote for Jerry Levin for a decade, my longest stint with any of my several suzerains. I rode in planes and limousines, and the occasional helicopter that lifted us over traffic-clogged roads to the Marine Air Terminal and the corporate jet.

I sat across from him at the same table on flights to L.A. He was comfortable with long silences. Our conversations were about politics or business or upcoming speeches. He never touched on his upbringing or family background or asked about mine.

I never heard him tell a joke that wasn't scripted. Sometimes when I came into his office, he was welcoming and warm. Other times, he was brusque or didn't bother looking up. Engaging one minute, he could be indifferent or distant the next. Peter W., who spent more time around him than practically anyone else, said that Jerry's moods were "about as predictable as a roulette wheel."

I was by no means alone in perceiving the psychic distance he maintained, the self-protective core. People who thought they were close to him and enjoyed a special relationship discovered they didn't. No one was unexpendable.

His first wife was quoted as saying you could sit beside him for a two-hour heart-to-heart and come away without the slightest idea what he was really thinking. After a speech at a National Cable TV Association convention in Chicago, he stayed to chat. When an old friend from HBO came over to greet him, he swept right past.

His emotions, raw and unfiltered, were on full display when his son was murdered. Jonathan Levin taught at Taft High School in the Bronx. By all accounts, he was a sensitive, highly effective teacher, dedicated to his students. Jerry never hid his admiration. Jonathan was doing the socially significant work he once considered for himself.

Jonathan made himself available after hours. He let a student into his Manhattan apartment who tortured him for his PIN and killed him. Jerry's grief seemed too deep a wound to heal. He had to be helped into the synagogue for Jonathan's service.

A friend who lost his son told me you don't get over it. You go on and take what comfort you can from the distractions of the everyday. "Drugged by time" is how he put it, "but never near anesthetized." Those of us who worked closely with Jerry weren't sure he'd come back. The only time I was present when he mentioned Jonathan in public was when he accepted an honorary Emmy from the Television Academy.

He asked me to draft remarks. He wanted to pay tribute to Jonathan, who saw it as part of his mission to equip his students with the mastery of media that people outside poor and underprivileged neighborhoods took for granted. Jerry never got back to me about the draft.

The ballroom of the New York Hilton was filled for the dinner. I sat in the back at one of the several Time Warner tables. Jerry took several folded yellow pages from his pocket and flattened them on the lectern. He said that while he had a speechwriter, this was a speech he had to write himself. He read verbatim what I wrote.

My colleague Ed A., to whom I gave the draft, looked across the table for my reaction. I shrugged. If I helped Jerry express his mixture of grief and pride, I was glad.

Jerry's focus on Time Warner's future was more intense than ever. For a while, his grip on his job seemed shaky. Now it was firm. The stock was moving.

The company's businesses sprawled from *Time* to *Progressive Farmer* magazine, from HBO to the Atlanta Braves, from some of the country's largest cable systems to amusement parks and Book of the Month Club and Little, Brown. The Time Inc. of 20,000 employees in which I started ballooned to around 90,000.

In its ownership of HBO, Warner Bros., Warner Music, and the Turner

Networks, Time Warner possessed some of the world's most recognized and valuable media brands. Between Time Inc. and Time Warner Cable, the company's subscriber base was unmatched.

The company began an extensive series of "Leadership Forums" that brought junior managers from across the company to New York for two days of lectures and discussion on the art of taking charge. I sat in on several. They were a circus of clichés lifted from the spiraling proliferation of self-help and how-to-get-ahead bestsellers.

I suggested in passing that since only a small number would end up in leadership positions, what was needed were "Followship Forums." It got a laugh. I laughed along. I was only half-kidding. Soon enough, the fate of Time Warner rendered the exercise moot.

The rising fortunes of Time Warner coincided with the seventy-fifth anniversary of *Time* magazine. Though a fading version of the opinion shaper it once was, it retained a measure of respect from its glory days.

The celebratory extravaganza was held at Radio City Music Hall in March 1998. A platform was constructed atop the seats that transformed the grand Art Deco space into a giant dining hall. Every living person featured on the cover was invited. In a surreal moment, I watched Leni Riefenstahl walk in on the arm of Muhammad Ali.

Per his instructions, Jerry's remarks honored Henry Luce and the magazine's past while emphasizing its importance to Time Warner and the success and influence it would enjoy over the next seventy-five years.

Despite the happy talk about the future, an aura of nostalgia hung over the festivities. It didn't take Nostradamus to perceive that *Time*'s best years were behind. An unofficial last hurrah, it was enjoyable and memorable, especially in light of the debacle to follow.

If Time Warner was back on its feet and the stock was moving ahead, the ground beneath rumbled and shook with Vesuvian tremors set off by the exponential rise of dot-com start-ups. All promise and no profits, their sky-high valuations baffled old-time investors, many of whom withdrew from the markets.

Jerry hosted an analysts' meeting at Warner Bros. Studio on the set of the sci-fi box-office hit *The Matrix*. Meant to impress, the message echoed the movie's plot—the bewilderment suffered by those caught between the twilight of old certainties and the confounding, disruptive possibilities of a new digital age.

A "new economy" was coming to birth. Old rules didn't apply. The law of what goes up must come down was repealed. Unfortunately, Murphy's Law wasn't.

On the morning after the millennial New Year, Kathy and I went to breakfast at the Center Diner in Hastings. In the famous (and, as it turned out, delusional) formulation of political economist Francis Fukuyama, it was the "end of history" moment—when the triumph of free markets and liberal democracy ushered in a brave new world of peace and prosperity. For a brief, shining moment, optimism reigned.

I shared with Kathy the thought that in two years Jerry would reach retirement age. I'd inferred from several conversations that he didn't plan to leave entirely but would graduate to chairman emeritus.

My expectation was that I'd go with him to the corporate equivalent of Golden Pond. I'd have a generous pension (I was a member of the last generation to enjoy that beneficence), a 401(k), and a plentitude of stock options—all in all, a cozy retirement. We could travel. I'd have plenty of time to write.

"If you want to make God laugh, tell him your plans for next week," the Hasidic adage goes.

That Friday, I was summoned to Jerry's office and hit with stunning news: Time Warner was merging with AOL. In barely a decade AOL had grown to become the world's largest online service with 22 million subscribers and a market cap of $222 billion. Afraid the news might leak, we weren't allowed to leave the building and worked all weekend.

I didn't feel qualified to judge, but people I respected felt the combination couldn't work. The world's largest "content provider" (the irritatingly vacuous moniker for print, movies, music, and programming), Time Warner was an institution with set procedures and financial strictures. People came with the prospect of spending their careers.

AOL came across as a one liner: "You've got mail!" It gave the impression of being a casino as much as a corporation where employees used stock options like chips, getting them one day, watching them skyrocket, then cashing in.

A tech-savvy acquaintance told me the dial-up basis of AOL's business was yesterday's technology. "The trouble with companies like yours," he said, "is you've got sixty-year-old relics on your board when what you need are wired-in twelve-year olds."

Sunday night, after minimum deliberation, Time Warner's board of directors supinely approved the merger. The thing to remember about present-day boards is they're an update of the sultan's *seraglio*, a select circle valued for its ability to go along, the ultimate pleasures bestowed by the compensation committee's pliant willingness to provide obscenely recompensed executives a monetary orgasm.

Ted Turner asked the only question: "What the hell do we get out of merging with an e-mail company?"

The next morning, when Jerry and AOL's dour, charmless CEO Steve Case officially unveiled the merger, the capacious auditorium of the nearby Prudential Building was packed with schools of reporters from Japan and Europe as well as the United States who devoured the news like frenzied piranhas.

It took a year to get all the government approvals for the merger to close. The morning of January 12, 2001, the day shares of the newly formed company debuted, I and a small band from newly formed AOL Time Warner accompanied Jerry to the balcony of the New York Stock Exchange to ring the opening bell.

The next morning, the *Financial Times* ran a front-page photo of Jerry smiling and clapping after just ringing the bell to open "the first day of trading in the $105 billion merged company."

A short distance away, Bob Pittman, the progenitor of MTV and the company's flashy co-COO, is doing the same. In a *Zelig* moment, I'm between them, as if part of the troika running the company. In the uncropped souvenir photo we were provided, the whole group is visible. Kathy said it reminded her of the defendants' box at the Nuremberg trials.

Before the bell ringing, Dick Grasso, NYSE's gnomish CEO, hosted a breakfast in a room lined with portraits of the solemn-faced high priests who'd served Plutus, the god of wealth, and maintained the Temple of High Finance. (Grasso, whose reputation soared after 9/11, floated back to Earth in 2003 with a $188.5 million golden parachute.)

The dining room exuded certainty, stability, prosperity. There'd be little of that for Time Warner in the days ahead.

Eight months later, from an office high in 75 Rock, we watched as the World Trade Center's Twin Towers vanished in paroxysms of smoke and ash. I'd worked in the governor's office on the fifty-seventh floor in Two World Trade Center for almost three years. I rode elevators filled with people on their way to their everyday jobs. I felt a special horror.

In the aftermath of the attack, I listened from my office, which looked down on St. Patrick's Cathedral, to bagpipes' dolorous bleat as they escorted fallen firefighters and police to their requiems. They were the first casualties in what turned out to be America's longest war.

History was rebooting, not ending.

▞

There's no need to recount the denouement of the dot-com daze. There are whole books dedicated to it. Fueled by hubris, shortsightedness, and the will to believe, it contained the same ingredients as every financial mania in history, from tulips to eToys.com. The scent of easy money, gobs and gobs of it, was everywhere, an aroma that, like Circe's potions, turned humans into pigs.

The merger of AOL and Time Warner was the dreamed-of juncture of dough and destiny. The term of art wasn't "filthy rich" or "wealthy" but "net worth," the full Monty of assets, liquid and fixed—cash, stock options, real estate, bonds, whatever was saleable or negotiable.

You didn't add incrementally to your net worth. You sprinkled Miracle-Gro, stood back, and watched. The bigger it was, the faster it grew. The invocation of a garden—green, lush, fragrant—wasn't accidental.

The golden apples dangled in reach: the ripening prospect of the Tribeca triplex, the castle-sized beachside home in Southampton, pampered stays in sumptuous spas, frictionless travel in limousines and private jets, the fleeting glance on the beach at Cannes by the passerby who recalls the two-page profile in *Vogue*, the incised name on the architecturally significant additions to philharmonics and Ivy League dorms and libraries.

It was hard not to get giddy. AOL's 30 million subscribers would rise to 60 million. Behind its "walled garden," Time Warner's movies, programming, and print would be available to subscribers only. The advent of AOL Television would revolutionize the medium. AOL Time Warner would grow at an annual rate of 25 percent.

Ed A., close friend and longtime survivor like me, and I walked back from a cheerleading session that left no doubt we'd enjoy the lifestyles of the rich and famous, or at least the rich. A young woman from the finance department accompanied us. She said the whole thing smelled to her like a bubble. She mentioned an article in *Fortune* that pointed out if Time Warner grew at the rate it claimed, it would be worth more than the E.U.

She was cashing in her stock options and moving on. We silently pitied her inability to heed the prophets who divined the swelling profits that would pave the way to The Promised Land.

It's almost impossible to recognize a bubble from inside. Once it's burst, you're out of luck and out of money.

While the storm clouds piled up, the merger was touted by true believers. "Change is good" was the cheerleading slogan. I told one youthful AOL enthusiast that I didn't regard the change from the Weimar Republic to the Third Reich as good. He flashed an undiscouraged smile. I deduced he had no idea what the Weimar Republic was.

The handwringing was on the wall. The alliance of AOL Time Warner went from "defining transaction of the twenty-first century" to "worst merger in history." The combined company posted a loss of $98 billion, to this day the largest corporate write-down in the history of American business.

I was far from alone in employing a loser's logic to hold on to his stock options as the company's prospects tumbled from celestial to cloacal. Ted Turner's net worth sank from $10 billion to one. Stony-faced, humorless AOL founder and CEO Steve Case took a bath. Employees watched their retirement be vaporized.

Jerry lost his reputation as well as his wealth. CNBC ranked him as one of the "10 Worst CEOs of all time." Other outlets concurred. Formerly hailed as a strategic visionary, Jerry was booed as he walked through the lobby of the Time Warner Building.

The money had never been real to me. Beyond a pledge I made to my alma mater (and had to renege on), it never figured into any of my plans. I told Dick Parsons, who took over as chairman and CEO, that I wanted out. He said if I stayed for three years, he'd allow me to stay on as a consultant for two. I'd gone from a lucky hire to family heirloom.

Easygoing, accessible, and astute, Dick was the fifth chairman I worked for. Twice in my career I excused myself from an assignment, both times with Dick.

Philip Morris, a global leader in the manufacture and distribution of cancer and emphysema, invented some bullshit award—corporate awards almost always are—to present to former British PM and Tory autocrat Margaret Thatcher, who'd been hired as a shill for the tobacco industry.

Dick was asked to speak. I told him that my father, once a heavy smoker, had died of lung cancer. Also, I regarded Dame Thatcher as a stone-hearted imperialist relic and Tory reactionary. I couldn't be part of any encomium. Dick said while he didn't share my feelings, he understood them. He'd get someone else to write his remarks.

Dick was appointed by President George W. Bush to co-chair with Senator Daniel Patrick Moynihan a commission on changes to Social Security that would have allowed workers to open "personal savings accounts" and invest part of their contributions in the stock market. He asked me to draft an op-ed for the *Wall Street Journal* that argued for the change.

I said I saw it as a Trojan Horse designed to turn a defined benefit into a bet—rewarding when the market soared, punishing when it crashed—another attempt to undo a building block of the New Deal that provided the elderly with a guaranteed level of support. The biggest beneficiary would be the financial services industry.

An old-fashioned Rockefeller Republican, socially liberal and a free-market enthusiast, Dick was less understanding than previously. My objection was a matter of politics, he said, not conscience. He didn't pursue it. The op-ed was prepared by the senator's staff. I looked at it when it was finished. Dick left it at that. It wasn't his way to hold a grudge.

At the same time the merger came together, Helen Ross retired. We'd been together for twenty years. I said we'd stay in touch. She said she'd like that.

Soon after, she developed cancer. I usually called her every other day. When several days went by and she didn't answer, I called the 52nd precinct close to where she lived in the North Bronx. The police got the super to open the door and found Helen's body. She'd died of heart failure. Her sister took her back to Chicago.

Helen was the proudest, most independent person I ever met. Content by herself, she lived a solitary life but, as far as I could tell, was never lonely. I still grieve at not having the chance to say goodbye.

The offices in which I started my career wouldn't have been entirely unfamiliar to Bob Cratchit and Bartleby the Scrivener. No quills or candles, it's true, but computerless desks cluttered with papers and pencils.

I'm struck by the leap in technology that's transforming office life. Work is done more and more by remote. People FaceTime and Zoom. Moments well spent in hallway show and tells, sympathizing, conspiring, kibitzing, celebrating promotions, engagements, and retirements—the subtle and not-so-subtle ingredients of trust—seem doomed to the fate of the carrier pigeon.

The pandemic has supercharged the transformation. But without the mundane interaction with Helen and people like her—the in-the-flesh back and forth, the eccentric and the everyday captured so brilliantly in "The Office"—my working world would've been impoverished.

AOL Time Warner was a deflated, dejected place, which didn't mean the politics couldn't be vicious. I quickly learned that in the reconfigured AOL Time Warner hierarchy, the person I nominally reported to was trying to get me fired, the first time this had happened in my career.

People with no identifiable skills are most often skilled in working the politics of the organization to their advantage. As one longtime colleague lamented, "People who aren't good at their jobs are usually good at fucking up yours."

I dubbed my nemesis Beelzebub. He summoned me to his office to talk about a speech. First, he called the company in Bermuda where his boat was being repaired. After ten minutes, he told me I'd have to come back because he had to stay on the call.

Another time, he let me sit there while he talked to a veterinarian about his daughter's horse. He said he was unsatisfied with my speeches. They weren't aggressive enough. He had an assistant make a list of all the "active verbs" that analysts used in covering the company. I was to restrict myself to them in future speeches.

It was all classic alpha-dog tactics. Still, I wondered at his determination to show me the door until I realized that I interacted face-to-face with the company's top executives, without his presence or permission. Predictably paranoid, Beelzebub couldn't abide the implied lack of control.

One of his methods of control was to designate people as "stars." He lavished them with praise and raises. Then, for no apparent reason, he cut them off. They slaved and groveled to salvage their stellar status.

Late one Friday, I got back a draft Beelzebub intercepted on its way to Dick. Comments in red were scribbled in the margins. "Dull." "Doesn't sound like Dick." "Needs work!!!" I was seasoned enough to take legitimate criticisms. But I knew this was another piece in the power game.

I showed the draft to Dick. He told me to ignore it. Beelzebub was trying to be helpful, that's all.

Monday morning, I went into Beelzebub's office and told him if he had been in the building when I got the draft back, I would have shoved it up his ass. He acted shocked. He protested he had no ill intent. He wanted our relationship to work. In the future, he'd do everything in his power to keep things right between us.

We shook hands. An hour later, one of his assistants confided that he was telling everyone I was "mentally unbalanced."

I told her to assure him that I was.

Beelzebub went right back to work to make sure my days were numbered. It turned out his were. I was far from the only one who complained to Dick. Beelzebub was eased out with enough money to soothe the sting.

My mother told me to never take pleasure in another person's pain. In Beelzebub's case I made an exception. He found solace of his own. He went on to make a fortune in a digital publishing venture.

⁂

I never gave up my writing routine. My original intent was for *Banished Children* to be the first in a New York trilogy that would unfold across the century between the Draft Riots and the assassination of JFK. When I didn't have the monetary success I hoped, I decided I needed to write shorter books that wouldn't take up significant chunks of my shrinking lifespan.

In 1998, I was accepted for a month's stint at the artists' retreat at Yaddo in Saratoga. Yaddo is a writer's dream. There are no assignments or deadlines or expectations other than spending the time as you feel best— working, sleeping, thinking. Evenings, the guests, who include sculptors, musicians, painters, et al., gather for, as a fellow resident commented, "mastication, conversation, and inebriation."

(Years later when I shared the comment with a friend who'd been at Yaddo, she added, "You forgot fornication.")

In my years as a writer, the luxury of such mental space was never mine. It consisted of what I could squeeze or steal from work. Although I never saw apparitions of the famous writers who'd resided at Yaddo, I had a close encounter with the bats that besiege the building at night.

I was awakened by screams and a pounding on my door. Molly O'Neill, the food writer for the *Times*, had locked herself out of her room. A wing-flapping bat madly zigzagged its way up and down the hallway, divebombing Molly's head before a last-minute pull away.

Unthinkingly, I snatched one of the nets stationed on each hallway for bat-catching. I lunged and snagged it. I know bats are intelligent and serve useful purposes, but they also resemble the spawn of Hell. In an instant, the bat freed itself from the net and resumed its aerial attacks.

Molly and I sprinted helter-skelter down the corridor like the terrified children in *The Amityville Horror* until we made it safely to a lower floor.

There were no more bat blitzes. Molly and I made it a point to stay in our rooms at night.

In the weeks that followed, I finally began my second novel. A devotee of Raymond Chandler, I read his books in part or whole more than once. No longer pigeonholed as a mystery writer, he's recognized as a prose stylist of the first rank.

I was enamored of his detective protagonist, Philip Marlowe. It was hard to think of L.A. without his hardnosed hunt for the serpents slithering through Hollywood's Eden.

Fintan Dunne showed up in a daydream. I immediately recognized him as the protagonist I was after. He looked back at Marlowe but was his own man. A former inmate of the Catholic Protectory, veteran of World War I, ex-NYPD, he roamed Depression-era New York, knew every manhole and pavement crack, mixed with the guilty and wrongly convicted, good cops, rotten ones, grifters, hookers, and highbrows.

I welcomed his companionship. I listened to his story. A simple homicide led to a secret program of eugenic murders. It got complicated. A parallel plot unfolded in Berlin where Admiral Canaris, head of the Abwehr and his adjutant, Hans Oster, led a plot to remove Hitler before he attacked Czechoslovakia and set off another war.

Al Silverman told me to get him my next novel before he retired. I wasn't close. After a deceptively fast start at Yaddo, the story came in its own time, at its own pace. My quick book took seven years. I got happily lost in the research. The hours I spent with Fintan Dunne were an antidote to merger-induced delirium and the manic composition and revision of corporate expectations and evasions.

I had no regrets. Writing *Hour of the Cat* comforted me through turbulent years. Peter Mayer, CEO at Viking Penguin when *Banished Children* was published, started his own imprint, Overlook. He bought the new novel. It did well domestically and was sold to publishers in France and Australia. We agreed to turn it into a trilogy.

As I graduated into my consultancy, I received offers to teach courses in speechwriting. I recalled what Al Silverman told me. He'd made a study of writing programs. He concluded that for those gifted with talent, the courses helped focus and deepen their skills; for those without, they didn't make a difference.

I've no idea if he was right. Some people are blessed from birth, for sure. The same could be said of ballplayers and musicians. For whatever reason, their innate abilities, however unearned, give them a critical advantage.

But age and experience change people in profound ways. Isn't it possible the abilities of an unpromising beginner might be dormant rather than absent? Who's to say?

I turned down teaching speechwriting courses not because I was convinced they were useless but because I had little to teach, certainly not enough to justify being paid. If pressed, all I could offer was a few suggestions.

Write badly. All writing is rewriting. Calvin Trillin said he always ripped a first draft into small pieces so the cleaning lady wouldn't find it and wonder how anyone could be paid to produce such crap. Be a writer first, an editor second.

Read promiscuously, voraciously, constantly. Newspapers, novels, biographies. Be on the lookout for original anecdotes, quotes, well-told stories. Copy sentences and paragraphs that stand out to you. A writing style is a process, not a gift.

Listen intently. Songs, plays, poems, movies. The spoken word must flow in ways words on the page don't. Always read aloud what you write. Search and destroy clichés. Avoid vocabulary or references that don't fit with the person you're writing for. (A writer I know almost lost his job for including a reference to Proust in a speech for a studio head.)

If you can't learn from your failures (which are inevitable), accept them and move on. The writing life is the business of moving on.

If none of these work for you, find your own.

In the late afternoon of my career, I packed up to leave the Time Warner Building at 75 Rock for a twilight spell in the new AOL Time Warner headquarters, a doomed Ozymandian monument to corporate hubris on Columbus Circle.

Rene T., my gifted, multi-talented assistant who filled the gap Helen left, helped me load box after box of materials dating back to the beginnings of my career. When we finished, she said in the solicitous voice of an intensive-care nurse, "Peter, you're carrying around a dead man."

Possessed of a genetic aversion to confrontation, I avoided an in-your-face rebuttal in favor of an e-mail excoriating her inability to grasp my historically significant trove of corporate/political documents.

As I typed my response and set my laptop afire, the truth sank in. Who was I saving them for beside myself? Who'd really miss them? What purpose would they serve? Weren't the world's archives bursting with unconsulted manuscripts?

Next day, we parked a bin outside my office. In went the Dead Sea Scrolls of my scribal life: graduations, keynotes, States of the State, fundraisers, eulogies, op-eds, groundbreakings, shareholder letters, annual meetings in Atlanta, New York, Burbank. The merger of Time and Warner. The merger with Turner. The catastrophe of AOL. The whole *megillah*.

I chose an office in the new headquarters in an obscure corner at the end of a row of empty offices that looked as if it was hit by a neutron bomb. It once housed the ill-named Risk Management Department, the first fatality of a company that took one too many.

I was sixty. It was *sayonara* time. I'd been a speechwriter for almost thirty years, half my life. My longevity was partly attributable to the fact that few coveted my job. It was brutally simple: You produced the speech on time, or you didn't. There's no way to postpone a deadline. If several speeches in a row bombed, it was time to look for another line of work.

More than once, I was approached by someone who told me that when he retired he intended to write. They made it sound like a pastime, a respite from playing golf. I didn't discourage them. I'd let them find out for themselves.

I came through elections, mergers, stock market crashes, terrorist attacks. On the last day of the year, as I left the building for good, I thought of Abbé Sieyès's response when queried what he did during the French Revolution. "J'ai vécu," he replied. *I survived.*

I had no regrets, no twinge of nostalgia. I felt gratitude at how it all worked out.

With retirement, the days again belonged to me. I traveled to Ireland with Frank and Ellen McCourt. Frank took me to the Redemptorists' church in Limerick, where as a boy he'd heard Ernest Hemingway's books denounced from the pulpit. "I had no idea who Hemingway was," Frank said. "At that point, I made a promise to myself to read them all."

A woman watched as we came down the steps of the church. She asked incredulously, "Are you Frank McCourt?" When Frank said yes, she snapped, "Your book is filled with lies."

"Name one," Frank replied.

"There were no cobblestones in Limerick," she said as she stormed away.

No hostile takeover to get in the way, Kathy and I made it at last to Venice. We added Florence and Rome. We traveled to Assisi on the Feast of St. Francis. Free to travel in the off-seasons, we enjoyed leisurely trips to Paris and Barcelona, the wine country of California, and Tuscany.

We went with Genevieve, Daniel, and our nephew Michael to Ireland. Genevieve and Daniel don't have the same bond with Ireland as I. They're firmly on the American side of the Irish-American equation. But the country cast its spell. They felt the pull of ancient roots.

I drove cross-country with my brother-in-law John. He was an ex–Green

Beret, the kind of fellow traveler who made an effete Easterner feel secure no matter how down-and-dirty the dives we patronized.

We spent a late September afternoon in a deserted Monument Valley circling around the East and West Mittens, the two buttes Ford made into the the *omphalos* of the American West.

John and I took our sons to Cuba. We followed Hemingway's trail. Soon after his first wife died, my father's father went to Cuba. He told my father that the Cubans were the handsomest people he ever encountered. I saw nothing to contradict him.

When I finished the Fintan Dunne trilogy with *The Man Who Never Returned* and *Dry Bones*, Tom Nolan, the *Wall Street Journal*'s reviewer of mystery/detective fiction, devoted his entire 11/1/13 column to the trilogy.

In part he wrote, "'The best men are left on the battlefield,' an aging Wild Bill Donovan is heard to say in *Dry Bones*. 'That's the trouble with war. The real heroes never make it home.' In his bracing Fintan Dunne trilogy, Peter Quinn has created a notable exception."

I took it as a fitting eulogy for Dunne; I was grateful for his company but didn't want to spend the rest of my career accompanying my fictional companion through history. We parted good friends. I promised to stay in touch.

▗▖▖

Noel Kilkenny, the Irish Consul General, and his wife, Hanora, hosted a reception to celebrate the trilogy's completion.

As I entered, he said, "The governor is here." I was confused. The governor was Andrew Cuomo. We were cordial, but I was never part of his circle, nor did I want to be.

One staffer labeled the coterie of obedient aides around him "Androids." They usually looked like they'd been in a ten-round prizefight—and lost.

"Andrew is here?" I asked. "No, it's Mario," Noel said. He explained that he'd sat next to the ex-governor at a luncheon and mentioned the reception he was planning. "The governor asked to come," Noel said.

He came with Matilda. They stayed the whole time. He told Daniel and Genevieve how much "your father's writing meant to me." He said he regretted never having the chance to thank me in public, a statement I left unexamined. I deeply appreciated his generous gesture.

I had lunch at his Sutton Place apartment soon after. It was our first conversation in twenty years. We reminisced about Albany and the way things were. It seemed a faraway time. He died the following year.

"He acted from honesty and for the general good," Mark Antony says of Caesar in Shakespeare's play, ". . . the elements mixed so well in him that Nature might stand up and say to all the world, 'This was a man.'" The same could be said of Mario Cuomo. Flawed as he was, he stood up for his beliefs. He was a man.

If his accomplishments as governor were less than memorable, his heart was always in the right place. When it came to the country's slide into economic inequality and the rise of predatory capitalism, he was also a prophet.

I followed at a distance the dismemberment and disappearance of Time Inc. and Time Warner. The fallen behemoth was sold for body parts. AT&T devoured the largest chunk, which was renamed WarnerMedia.

In proposing the acquisition of WarnerMedia, AT&T CEO Randall Stephenson hailed it as "the deal of a lifetime" that would offer "a unique customer experience." He said, "It's all about execution."

He was as good as his word. Under the familiar corporate fig leaf of "synergy," the heads of several thousand employees went on the chopping block. Three years later, roughly the lifespan of a hedgehog, it was Stephenson's head on the block. His severance package was worth $65 million.

The CEO of the new company, which resulted in another synergistic merger (and several thousand fewer employees), was awarded an annual salary of $45 million.

The fees for these wheeling-dealing, casino-style mergers, un-mergers, and re-mergers approached a billion dollars. A new crop of palatial mega-mansions emerged on Hampton beaches and the manicured swards of Beverly Hills.

The Time & Life Building, a Modernist embodiment of the confident expectations of a vanished age, was gutted and retrofitted. So was 75 Rock, the headquarters of Warner Communications, Time Warner, and—o! so briefly!—AOL Time Warner.

Kathy and I have the house to ourselves. Her company is more important to me than ever. Genevieve and Daniel are out of college, with careers of their own, and wed to spouses we treasure. Last year, Genevieve and her husband, Sam, made us grandparents of an impossibly beautiful baby girl, Lila Viola Clarke.

Tom and I spend more and more time together talking about religion and politics. We periodically revisit our Bronx haunts and try to puzzle out our childhood.

In the wake of the passage of President Biden's trillion-dollar infrastructure legislation, there's talk of covering over large sections of the Cross Bronx and building parks and housing on the newly redeemed space. Justice would be done if the underground sections were flooded and turned into a version of Mario Cuomo's canal.

A memoir isn't a rearview mirror. It's a scrim on which a mélange of images is projected, some clear, some blurred, some amusing, others painful, an unfolding of revelations, indictments, vindications, a confrontation with "all I've done and failed to do."

Looking back, what I'm struck by most is luck. Don't kid yourself, whether it comes to love, or writing, or staying alive, luck—good and bad—has as much to do with it as anything. My good luck includes the family I was born into, the friends I've made, the woman I married, the opportunities I stumbled into.

Why I've enjoyed such luck while others, hobbled and wounded by circumstances beyond their control, have never had a chance is among the many questions I can't answer.

Most mornings, I go to my attic office, sit at my desk, daydream, read, and write.

Out the window to the west, the Palisades rise like a giant protective wall. The foliage changes color each season, from winter silver to spring green to fall's carmine and gold.

As the leaves fall, the sliver of the Hudson I can see grows wider.

What I feel most is gratitude.

EPILOGUE

IN MY EARLY DAYS as a speechwriter, I fell in with a circle of writers and wannabes who met for lunch on the first Friday of every month at Eamonn Doran's, a lively Second Avenue eating-and-drinking establishment gone too soon and interred, like so many of its kin, beneath a luxury high-rise.

The first items on the First Friday Club menu were talk and drink. (Not always in that order.) Lunch was sometimes an afterthought. The participants varied month to month. Among the stalwarts were Frank, a high school English teacher; his brother Malachy, an actor whose steady work was in soap operas; Terry, an ex-Marine turned NYU professor; Dennis, an FDNY veteran and the group's only published author; and Isaiah, West Side impresario and founder of Symphony Space.

The observance of the First Friday custom was a genuflection to the tradition many of us grew up with, which promised those who attended Mass nine First Fridays in a row the presence of a priest at their deathbed. The secular equivalent for nine consecutive First Friday lunches was the presence of the bartender from Eamonn's to see them off on their final passage with an Irish coffee.

I attended when I could. Lunch often stretched well beyond lunch. There was general agreement that nobody could agree on anything. The arguments were often fierce, but never physical and never dented anything beyond friendships.

Depending on the time of the year, I found myself stuck in Albany and unable to attend. Since I couldn't be at Eamonn's, I conceived an idea to bring First Friday to the state capital and invite William Kennedy to join us.

With *Ironweed*, his fourth novel, little-known Albany writer William Kennedy hit the trifecta—the National Book Award, the Pulitzer, and a MacArthur "Genius" Award. He emerged as one of the country's premier novelists and put his hometown on the literary map.

A while earlier, I almost met Kennedy. I became friendly with Joe Persico, Nelson Rockefeller's longtime speechwriter who went on to success as a novelist and nonfiction writer. We had dinner a few times and traded speechwriting anecdotes unfit to print.

Joe couldn't say enough good things about Albany novelist Bill Kennedy, who wrote brilliant novels that never had commercial success. He sent a few speechwriting assignments his way. He gave me his address. He said I should look him up

Thanks to my topsy-turvy, upstate–downstate existence, I never did. Now I wrote him that the First Friday Club, a group of New York City literary enthusiasts, was interested in coming to Albany to host him at a lunch where his novels would be discussed.

Kennedy imagined a band of retired academics and senior-citizen *littérateurs* eager to explore the Jungian nuances in *Ironweed*. He thought if they were willing to take the midwinter, three-hour train ride to Albany, the least he could do was let them buy lunch.

We met at Lombardo's, an Albany landmark on Madison Avenue, down from the Cathedral, where in *Ironweed* Billy Phelan takes Francis, his homeless, down-at-the-heels father, after bailing him from jail for registering to vote twenty-one times (an Albany record, maybe).

Kennedy barely got a word in. Frank and Malachy put their skills as songsters and story spinners to full use. It was a hilarious, outrageous afternoon of jokes, ballads, and dueling soliloquies. We never got around to lunch. Day retired into evening. The proprietor arranged transportation across the river in time for us to catch the last train to the city.

It would be a decade before *Angela's Ashes*, Frank's memoir of a sodden, impoverished childhood, brought him international acclaim. The First Friday Club melted away beneath the glare of his success.

I remained friends with Bill Kennedy. He was kind and helpful, which some writers are, and others not. I loved all his novels, especially *Legs*. He purchased the house on Dove Street, not far from the Capitol, in which Legs Diamond was shot to death. He used it as a writing den.

He invited me to stop by for a glass of wine—truth be told, on occasion something stronger—in the late afternoons when he was done with his day's work. I tried not to abuse the invitation, which wasn't easy.

I talked to Kennedy about the theory of the novel and what distinguishes good novels from bad. He listened patiently, until he couldn't. "Forget theories," he said. "Good novels endure. The bad go away."

Legs Diamond was an Irish-American gangster, a violent criminal and stone-cold killer, who did a lot of bad things. By breathing his last in the house on Dove Street, he gave me the chance to get to know Bill Kennedy. For that, I owe him.

My last full day in Albany, before I left for good, I took a bottle of Jameson and a tape recorder to Kennedy's house in Averill Park. We talked all day and did serious damage to the Jameson. (The next morning, it returned the favor.)

The interview was published in *The Recorder: The Journal of the American Irish Historical Society* and republished in *Riding the Yellow Trolley*, his collection of nonfiction, under the title "Tap Dancing into Reality." (An edited version follows.)

What I learned that afternoon were things essential to writers, the effrontery to believe they have something to say; the hope they can say what's been said before in ways that make it new and different and worth a reader's time; the willingness to see their work rejected, torn apart, ignored, and stomped on; and the strength to endure, persist, and—in Kennedy's words—"to renew your vulnerability."

It was an epiphany or, at another level, a good boot in the ass, intimidating and inspiring at the same time. What I learned about writing novels influenced me more than anything before or since. I don't think I'd have ever finished a novel if not for that afternoon.

"All of *Ironweed* is this tap dancing into reality, trying to figure it out," Bill explained in the interview. "How am I going to do it?'"

The image resonated. I remembered returning from Bill's house on a freeze-your-ass-off January in Albany. It was two or three o'clock in the morning and two or three degrees. He was taking me back to my hotel. He pulled over on Broadway, across from the old Union Station. I followed him out of the car to the steps of a long-defunct bank.

He said this was where Francis Phelan stood, during the trolley strike, when he threw the stone that hit the scab driver between the eyes and killed him. It was as if the fictional scene from *Ironweed* was playing out for real in front of our eyes.

Spry and light-footed, more like someone in his forties than his late sixties, Bill danced up the two or three steps and hurled an imaginary stone, then back down with an equally graceful movement, an abbreviated combination of jitterbug and Irish step dance. Bill would be the first to tell you, he's an excellent dancer.

He was tap dancing, I thought, from the real world into the reality of fiction and back from the reality of fiction into the real, *one step down, two back up*, the effort made to seem effortless, the special hocus-pocus of art, making the hard work disappear, the writer's back and forth, up and down, tap dancing into reality.

An Interview:
Tap Dancing into Reality

It's the writer's dream: the National Book Critics Circle Award for fiction; a MacArthur Foundation "Genius" award of a quarter of a million dollars; the Pulitzer Prize for fiction; movie deals, fame, acclaim, wealth, a success story so improbable that even Frank Capra might have turned it down.

But it's true. It's as real as this man sitting on the porch of his house outside Albany, a novelist whose life reads like a novel, who spent years of struggle and anonymity, writing books that, despite praise and plaudits, never seemed to sell.

"I was broke," Kennedy says. "I didn't have any future. I didn't have anything." Nothing, that is, but the writer's craft, nothing but the redemptive satisfaction of his own creativity as he came "to understand that the writing itself was the most important element in my life."

Kennedy's literary odyssey began in good Irish fashion when he turned his back on the parochial world of pols and prelates and left Albany for Puerto Rico. But, also in good Irish fashion, he remained a prisoner to the place, with a knowledge of himself now as "a person whose imagination has become fused with a single place. And in that place finds all that a man needs for the life of the soul . . ."

Bill Kennedy has it all now. But sitting with him on a soft summer afternoon, warmed by the sun and the smooth assurance of a glass of Irish whiskey, you realize that the work goes on, that while the fame and good fortune are welcomed and even relished, they are still beside the point. For Bill Kennedy the point is what it always has been—the sentence: words strung together into complexity, words transubstantiated into life, words that jump off the page.

What follows are some of Bill Kennedy's reflections on life, art, and the Irish-American experience, a self-portrait of an artist in progress.

Quinn: John Updike in a recent piece in the *New York Review of Books* mentions a story that he wrote called "The Happiest I've Ever Been." He says that "while composing a single paragraph I had the sensation of breaking through a thin sheet of restraining glass to material previously locked up." Did you ever have a similar experience, a moment—an epiphany—when you knew you were going beyond the material?

Kennedy: Yes, I wrote something once and showed it to a friend. When he asked, "*Who* wrote this?" I knew I was on to something. But it happened to me seriously when I was in Puerto Rico. I was working on a first novel that has never been published. When I read back what I'd written the day before, I knew I had done *something*, probably just as Updike knew he had. It's when you discover there's something else going on in your head, when you find the right metaphor, or symbol, or whatever it is you're groping for—and suddenly the work begins to blossom in directions you couldn't conceive before.

That's precisely the way I felt with *Ironweed*. You create the structure, the character, and a number of events, and then you find out that what you've done is beyond what you intended. Of course, you understand the new developments as soon as you touch them. In my reading of that paragraph back in Puerto Rico, I realized I knew more than I gave myself credit for. It comes out of your fingertips as you write, the unconscious becoming conscious at the instant you need it. It first seems a happy, wonderful accident, but it's not—it's everything you always were and hoped to do that emerges.

Quinn: What about the "muse," the sense of something speaking through you? Some writers seem to experience this presence. Have you?

Kennedy: I never understood the muse. I used to wait for her when I was a kid. But it was her day off, and mine too. But I liked the stuff I wrote anyway. Nobody ever bought any of it, so I felt there was some other element in writing that I didn't understand. That was a question

I asked in *The Ink Truck*: "What is it that I don't understand? What is it that I can't figure out?"

With *Legs*, I began to understand writing a little more clearly. I would work for hours and nothing would happen, but then, after ten or maybe eleven hours, suddenly, something *would* happen. I used to go to a friend's lake house and put in time. I knew what I wanted to say—I had all the material, but nothing would come together. I couldn't figure out what to do or how to do it. But after those long hours, I would begin to write, and feel very good about what I'd achieved by day's end.

I came to understand that writing itself was what was important. It was enough. I mean I was broke, didn't have any future, didn't have even a prospect. But I would come away from those sessions at the lake house feeling quite happy. It was amazing. I went to Cape Cod. I went up to the Adirondacks, all by myself, and hung out and wrote. I would be ecstatic about the fact that I had produced whatever number of pages. I was somehow making something worthwhile out of nothing.

Quinn: There's a scene in *Legs* that strikes me as being one of those moments when you felt a sense of "breaking through." It's the scene when Legs's girlfriend, Kiki, is hiding in a closet. It's a tautly woven, exciting example of what—for lack of a better phrase—is called "stream of consciousness."

Kennedy: That's a true fact of her life. Kiki was actually arrested in a closet in her friend's house. She was hiding when the police came and got her. I guess I got to know Kiki. I felt it one afternoon when I was writing about her. That piece didn't get into the book, but it was a most ecstatic afternoon, another one of those moments when I felt I had done something I hadn't expected to do. I had gotten beyond the journalistic sense of who Kiki was into what she *truly* was, the kookiness of her life, the voluptuousness, and it was all in this page and a half that never got into the book. It was giving definition to something that had not been clear before, and that is what I really loved. It was a new sense of writing, a breakthrough in saying things obliquely.

Quinn: John Gardner has described the writing process as getting to the point where you look at your characters and let them act, let them live their lives. They're so real that you're writing down what they are doing, rather than attempting to invent. Have you ever had that experience?

Kennedy: That's the idea of the character running away with the writer. I've never really felt it. It was true for Gardner, I guess, but it's not entirely true for me. My way is to impose myself, my new information, my new interest, my new attitudes on anything in the book. Whatever I read tends to turn up in the next chapter. You may not know that I read it yesterday afternoon, it may be something that happened back in 1846, but quite possibly it can turn up in the writing as a brand-new perception.

Quinn: You spent several years writing *Legs*. How well did you get to know him? Was he a real person for you?

Kennedy: I believed I knew Jack Diamond, but it took me a long time. I tried to write him in the first person but couldn't, because I didn't know him. I started to write his life as a movie script, which would become a novel, but before I got very far, I was asking myself, "Where am I going to put the camera now?" All those artificial aspects of the constructed world, the stylistic world, were intrusive and ridiculous.

I wrote the story eight different times. I finally arrived at a narrator who could see Diamond in the round. When I did that, I began to see Diamond myself. I looked for him on the road. I figured he'd be a nervous hitchhiker and I'd pick him up. Dana, my wife, had a dream about him being on the front lawn after the book was finished. She went out on the porch and there was Diamond. He rolled around in the grass and kicked his legs up in the air. Dana asked, "What's going on?" Legs replied, "Bill got it just right." That's her dream, not mine.

Quinn: *The Ink Truck* was your first novel. It's said that there's a special relationship between authors and their first novels, a parent's pride in their firstborn. Do you feel that way about *The Ink Truck*?

Kennedy: Yes. I love it. Some people badmouthed it after the fact, and before the fact for that matter. Actually, it sold the first time out. My agent sent it over to Dial Press, where Ed Doctorow was the managing editor, and he bought it. It went out of print fairly quickly, but that's the nature of first novels. Writers who are serious about themselves don't worry about that.

If you're going to cut your wrists after your first novel, you're not a writer. After the twenty-eighth novel, and nobody will buy it, well . . . . But you think of James Farrell. His writing career essentially ended with *Studs Lonigan*, but he never quit. It's an admirable thing, because he was getting pleasure out of what he was doing. If there are enough people who understand that, if there are other writers getting some pleasure out of reading your twenty-eighth novel, then maybe that's enough.

Quinn: What about the influence of other writers on you? James Joyce must certainly be one of them.

Kennedy: Yes, absolutely. I've been re-reading him just lately. There's no end to the man. He's the greatest man of letters in the twentieth century. I don't think there's a close second. If there is, it's Faulkner.

But Joyce has transcendence. Leopold Bloom is someone who is never going to die in the history of literature. Faulkner did great things. But there's nothing like Leopold and Molly, the Blooms, in all of twentieth-century literature. I don't know where the hell you go to find their equal.

Quinn: What about the similarities between you and Joyce?

Kennedy: Similarities? I don't aspire to similarities.

Quinn: People have compared the opening of *Ironweed* to "The Dead" and the "Circe" chapter in *Ulysses*. Is there any validity to that?

Kennedy: I wish I had heard somebody say that, but I never heard that before. Joyce is Joyce. He's by himself, and I wouldn't make any comparisons. No, it's not an attempt at conscious imitation, if that's the question.

Quinn: Your careful reconstruction of Albany, your fascination with place, certainly evokes Joyce's obsession with Dublin.

Kennedy: That's true enough. Joyce made things easier for all of us. He prompted us to become aware of our entire heritage, including dishpans and the jakes in the back yard.

Quinn: You both are absorbed with the place where you grew up. And you both left it. Did you choose, as Joyce did, "silence, exile, and cunning," and set out to chronicle Albany at a distance? Or did you only gradually come to understand your relationship to Albany?

Kennedy: Silence was imposed on me by my editors. My might-have-been editors. Exile came because I couldn't stay in Albany any longer and still function effectively. I went to Puerto Rico, which is exile under the American flag. Cunning was not in my kit bag. I never felt that it was necessary. I was always aboveboard. I put out my work for stomping. And I usually got stomped. But I never felt it was necessary to nurse my wounds and never try again until I had a masterpiece. That was never my understanding of how to write, or how to live as a writer.

Somewhere along the line I came across a phrase about "renewing your vulnerability." And that seemed to me a most important thing for a writer. You renew your vulnerability. Constantly. You start out feeling so vulnerable that you're afraid the criticism will kill you. But if you're not afraid of being vulnerable, if you say, "Go ahead, hit me again, I can take it," you get a thick skin.

You get that as a journalist. Letters to the editor demanding "Throw this guy in the river." Or "Why did you hire him to begin with? This man should be destroyed." Or "This is a radical," or "This is a liberal"—or some other dirty word. You get to live with that.

Quinn: Your first three novels are set in Albany in the Depression, which really seems to have captured your imagination. Why?

Kennedy: *Legs* was 1931, and that was researched to discover that era. And once I got into the twenties and Prohibition and the gangland world, I was hooked. I began to see that it had tentacles that went forward, that people I was writing about in *Legs* were going to be significant in future books I wanted to write. When I got around to writing *Billy Phelan*, which was the next one, it should have taken place in 1933, which was only two years after Diamond died, but I felt what I needed to do was to move deeper into the Depression, into the grit of it, into the end of it, the feeling of coming out of it.

Quinn: Do you see a resemblance between Legs Diamond and Jay Gatsby?

Kennedy: *Gatsby* is a great book. I wouldn't want anyone to think I was cavalierly using the narration of Marcus Gorman about a gangster without understanding the precedent. But I also feel that the narrator in *Gatsby* was boring as a character, and I don't think Marcus is. Fitzgerald's narrator came to life only when he let him stop talking about himself and let us see him in action. That was when he leaped off the page for me.

Quinn: *Legs* and *Gatsby* are both about outsiders trying to force their way into America. Is that right?

Kennedy: Right. But you never see Gatsby doing it seriously. There are some who have made the analogy that Diamond *is* Gatsby, but I don't think Gatsby was like Diamond. I don't think Gatsby was a gangster. I think he was a thief, not a killer. People said he killed a man once, but they said that about a lot of people in the twenties.

Quinn: That's the great American saga. The immigrant or his son forcing his way in.

Kennedy: The ambition was always to reach fame and fortune. Like Legs Diamond or Cagney in *Public Enemy*, or Edward G. Robinson in *Little Caesar*, the tough guys who tried to shoot their way in. Some survived, got rich, and went straight. Big Bill Dwyer did that. He was one of the great rumrunners, and he wound up in café society, Palm Beach, racetracks, hobnobbing with the rich, hanging out in tuxedos.

In America, everybody is a climber. Everybody is trying to come up from below. That's the first law of motion in America. Nobody wants to live in the Five Points forever. Nobody wants to live the stereotypes associated with poverty and gangs, the shame of being seen as an out-sider, the sense of not being worthy enough to be let in. The Irish and every immigrant group faced it. Nobody worse than African Americans, who were dragged here as slaves. For them, the barriers never went away, not entirely.

Quinn: *Ironweed* is the latest part of the Albany cycle. You said in a recent interview that it came "like a bullet." Is that because you had lived in that world for so long, were so familiar with it from all the research you'd done, that you already knew the characters?

Kennedy: No. *Ironweed* was something else. It had a preexistence in both journalism and early fiction. In that unpublished novel I wrote in Puerto Rico I created Francis Phelan, just one of several characters in a family chronicle. Then, in 1963, I wrote a series of articles on a wino couple for the *Albany Times-Union*, and I fused the fiction and nonfiction when I started to create Francis Phelan for *Billy Phelan*.

The early work was dead at this point, which is what usually hap-pens when you leave it in the drawer, so I began from scratch. Francis emerged as a new and more complex character in *Billy*, so much so that I knew he should have his own book. By the time I got to him in *Iron-weed*, I knew far more about the history of the city, and I was reflecting a complexity of life I had not been able to reach in the first novels. I felt I really knew this man. The book was written in just about seven months.

Quinn: One reviewer has seen in *Ironweed* a parallel between the liturgy of the Catholic Church and the events of the three days the book encompasses. Is he right?

Kennedy: Absolutely, but not for the reasons of celebration and liturgy. In *Ironweed*, it was all accidental because I had already created the time frame in *Billy Phelan*.

I created it because I had to have it all happen during the pre-election period. That was the whole purpose in *Billy Phelan*. So I made the kidnapping take place in an election year, then moved forward into the campaign. Once I had that, I went back, and if you notice, *Billy Phelan* and *Ironweed* end the same day. That is because having created the dynamics of Billy meeting his father, the logical thing when I dealt with Francis was to see him in those post-confrontational days with Billy—to discover what it was that made him go home.

Francis Phelan wouldn't go home until he knew Annie, his wife, never condemned or blamed him for the death of their infant son. So first come these two things: the invitation from Billy and the knowledge about Annie. They stay in his mind. He dries out. He wants to go home. All of

Ironweed is this tap dancing into reality, trying to figure it out, "How am I going to do it?"

Quinn: Editors kept turning down *Ironweed* because they said it was too depressing. Nobody would want to read a novel about bums. But it's actually a very hopeful novel, isn't it? A novel about redemption? And forgiveness?

Kennedy: *Redemption* is the key word. That's what it's all about. It parallels the *Purgatorio*. When you talk about the liturgy or Catholic thought, you think of Dante, and eventually you think of the *Inferno*, and the *Purgatorio*, and the *Paradiso*. From the epigraph, you enter my book with Dante, and it's a journey through planes of escalation into a moment of redemption. Francis cleanses himself. It reflects something I think is profound about human behavior.

Quinn: All Saints' Day is taken from Irish mythology. It's based on the Celtic feast of Samhain, when the barriers between the living and the dead disappeared. Was Irish mythology a conscious part of the cemetery scene at the opening of *Ironweed*?

Kennedy: No, it was not. I didn't know that about All Saints' Day. I just grew up with it as a holy day. But I'm finding out all kinds of things about myself, things that are pushing me, nudging me into places I'm not yet fully aware of.

Quinn: The Irish poet Patrick Kavanaugh has written that he lived in a place where literature wasn't supposed to happen. It was too conventional, supposedly. Did you ever face that stumbling block? The thought that literature happened in places grander or more exotic than Albany?

Kennedy: Oh yes, from the very outset. I understood that Melville went to school here. I understood that Henry James touched down here and left immediately. Those kind of moments were about as much as you could expect out of Albany. But then, I began to figure that it couldn't be all that bad. I found out that Albany was, and is, a great place. Not that it was a cultural hotbed filled with artists and writers whose works would endure through the ages. But there was a sense of the place being valuable, home to uniquely interesting human beings, and this was *tremendously* important. As soon as I began to understand this, I realized that the town was unexplored.

Quinn: Was it out of the newspaper articles you wrote about Albany that you began to sink yourself into its history? To sense its depths?

Kennedy: I was writing in Puerto Rico about myself and my wife, who's from the island, and my ancestors, trying to understand it all, and then I realized I didn't understand, and that was it. That ignorance drove me to come back, settle in, and do research in the library, and try to understand. I never expected that I would stay forever.

But how can you write about a place if you don't understand what the street names signify, or who the mayor is, or what the machine was all about? I was writing from Puerto Rico at a point when I didn't really understand the nuances and historical roots of machine politics and bossism in Albany. I hadn't paid sufficient attention when I was working at an Albany newspaper. I just said, "I'm *mildly* opposed." I was very self-righteous.

Quinn: Albany's all-powerful Democratic machine was an Irish-American machine. For the Albany Irish, you've written, "politics was justice itself; politics was sufficient unto itself." What did you mean by that?

Kennedy: Old-timers used to proclaim that the motto of O'Connell's machine was "Honesty is no substitute for experience." It was a joke, only they meant it. When I grew up, if you were Irish, you were a Democrat. If you were a Democrat, you were probably a Catholic. If you were a Catholic, you gave allegiance to the church on the corner, and to Dan O'Connell, who was a pillar of the church, inseparable from the bishop and the priests, and who was revered and prayed for. But Dan was also profiting from the whorehouses, the gambling joints, the all-night saloons, and the blackout card games. He was in collusion with the grafters and the bankers, getting rich with the paving contractors.

No matter what it was in town, wherever you could make an illegal dollar, that's where the Irish were, that's where the politics were, that's where the church was, that's where the morality was. And it was all fused. You couldn't separate it because the families were so interlocked, goodness walked hand-in-hand with evil. But it wasn't viewed as evil. It was viewed as a way to get on in the world.

Objective morality didn't interest Albany. The Irish didn't care about it. They understood that they had been deprived and now they were not. Now they were able to get jobs. In the previous era, when the Irish were not in power, they couldn't get jobs. Their families were starving, and starvation for them was immorality.

Quinn: Albany is more than a setting for your novels. It becomes kind of a character. But do you think of yourself as a regional writer in the way that Flannery O'Connor thought of herself as a southern writer?

Kennedy: Yes and no. All regional writers are trying to capture the uniqueness of their region, obviously. And most writers who use regions are trying for universality, to speak to life outside the region. It depends,

I suspect, on how well you are able to make your cosmos, however small—Milledgeville, Georgia, or Yoknapatawpha County, or Dublin, or the *Pequod*—a center of vitality, of universality, of spiritual life that transcends the limitations geography imposes. If you never find that center, all you're doing is floating free. Until you have a Yoknapatawpha, or unless you're a genius like Beckett, you can't coalesce your meaning. Creating life in an abstract place—that's very hard to do, you have to really have genius.

You can do all the navel-gazing you want, and until it's centered on a place, it seems to me a vagrant pursuit, a Sunday in the park, a soap opera. It's an absence of significance. If you don't have the place, you don't have the dynamics of the society that exists in that place, the context that contains people, that they spend their lives confirming or confronting or trying to escape.

Quinn: What about Ireland? Does it ever tug on your imagination? Any of the Albany cycle spinning its way back there?

Kennedy: I've been to Ireland several times. I'll go again in quest of my ancestors, like so many other Irish in this country, to comprehend origin and consequences. But Ireland is a foreign country to me. I feel I don't know enough about any particular place to give me what I'd need for a novel. I'd be a fraud if I tried to write significantly about somebody there. Albany belongs to me and vice versa.

For me, fiction exists, finally, in order to describe neither social conditions nor landscapes but human consciousness. Essays, documentary films, editorials in newspapers can persuade you to a political position. But nothing except great fiction can get to the heart of what it means to be alive. Great fiction, great films, great plays, they all center in on consciousness, which always has a uniqueness about it, and that uniqueness is what a novelist can give you that nobody else can: a sense of having lived in a certain time and understood a certain place, a certain consciousness, a certain destiny, the known and unknown, all the squalor and all the glory of being alive.

And if you reduce fiction to political or social argument, or to a kind of sociological construct, you lose its real strength. When you think of Chaucer or Boccaccio, you remember the individualistic elements of their characters in the same way you remember the people in, for example, Sherwood Anderson's *Winesburg, Ohio*. Forget theories. Good novels endure. The bad go away.

Quinn: Do you write with a certain audience in mind?

Kennedy: I write for people like me who used to appreciate Damon

Runyon sentences, people who appreciate writing first, who understand the difference between an ordinary sentence and a sentence that jumps off the page when you read it.

I'm working on a preface for a new book about the state capitol. As always when I do research, I read an incredible amount of horseshit that's been published on the subject. The same old stuff rehashed every which way. But every once in a while a historian gets hold of something and creates a real sentence, maybe one in a whole book of essays, but it stops you. You look at it and say, "Terrific sentence." That's the reaction I'm looking for.

Quinn: Does writing—the creation of a "terrific sentence"—ever get easier?

Kennedy: Some things get easier. Journalism gets easier. I'm not sure it gets better. Fiction, at least for me, seems to get more complicated. Not that it's hard to write a sentence or a paragraph, but it's hard to believe that the current sentence or paragraph is new, that I'm not just saying something that's been said a hundred times before.

When I begin to write, I begin to confront things that I never confronted before. I begin to invent things, willfully going into the unknown. As I face the challenge of an empty page tomorrow morning—and that's what I live for—what I need to do is discover something that will surprise me, something that I've never done before, written before, seen before, heard before.

You start with an ordinary story. But you must penetrate something beyond. You have a man or a woman moving quietly through life. A man and a woman in trouble, both of them. And there's a classical way to create the clichéd situations about how they meet and get back together, or how they stay together for forty years. But you can't do any of those things.

You must do something that you have never done before. And how do you do that? Mostly, it seems to me, through language. It can happen through dialogue. When your language leads you in, it's like watching the sea, and the sea is never the same. And it's never the same sentence. And as long as it isn't, you're in good shape. As soon as it becomes the same sentence again, you're all washed up.

Quinn: Your next project, besides the new novel, is to write screenplays for *Legs*, *Billy Phelan*, and *Ironweed*. Any trepidations? Any fear that Hollywood might hurt your writing?

Kennedy: No, I don't have that kind of conflict. I love movies. I'm glad to be part of the movies. I don't confuse them with novels. I don't see them as competition. I think the novel is far superior to film because of its complexity. But I think film can also do many things that engage you in ways no novel can. You can't get quite such an exciting vision of womanhood from a book as you can with Garbo or Monroe or Ava Gardner on the screen. When you see these people idealized up there, there's nothing quite equivalent to it in literature. Literature is an extension of your imagination, but here's an incomparable illusion of visual reality to film.

Quinn: How different is screenwriting from writing a novel?

Kennedy: Very different. I'm glad to write the screenplays for the films that are going to be made out of my books, since I've got some control. I respect films very much. I think film can be a tremendously exciting medium. It's been that way all my life, from when I was a kid at the time I began discovering Ingmar Bergman. The whole idea of the translation of any kind of life into cinema is important, because it's a medium that reaches so many people. And if you can reach those people with something that's valuable to you, it's the same as reaching them with your novel in a certain way.

Quinn: What do you most want to preserve from your novels when they're made into films?

Kennedy: I'd like to preserve the whole novel, but you can't. Movies can only do so much. The novel is the supreme form of explaining how it is that any human being exists on this planet, the intensity and complexly, with a history, with a soul, with a future, with a present, in a particular place or places. You can get some of the environment, you can get a bit of the language, you can get the look of things in the movies. But you can't encompass the depth and density of the unconscious, you can't get the ineffably complex element of what it means to be alive. It's all but impossible in the movies.

Quinn: Do you ever look back at what you've written and say, "I've learned so much since then. I know so much more now"?

Kennedy: Yes, absolutely. But that doesn't mean it gets easier just because you know more now. Often, it makes it more complicated. What you have to do constantly is not repeat yourself, at least try not to. You feel that maybe you're in better command of the language, of your ability to write a sentence, to conceptualize, to create a new character. But the process is problematical. It's still a great game.

As far as I'm concerned, that's what the whole thing is about, what writing is all about, what it's always been about: the invention of something out of nothing. I believe this is the whole satisfaction that comes from writing: That you're able to spin something out of nothing, that seems new to you and that you make new for the reader. Making it new, that's what's hard. I don't expect it will ever get any easier. I'm not counting on it.

Peter Quinn
1985

INDEX

Peter Quinn is a novelist, political historian, and foremost chronicler of New York City. He is the author of *Banished Children of Eve*, American Book Award winner; *Looking for Jimmy: A Search for Irish America*; and a trilogy of historical detective novels—*Hour of the Cat*, *The Man Who Never Returned*, and *Dry Bones*.

EMPIRE
STATE
EDITIONS **SELECT TITLES FROM EMPIRE STATE EDITIONS**

Andrew Feffer, *Bad Faith: Teachers, Liberalism, and the Origins of McCarthyism*

Colin Davey with Thomas A. Lesser, *The American Museum of Natural History and How It Got That Way*. Forewords by Neil deGrasse Tyson and Kermit Roosevelt III

Wendy Jean Katz, *Humbug: The Politics of Art Criticism in New York City's Penny Press*

Mike Jaccarino, *America's Last Great Newspaper War: The Death of Print in a Two-Tabloid Town*

Angel Garcia, *The Kingdom Began in Puerto Rico: Neil Connolly's Priesthood in the South Bronx*

Jim Mackin, *Notable New Yorkers of Manhattan's Upper West Side: Bloomingdale–Morningside Heights*

Matthew Spady, *The Neighborhood Manhattan Forgot: Audubon Park and the Families Who Shaped It*

Robert O. Binnewies, *Palisades: 100,000 Acres in 100 Years*

Marilyn S. Greenwald and Yun Li, *Eunice Hunton Carter: A Lifelong Fight for Social Justice*

Jeffrey A. Kroessler, *Sunnyside Gardens: Planning and Preservation in a Historic Garden Suburb*

Elizabeth Macaulay-Lewis, *Antiquity in Gotham: The Ancient Architecture of New York City*

Ron Howell, *King Al: How Sharpton Took the Throne*

Phil Rosenzweig, *Reginald Rose and the Journey of "12 Angry Men"*

Jean Arrington with Cynthia S. LaValle, *From Factories to Palaces: Architect Charles B. J. Snyder and the New York City Public Schools*

Boukary Sawadogo, *Africans in Harlem: An Untold New York Story*

Alvin Eng, *Our Laundry, Our Town: My Chinese American Life from Flushing to the Downtown Stage and Beyond*

Stephanie Azzarone, *Heaven on the Hudson: Mansions, Monuments, and Marvels of Riverside Park*. Photography by Robert F. Rodriguez

Ron Goldberg, *Boy with the Bullhorn: A Memoir and History of ACT UP New York*

Jill Jonnes, *South Bronx Rising: The Rise, Fall, and Resurrection of an American City*, Third Edition

For a complete list, visit www.fordhampress.com/empire-state-editions.

Printed in the USA
CPSIA information can be obtained
at www.ICGtesting.com
JSHW011657141024
71662JS00005B/74